The Age of Reptiles

EDWIN H. COLBERT

DOVER PUBLICATIONS, INC.
Mineola, New York

Copyright

Copyright © 1965, 1997 by Edwin H. Colbert.
All rights reserved under Pan American and International Copyright Conventions.

Published in Canada by General Publishing Company, Ltd., 30 Lesmill Road, Don Mills, Toronto, Ontario.
Published in the United Kingdom by Constable and Company, Ltd., 3 The Lanchesters, 162–164 Fulham Palace Road, London W6 9ER.

Bibliographical Note

This Dover edition, first published in 1997, is an enlarged and corrected republication of the work originally published by W. W. Norton & Company, Inc., New York, in 1965. A preface and an addendum have been specially prepared for this edition by the author.

Library of Congress Cataloging-in-Publication Data

Colbert, Edwin Harris, 1905–
    The age of reptiles / Edwin H. Colbert.
        p.   cm.
    "An enlarged and corrected republication of the work originally published by W. W. Norton & Company, Inc., New York, in 1965. A preface and an addendum have been specially prepared for this edition"—T.p. verso.
    Includes bibliographical references (p.   –   ) and index.
    ISBN 0-486-29377-7 (pbk.)
    1. Reptiles, Fossil.   I. Title.
QE861.C72   1997
567.9—dc20   96-31472
                                                                         CIP

Manufactured in the United States of America
Dover Publications, Inc., 31 East 2nd Street, Mineola, N.Y. 11501

Contents

	Preface to the Dover Edition	xiii
	Preface to the First Edition	xv
I	TIME, TETRAPODS AND FOSSILS	I
2	BEGINNING OF THE AGE OF REPTILES	33
3	EARLY REPTILIAN RULERS OF THE LAND	49
4	THE TRANSITION	64
5	SUPREMACY OF THE REPTILES	86
6	THE FIRST WAVE OF EXTINCTION	106
7	NEW RULING REPTILES	116
8	DOMINANCE OF THE DINOSAURS	130
9	A NEW WORLD FORESHADOWED	147
10	ZENITH OF THE DINOSAURS	161
11	THE GREAT EXTINCTION	191
	Bibliography	208
	Addendum	221
	Index	245

Acknowledgments

With the exception of figures 2 to 19 inclusive, all of the figures were drawn especially for this book. The restorations, figures 22, 24–27, 29–32, 35–43, 46–48, 50–52, 54–58 and 61–65, were made by Margaret Matthew Colbert under the supervision of the author. The four maps, figures 23, 34, 49 and 59 were drawn by George Matthew Colbert under the supervision of the author. The charts, figures 1, 20, 21, 28, 33, 44, 45, 53, 60, 66 and 67 were drawn by Michael Insinna under the supervision of the author.

Acknowledgments for figures not listed above are as follows.

Figures 2, 4 and 5 are from Gregory, W. K. (1951) *Evolution Emerging*, New York, Macmillan, vol. 2, p. 371, fig. 11.31; p. 387, fig. 12.9; p. 417, fig. 12.34. Figure 3 is from Olson, E. C. (1951) *Fieldiana: Geology*, Vol. 11, No. 2, pl. 4. Chicago Natural History Museum. Figure 9 is from Olson, E. C. and Robert Broom (1937) *Journal of Paleontology*, Vol. 11, No. 7, p. 615, fig. 3. Figures 6 and 8 are from Andrews, C. W. (1910) *A Descriptive Catalogue of the Marine Reptiles of the Oxford Clay*. Part 1, p. 62, fig. 42; p. 118, fig. 66. Figure 7 is from Gregory, J. T. (1945) *University of Texas Publ. 4401*, Pl. 33. Figure 10 is from Walker, A. D. (1961) *Philosophical Transactions of the Royal Society of London, B*, Vol. 244, p. 161, fig. 22. Figure 11 is from Osborn, H. F. (1917) *Bulletin of the American Museum of Natural History*, Vol. 35, Pl. 26. Figure 12 is from Brown, Barnum (1917) *Bulletin of the American Museum of Natural History*, Vol. 37, Pl. 13. Figure 13 is from Reese, A. M. (1915) *The Alligator and its Allies*. New York, Putnam, p. 50, fig. 16. Figure 14 is from Williston, S. W. (1925) *Osteology of the Reptiles*. Cambridge, Harvard University Press, p. 297, fig. 188. Figure 15 is from Romer, A. S. and L. I. Price (1940) *Geological Society of America, Special Paper No. 28*, p. 324, fig. 59. Figure 16 is from Colbert, E. H. (1948) *Bulletin of the American Museum of Natural History*, Vol. 89, p. 393, fig. 22. Figure 17 is from Young, C. C. (1947) *Proceedings Zoological Society, London*, Vol. 117, p. 543, fig. 2. Figure 18 is from Heilmann, Gerhard (1927) *The Origin of Birds*. New York, Appleton, p. 33, fig. 23. Figure 19 is from Simpson, G. G. (1928) *American Museum Novitates, No. 329*, p. 6, fig. 3.

The four double-page plates, showing reconstructions of Permian (Plate 3), Triassic (Plate 8), Jurassic (Plate 13) and Cretaceous (Plate 18) scenes, were drawn by Margaret Matthew Colbert under the supervision of the author. Plates 1, 2, 4–7, 9–11 and 15 are from photographs taken by the author. Plates 12, 14, 16, 17, 19 and 20 are from the photographic files of the American Museum of Natural History in New York.

Plates

[*Between pages* 148 *and* 149]

1   The Lower Permian Wichita beds of northern Texas
2   The Upper Permian *Cistecephalus* zone in the Lower Beaufort beds of the Karroo Series of South Africa
3   Life of Early Permian time in Northern Texas
4   The Upper Triassic Red Beds and Cave Sandstone of the Stormberg Series of South Africa
5   A gully or *sanga* exposing the bright red sediments of the Upper Triassic Santa Maria formation in the state of Rio Grande do Sul, Brazil
6   The Upper Triassic Chinle formation, as exposed in Arizona
7   The Mesozoic sequence at Ghost Ranch, northwest of Abiquiu, New Mexico
8   Life of Late Triassic time in Western North America
9   The Lower Jurassic or Liassic cliffs of the Channel Coast near Charmouth, Dorset, England
10 The Upper Jurassic Oxford clays, as exposed in a quarry in Dorset
11 The Upper Jurassic Morrison formation, at Dinosaur National Monument, Utah
12 Excavating Jurassic dinosaurs at the turn of the century in the Bone Cabin Quarry, at Como Bluff, Wyoming
13 Life of Late Jurassic time in western North America
14 The Cretaceous Djadochta formation at Shabarakh Usu, Mongolia
15 The white Upper Cretaceous chalk cliffs of southern England
16 Hauling dinosaur bones out of the valley of the Red Deer River, Alberta, from exposures of the Cretaceous Belly River beds
17 Exposures of the Upper Cretaceous Edmonton formation, Red Deer River, Alberta
18 Life of Late Cretaceous Belly River time in western Canada
19 Excavating the skeleton of a duck-billed dinosaur
20 The Upper Cretaceous Hell Creek beds of Montana

Figures

1   The classes of vertebrates   8
2   The skeleton of *Eryops*, a Permian labyrinthodont amphibian   13
3   The skull of *Diplocaulus*, a Permian nectridian amphibian   13
4   The skeleton of *Diadectes*, a Permian cotylosaurian reptile   14
5   A turtle skeleton, showing the neck extended and retracted   15
6   Skeleton of a Jurassic ichthyosaur   16
7   The skeleton of the Triassic protorosaur, *Trilophosaurus*   16
8   The skeleton of the Jurassic plesiosaur, *Muraenosaurus*   17
9   The skull of *Youngoides*, a Permian diapsid reptile   17
10   The skeleton of *Stagonolepis*, a Triassic thecodont reptile   18
11   The skeleton of the Upper Cretaceous saurischian dinosaur, *Ornithomimus*   18
12   The skeleton of the Upper Cretaceous ornithischian dinosaur, *Monoclonius*   19
13   The skeleton of a modern alligator   19
14   The skeleton of the Jurassic pterosaur, *Rhamphorhynchus*   20
15   The skeleton of the Permian pelycosaur, *Sphenacodon*   21
16   The skeleton of the mammal-like reptile, *Lycaenops*   21
17   The skull of *Bienotherium*, a Triassic tritylodont   22
18   The skeletons of *Archaeopteryx*, a Jurassic bird, and of a pigeon   23
19   The skull of a Cretaceous placental mammal, *Zalambdalestes*   24
20   A phylogeny of the late Paleozoic and Mesozoic tetrapods   28
21   The duration through time of the orders of tetrapods that lived during the Age of Reptiles   31
22   The tetrapod-like fish, *Eusthenopteron*, and the primitive amphibian, *Ichthyostega*   36
23   World map showing localities at which Permian tetrapods have been found   39
24   The North American Lower Permian amphibian, *Eryops*   42
25   *Diadectes*, a cotylosaurian reptile from the Lower Permian red beds of Texas   43
26   The North American pelycosaur, *Dimetrodon*   45
27   A gigantic pelycosaur, *Cotylorhynchus*, from the Middle Permian of Oklahoma   47
28   The evolution of the therapsid reptiles   51
29   The Middle Permian pareiasaur, *Bradysaurus*, from South Africa   53

30 The Permian dinocephalian, *Moschops*, from South Africa 54
31 *Endothiodon*, a small anomodont from the Permian of South Africa 55
32 The Permian gorgonopsian, *Lycaenops*, from South Africa 56
33 A comparison of the number of tetrapod genera in the Upper Permian and Lower Triassic sediments 66
34 World map showing localities at which Triassic tetrapods have been found 73
35 The Triassic marine reptiles, *Nothosaurus* and *Placodus* 79
36 The Lower Triassic dicynodont, *Lystrosaurus*, of South Africa and Asia 81
37 The Lower Triassic theriodont, *Cynognathus*, from South Africa 83
38 *Tanystrophaeus*, a Middle Triassic lizard-like reptile from Europe 88
39 *Triassochelys*, a Triassic turtle from Europe 91
40 *Henodus*, the last of the placodonts, from the Upper Triassic of Germany 91
41 The large rhynchocephalian, *Scaphonyx*, from the Triassic of Brazil 93
42 The Triassic dinosaur, *Plateosaurus*, from Germany 96
43 *Bienotherium*, an Upper Triassic tritylodont from China 99
44 A comparison of the number of tetrapod genera in Upper Triassic and Lower Jurassic sediments 109
45 The range and abundance of tetrapods that lived during the Age of Reptiles 112–113
46 A Jurassic ichthyosaur 121
47 The plated dinosaur, *Scelidosaurus*, from the Lower Jurassic beds of England 122
48 *Dimorphodon*, an early Jurassic pterosaur from Europe 123
49 World map showing localities at which Jurassic tetrapods have been found 124
50 The Upper Jurassic pterosaur, *Rhamphorhynchus*, from Europe 137
51 The first bird, *Archaeopteryx*, from the Upper Jurassic of Germany 138
52 The Jurassic marine crocodile, *Geosaurus* 139
53 The expansion of teleost fishes and flowering plants in early Cretaceous time 149
54 The ornithischian dinosaur, *Iguanodon*, from the Lower Cretaceous of Europe 153
55 *Hypsilophodon*, a primitive ornithischian dinosaur from the Lower Cretaceous of England 154
56 *Polacanthus*, a plated dinosaur from the Lower Cretaceous of England 155
57 A possible ancestor of the horned dinosaurs, *Psittacosaurus*, from the Cretaceous beds of Mongolia 157
58 The gigantic Cretaceous plesiosaur, *Kronosaurus*, from Australia 158
59 World map showing localities at which Cretaceous tetrapods have been found 166
60 The evolution of the duck-billed and horned dinosaurs 170–171
61 The Upper Cretaceous plesiosaur, *Elasmosaurus*, from North America 181

62 The gigantic Upper Cretaceous marine lizard, *Tylosaurus*, from North America   182
63 An Upper Cretaceous diving bird, *Hesperornis*, from North America   183
64 The largest of the pterosaurs, *Pteranodon*, from the Upper Cretaceous of North America   184
65 One of the first of the horned dinosaurs, *Protoceratops*, from the Cretaceous of Mongolia   187
66 An example of the decline of dinosaurs during the final stages of Cretaceous history in North America   199
67 A comparison of the number of tetrapod genera in Upper Cretaceous and Lower Tertiary sediments   202

Preface to the Dover Edition

THIRTY YEARS and more have elapsed since *The Age of Reptiles* was published simultaneously in 1965 by Weidenfeld and Nicolson of London and by W. W. Norton & Company of New York (Norton also published a paperback edition in 1966).

During the past three decades a monumental body of knowledge has appeared pertaining to late Paleozoic and Mesozoic tetrapods (the air-breathing, four-footed backboned animals), much of it based upon new paleontological discoveries made throughout the world. At the same time our concept of past intercontinental relationships has been profoundly revolutionized by the facts of Plate Tectonics. Since many details of fact and interpretation have been added to or have superseded the information on which the original text of this book was based, some recognition and discussion of our new knowledge are needed, if a reprinting of *The Age of Reptiles* is to be valid and useful to the present generation of readers. These desiderata are attempted in an Addendum to the original text, kindly authorized by Dover Publications.

It is to be hoped that this Addendum will be satisfactory to the reader and will provide a summary of sorts, outlining our modern understanding of the evolution of tetrapods, and of the continents and the oceans on which and in which they lived during some 200 million years of earth history.

Flagstaff, Arizona   EDWIN H. COLBERT
1996

Preface to the First Edition

IN 1831 Gideon Algernon Mantell, an English physician living in Lewes, published a three-column communication in a local paper, the *Sussex Advertiser*, entitled 'The Age of Reptiles'. Mantell, one of the small, dedicated group of men who did so much in their so-called spare time to help found our modern sciences, had come to realize that during a long span of geologic history the earth was ruled by great reptiles. This interesting phase in the history of the earth and the evolution of life, so much of it marked by the dominance of the dinosaurs, has since Mantell's day been the subject of extensive study in field and laboratory by men of many nations on all of the continents. It is a subject that has attracted much popular attention.

The purpose of the present book is to attempt a review, and it is to be hoped a concise one, of the Age of Reptiles, with particular emphasis on the tetrapods, the four-legged vertebrates, that lived during the years of reptilian supremacy. It is intended as a story of the tetrapod life of an ancient age, of the interrelationships between amphibians and reptiles, between birds and mammals, and between all of these animals and their environments, at successive times through some two hundred million years of earth history. It is a story of faunas that followed one after the other through time, and changed as they developed – as they mirrored evolution through the years, as they recorded the origin and the extinction of species. The story is not concerned in its primary aspects with descriptions of the tetrapods which are the chief actors, but these are necessarily briefly described, in order that the reader who is not familiar with them from other sources may have some idea of their principal features and their relationships. It is hoped that the illustrations will be of much assistance on this score.

The story is a large one, and in a book such as this a great deal must be omitted. Even so, it may seem to some readers that parts of the account are filled with details. The author can only ask for the indulgence of such readers, with the assurance that no more details have been included than are necessary to tell the story of the Age of Reptiles in a meaningful way.

I am indebted to many sources and to many people for the background and the help that has made possible the writing of this book. First I wish to acknowledge my debt to paleontologists and geologists, who through their publications, and in many cases through their letters and conversations, have provided the base on which this present work has been erected. Specifically I wish to extend particular acknowledgments to Margaret Matthew Colbert for the restorations of animals and scenes illustrating this book, to George M. Colbert for the maps and to Michael Insinna for the diagrams and other illustrations. Richard Carrington read the original manuscript and offered many helpful suggestions. The manuscript in its several phases was typed by Mrs Catharine Minerly.

1964   EDWIN H. COLBERT

The Age of Reptiles

Chapter 1

Time, Tetrapods and Fossils

THE PAST is mysterious, ever more so the farther we look back from our vantage point in the twentieth-century world. As we follow the procession of years back through time the earth and its inhabitants seem to us less real and less substantial the more distantly they are removed from this age in which we live. How vague in our minds is the golden age of the Greek heroes, in spite of the Homeric legends that have come down to us through the generations, in spite of the tangible relics of that distant time, the ruined temples and statues, the shining black and white vases and amphorae, the exquisite gems and coins. How much more vague is the far more ancient age of the Magdalenian hunters in western Europe, in spite of the burials and the skeletons, the flint tools, and the incomparable paintings that these men left on the walls of their caves. And how very much more vague still is the age when reptiles ruled the earth, in spite of the fossil bones – relics of animals that lived on the continents and in the seas in a world of long ago.

Yet although there are many mysteries, there is much to be learned from the past. If we probe deeply and in detail it is possible to thrust aside some parts of the curtain of obscurity that comes between us and the vanished ages of history – human and prehuman – thus to bring a certain degree of life and reality to those years before there were men, even before there were mammals. Such is the intended purpose of this book; we are to explore the Age of Reptiles.

What was the Age of Reptiles ? It was, as the name implies, that portion in the story of the earth when reptiles were supreme. Let us look at it in its proper frame of reference, against the backdrop of life history.

When we trace the evolution of life back through time, so far back that the days of the ancient Greeks or even the years of the Magdalenian hunters seem as but yesterday, we can see the first grand entrance of animals on the stage of earth history, as abundantly revealed by the fossil record, about six hundred million years ago. At that far distant day the record of animal life, as preserved by the fossils in the rocks, bursts upon our view in almost full panoply, and we see before us a rich array of shelled animals that lived in ancient seas. Evidently there had been a vast preceding time span during a considerable part of the four or five thousand million years of earth history in which animals and plants were simple organisms, unprotected by outer shells, unsupported by woody tissues, and therefore seldom fossilized. Then, when animals had evolved to such a degree of complexity that many of them were protected by shells of various sorts, the Age of Invertebrates, as we know it, had begun.

Millions of years passed, and the first, primitive, jawless fishes made their appearance in the stony record of life. This event, followed by a long period during which the fishes multiplied in great diversity, marked the Age of Fishes.

While the fishes were evolving along lines that were to determine the course of their later success, the plants, heretofore simple marine forms, had migrated on to the land, to clothe the hills and valleys with a mantle of green, and accompanying the plants as early explorers of the land went various animals without backbones, particularly the ancestors of the insects. About three hundred million years ago some of the fishes, which had strong, leg-like fins and lungs to breathe with, ventured on to dry ground from the streams and lakes in which they lived. These were the progenitors of the amphibians, and the Age of Amphibians had begun.

The rule of the amphibians on the land, at the beginning quite unopposed, was relatively brief. These animals throughout their history have retained vestiges of their fish heritage, especially in their method of reproduction. In short, the modern amphibians (the frogs, toads and salamanders, and a group of tropical amphibians known as coecilians) generally lay unprotected eggs in the water, hatch as little fish-like tadpoles, and after an interval of a somewhat fish-like existence, these tadpoles change or metamorphose to become adult, four-legged animals. There is every reason to think that this method of reproduction was as characteristic of ancient amphibians as it is of those we know today. Animals that perpetuate their own kind in this way are and always have been tied closely to the water; it is and was in past ages necessary for them to return to the water or to moist places to lay their eggs. This has been a limiting factor in their lives.

So it was that not long after the amphibians had become established on the land that some of them trended away from this method of reproduction to become completely independent of the water. Thus arose the first reptiles, very much like their immediate amphibian forebears in many respects. But one very important thing distinguished the first reptiles from the amphibians, and this was the *amniote egg*. In these early reptiles, and in reptiles ever since, it was not and has not been necessary to return to the water to reproduce. These animals were freed from their ancestral habitat and could wander far and wide over the world, because they produced an egg that was protected from the environment. The reptile egg, in brief, is enclosed by a shell within which the developing embryo is bathed in fluids. One can say that the embryo lives in a sort of little pond of its own, in the dark world within the shelled egg. Then when the baby reptile breaks out of the crypt where life began, it appears as a miniature of its parents, ready to make a living in a strange and hostile world.

The rise of reptiles from their amphibian ancestors did not immediately usher in an Age of Reptiles, because for some time there was keen competition between amphibians and reptiles for living space on the earth. When the first reptiles arose the amphibians were well established and many of them were rather large and to a degree aggressive, so that the early reptiles had to fight their way upward. But in time the advantages of the shelled egg, together with improvements in the individual for life on dry land, did tell, and the reptiles came into their own.

The Age of Reptiles began something more than two hundred million years ago, and it continued until about seventy million years ago. It was a long and successful reign; in many respects the most spectacular phase of life history. It was the age when, through much of its extent, the dinosaurs ruled the land. And it came to an end only when the great dinosaurs and other large reptiles that lived with them became extinct. Since that event the world has been dominated by the mammals, and within the past few hundred thousand years one mammal, man, has established himself as the master of the globe. The Age of Mammals has recently passed, and we are living in the Age of Man. Being men we can do something that no animals in the past have been able to do: we can look forward and we can look back. We can look back to the Age of Reptiles.

Such a backward glance leads us through great expanses of geologic time. But how can one look back through the corridors of the years to long vanished ages, back to the Age of Reptiles and beyond?

Early in the last century one of the pioneers of geology, William Smith, an English surveyor, established the principle that each particular stratum of sedimentary rocks – of sandstones, shales or limestones – has enclosed within it (if it is fossiliferous) fossils that are distinctive for that layer. The sediments of the earth are piled up, one on top of another, in a great succession that records their deposition on the bottoms of shallow seas and ocean basins, in lakes, ponds, streams, and rivers, in the dunes of deserts or as the debris of glaciers.

It is obvious that the oldest sediments are at the bottom of this grand sequence, and that successively younger sediments follow in order. It is also obvious that the fossils in these sediments show a progression from oldest to youngest, and hence a record of the progression of life through the ages.

Of course it isn't nearly as simple as these few sentences might indicate. The story of earth history as recorded by rocks and fossils is incredibly complex, with parts missing at various places over the globe, with other parts confused by the processes of earth movements, by the upwelling of volcanoes and by other earth forces – in short with countless interruptions, modifications and the like that have taken place during millions of years of time. But as a result of long explorations and studies in field and laboratory, students of earth history have been able to put together many facts to make a reasonably orderly story. They have been able to draw up a table of geologic time, in which a sequence of periods has been established, each distinguished by its fossils, as well as by indications in the rocks of the physical events that took place while these rocks were being formed.

The table of geologic time is simply presented in Table 1. A few explanations are necessary.

The three eras in the Table are named on the basis of the general aspects of life through time: Paleozoic, ancient life; Mesozoic, middle life; Cenozoic, recent life. Geologic history before the fossil record has also been subdivided into several eras, but it is common practice to call this long early phase Precambrian time, and for the purposes of our book such usage is quite sufficient.

The periods within each era are named after regions where they were first studied, or according to attributes of their sediments. Cambria is the ancient name for Wales, where rocks of this age were first defined. The Ordovices and Silures were prehistoric tribes of southern Britain, inhabiting the regions where rocks of this age were originally studied. Devonian is named after Devonshire. Carboniferous, the term used by most European geologists, refers to the great carbon or coal deposits that typify these rocks. Mississippian

Table 1. *Geologic time* *

(To be read from the bottom up)

ERA	PERIOD	DURATION (IN MILLIONS OF YEARS)	TIME SCALE (IN MILLIONS OF YEARS)	
Cenozoic	Quaternary Tertiary	1 69	1 70	The Age of Mammals
Mesozoic	Cretaceous Jurassic Triassic	65 45 35	135 180 215	The Age of Reptiles
Paleozoic	Permian	45	260	
	Carboniferous*	80	340	The Age of Amphibians
	Devonian	50	390	The Age of Early Fishes
	Silurian	40	430	
	Ordovician	60	490	The Age of Invertebrates
	Cambrian	100	590	
Precambrian time—a span of several thousand million years				

* North American geologists recognize two periods here, the earlier one being the Mississippian, of about thirty-five million years duration, the later one being the Pennsylvanian, of about forty-five million years.

and Pennsylvanian, used by North American geologists, refer to the regions where these rocks are most completely exposed. Permian is from the district of Perm in northern Russia. Triassic refers to the threefold division of rocks of this age first recognized in central Europe. Jurassic comes from the Jura mountains in the Alps. Cretaceous is from the Latin *creta*, meaning chalk, a reference to the cliffs of southern England. Tertiary is based on an old classification of rocks, of which these are the third part. Quaternary similarly refers to an original fourth division of geologic history. These last two terms are retained for convenience, whereas the correlative terms originally used for earlier divisions of geologic time, the Primary and

5

*See 'Page Corrections and Emendations' and 'Tables and Diagrams' in Addendum.

Secondary, have long since been abandoned. All of which goes to show that man tries, but never quite succeeds, to be completely logical.

The duration of the various periods as shown in the Table are based upon careful studies made within the past few decades on radioactive elements. It is known, for example, that certain elements, such as uranium, break down through time, the end product of this process being lead. The rate of decay is known. By comparing in selected rocks, fortunately discovered at various levels through the geologic column, the ratios of radioactive elements and the end products, it is possible to reach figures that express with what is thought to be a considerable degree of accuracy the age of the rocks in years. On these studies our modern ideas about the duration of geologic time have been established and generally agreed upon.

As for the Ages shown in the chart, these are rather informal designations to indicate the types of animals that were generally dominant during the geologic periods to which the names apply. They are not to be taken too seriously, but they are useful.

For the purposes of this book the Age of Reptiles will be regarded as consisting of the Permian period, at the close of the Paleozoic era, and the Triassic, Jurassic and Cretaceous periods, making up the Mesozoic era. This is somewhat at variance with common geologic practice, which assigns only the three Mesozoic periods to the Age of Reptiles, thus making a neat coincidence of ages with the major geologic time divisions. Certainly such an orderly arrangement is very convenient to those interested in the large dimensions of earth history; but if we are to be concerned with the time when reptiles were truly dominant on the earth, we must include the Permian period within our Age of Reptiles.

This Age, so far as it concerns the evolutionary history of reptiles and amphibians, is readily divisible into two definite stages. The first of these, consisting of the Permian and Triassic periods, was the time when lands were ruled by large amphibians belonging to a group known as the labyrinthodonts, by primitive groups of reptiles, and by the mammal-like reptiles, which appeared very early in reptilian history. At the close of this Permian–Triassic stage of life history the labyrinthodonts, the primitive reptiles and the mammal-like reptiles became extinct. So it was that the second stage of the Age of Reptiles, composed of the Jurassic and Cretaceous periods, began, and new groups, most of them originating during the latter part of the Triassic period, became dominant on land and sea. These were the frogs, the various archosaurs, consisting of thecodonts, dinosaurs, crocodilians and flying reptiles, the turtles, lizards and snakes, the marine ichthyosaurs and plesiosaurs, and the primitive birds and mammals. Thus, instead of looking at the Age of Reptiles as a straight succession of four periods, Permian–Triassic–Jurassic–Cretaceous, we may look at it as a divided succession: Permian–Triassic/Jurassic–Cretaceous. If so regarded, the history of the tetrapods living during these several periods of earth history will take on a new significance.

Such is the setting of time within which our story takes place. Now let us become acquainted with the principal characters of the story, the reptiles, and the ancient amphibians, birds and mammals who were their contemporaries. What are reptiles? And what are these other groups of animals? In the first place, they are all tetrapods, a word which means 'four feet'. These are the backboned animals with a basic common inheritance of four legs (although in some of them the legs may be variously transformed into wings, or paddles, or they may even be lost) and lungs. They are the animals primarily adapted for life on the land, in other words the backboned animals other than fishes.

One way to compare modern tetrapods is on the basis of their body temperatures. Among the amphibians and reptiles there are no internal physiological mechanisms to regulate temperatures, so that the body heat in these animals varies more or less directly as does the temperature of the environment. Consequently the amphibians and the reptiles are often thought of as being ectothermic or 'cold-blooded' tetrapods, capable of continued activity only in warm or mild climates. In contrast the birds and the mammals, which are often designated as being endothermic or 'warm-blooded' tetrapods, do have internal physiological controls of their body temperatures, so that these temperatures remain more or less constant, however environmental temperatures may fluctuate. This distinction between the amphibians and the reptiles on the one hand, and the birds and mammals on the other, reflects something of their origins and past histories, for the amphibians and reptiles arose during Paleozoic time and retained their primitive lack of bodily temperature controls, whereas the birds and mammals arose from certain reptiles during Mesozoic times, and in the course of their evolutionary origins became endothermic animals.

If one compares reptiles downwardly with amphibians a crucial

7

difference between them, namely their different modes of reproduction, is at once apparent. As has been shown, the amphibians lay an unprotected egg and go through a tadpole stage in the water, whereas the reptiles, having lost this ancient tie with the ultimate fish ancestors of all land-living tetrapods, lay an egg protected by a shell, thus freeing them completely from dependence on water for continuation of the species. The distinction between the two groups on this basis

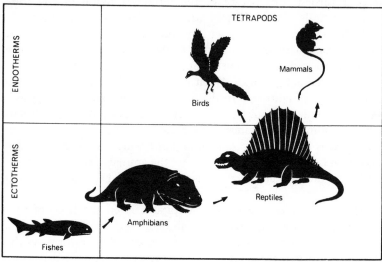

Figure 1. The classes of vertebrates.

is quite clear, but when we look at the diagnostic features of amphibians and reptiles as delineated by anatomical structure, which is necessary when studying the fossils, it is not easy to draw sharp boundaries between primitive reptiles and their amphibian ancestors. The emergence of the reptiles from their amphibian forebears was a gradual process, and as is so often the case when we have a rather good fossil record, the lines of demarcation between the groups tend to be rather fuzzy and ill-defined. The modern wanderer in field and woodland has no difficulty in distinguishing a frog from a snake, but the student of fossils does not always find it easy to separate early reptiles from their amphibian cousins.

In general terms, the reptile is more 'advanced' than the amphibian, which does not tell us much. Both are tetrapods, which means that they are basically animals that walk on four legs. Any departure from this mode of progression is a specialization. In a general way the reptile skeleton is more adequately developed for life on the land than the amphibian skeleton; the bones are on the whole more elegantly formed, and the joints between them are more efficiently arranged. One can usually see in comparing a reptile skeleton with an amphibian skeleton that the former could operate to better advantage than the latter, not only because of the superior bone forms and articulations but also because of the arrangement of the muscles in the reptile.

This greater efficiency of reptile over amphibian is exemplified by the trend toward consolidation and reduction of bones in the reptile skeleton as compared with the amphibian skeleton. This is particularly apparent in the skull, where it is advantageous to have a well-integrated structure for the protection of the brain and as a base for the operation of the jaws. It is also apparent in the feet, which in the reptile are more compact than those of the amphibian. To a considerable degree it is apparent in the backbone, the flexible girder from which the body is suspended. Here one can point to a very definite difference. In the ancient amphibians there is a single vertebra connected to the upper bones of the pelvis; in the most primitive of reptiles there are two, and in many reptiles there are more. This affords the reptiles an expanded connection between hind limbs and skeleton, a character of prime importance during the course of their evolution.

Both reptiles and amphibians have lowly brains, but the reptilian brain is proportionately larger and more advanced than the brain of the amphibian. This indicates a better degree of nervous control and co-ordination in reptile than in amphibian, again a matter of great importance in evolution.

Since these animals have no internal control of the body temperature, they have no external insulation for the conservation of heat as do the birds with their feathers and the mammals with their hair. So it is that amphibians and reptiles have naked skins, or are covered with scales or plates of various types.

If one compares modern reptiles upwardly with birds and mammals, the difference of ectothermy and endothermy, of cold-bloodedness and warm-bloodedness, is immediately apparent. But again when we look at the fossils and contrast them by their anatomical characters the lines of distinction become as vague as those between reptiles and amphibians. Birds and mammals arose from reptilian ancestors during Mesozoic times, and the fossils show this transition.

Consequently the most primitive birds are very close to their reptilian ancestors, and likewise primitive mammals resemble in many features the advanced mammal-like reptiles.

In general terms, the birds and mammals are more 'advanced' than reptiles, one indication of this being in the perfection of bone articulations among these warm-blooded tetrapods as compared with those of the reptiles. Just as the reptilian skeleton shows consolidation and reduction of bones as compared with the primitive amphibian skeleton, so do the bird and mammal skeletons show further consolidation and reduction of bones as compared with the reptile skeleton. Such advances are particularly well exemplified in the skull and in the feet. In birds and mammals, moreover, the connection between the backbone and the pelvis is much more expanded than in all but a few specialized reptiles. The bird brain and the mammalian brain is in each case developed beyond the reptilian brain, and in each case along different lines. Finally, birds and mammals are very active animals as compared with reptiles because of their relatively constant body temperatures and their resultant high degree of energy and physiological efficiency[*].

So much for the four great groups or classes of tetrapods. These are the animals, and among them in particular the reptiles, with which we will be dealing in the pages that follow. But discussions of the reptiles and the associated tetrapods living with them during the Age of Reptiles must be concerned with more than the primary divisions or classes. It is necessary to turn our attention to the lesser groups, and the detail with which the subject is to be considered depends to a large degree upon just how willing we are to follow down and down through the lesser categories of zoological classification. There is much to be learned from the fossils, down to genera and to species, and even to individual specimens, but if this account of the Age of Reptiles were to be carried to such detail it would stretch out to prodigious lengths and would be a monograph, not a book. Obviously only the larger categories of reptiles and other Paleozoic and Mesozoic tetrapods can be treated here. So let us examine the pertinent orders and other large groups of amphibians, reptiles, birds and mammals, to build a framework for the treatment of their various development through two hundred million years of time. If the broad features and relationships of these groups can be kept in mind, the descriptions and discussions pertaining to individual forms (genera for example) will fall into place and have some meaning.

[*]See 'Page Corrections and Emendations' in Addendum.

The remarks in the preceding paragraph touching upon the classification of tetrapods that lived during the Age of Reptiles have indeed been fleeting and informal. Therefore, before proceeding further, a digression may be made to consider a few important aspects of classification, a subject that is basic to our proper understanding and appreciation of the animals that will be described in the pages of this book.

Taxonomy – the classification of animals and plants – is supposed by many modern biologists to be a tedious and indeed a sterile field of endeavor. This is not at all true. Within the past two or three decades there has been developed a movement toward a dynamic approach to taxonomy, a treatment of the subject which includes diverse disciplines. Thus modern taxonomy is in part anatomical, in part evolutionary, in part genetic, in part behavioral, and in part other things as well. It is a subject that comes alive when approached and practised in this way. It makes animals and plants meaningful – not merely laboratory exercises in systematics or cell structure chemistry or other isolated disciplines. It brings a theme of unity into the great, diverse world of living things, past and present.

As perhaps most readers of this book know, our modern concept of animal and plant relationships goes back to the great Swedish naturalist, Carl von Linné, commonly known as Linnaeus, who lived in the eighteenth century. Linnaeus was a great scholar, primarily a botanist, who studied life assiduously in the field and in the laboratory, so that in time he possessed for that day and age an encyclopedic knowledge of plants and animals. He realized that if animals and plants were to be properly classified they could no longer be designated by single common names, such names being different in every language. So he devised the binominal system of naming organisms, whereby every species has its own specific or trivial name, and in addition a more inclusive or generic name. It is something like the forename and family name by which we are all known. Except that according to the binominal system the name expressing the larger relationships of the organism, the generic name (the name of the genus), comes first and is begun with a capital letter, whereas the trivial name expressing the specific relationships of the organism comes second and contains no capital letters. Both names are commonly italicized.

A species is a population of interbreeding organisms, the individual members of which do not cross in Nature with those of any other species. The species is designated by its binominal, its generic and trivial names. Thus *Equus* (the genus) *caballus* (the species) is the horse. *Canis familiaris* is the dog.

Of course it is not possible to distinguish fossil species by any criterion of reproductive behavior among its individual members. Such species must be distinguished almost entirely on their morphological characters (indeed, in practice most recent species are identified in this way) and their definitions are often rather subjective. In general discussions of fossil animals and plants it usually suffices to carry distinctions down no farther than the genera, which has been done in this book.

Groups of related genera belong to higher categories – families, and families may in turn be grouped into orders. Orders belong to classes, and classes to phyla*. Here the progression has been carried from the lesser to the greater categories. To reverse the order, one of the reptiles that plays a part in our account of the Age of Reptiles may be classified in this way.

PHYLUM Chordata: animals with notochords or backbones.
  CLASS Reptilia: reptiles.
    ORDER Saurischia: one group of dinosaurs.
      FAMILY Deinodontidae: large carnivorous saurischians.
        GENUS *Tyrannosaurus*: a deinodont of late Cretaceous age.
          SPECIES *rex*: the tyrannosaur found in the upper Cretaceous beds of Montana.

To return now to the consideration of late Paleozoic and Mesozoic tetrapods, we may first look at the early amphibians, descended from fish ancestors during the transition from Devonian to later Paleozoic times. These earliest amphibians, known as labyrinthodonts because of the labyrinthine pattern of the enamel in the teeth, were the progenitors of a very long and successful evolutionary line, continuing from this ancient origin to the end of the Triassic period, a span of more than one hundred million years[†]. These were clumsy tetrapods, to put it briefly, with rather heavy bodies, short, stubby legs, and solid skulls pierced only by the openings for the eyes, the nostrils and a single median orifice, the parietal or pineal opening, which housed

* Usually it is often necessary in detailed classifications to use additional, intermediate categories, such as subfamilies and superfamilies, suborders and superorders, and subclasses.

[†]See 'Page Corrections and Emendations' in Addendum.

what was probably a light-sensitive organ during life. The vertebrae in these amphibians were originally composed of interlocking blocks

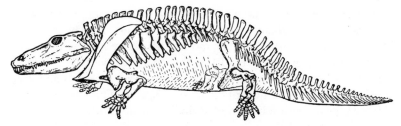

Figure 2. The skeleton of *Eryops*, a labyrinthodont amphibian of Permian age from Texas. Here we see a primitive tetrapod, about five feet long, with a large, solid skull, almost no neck, a rather undifferentiated backbone, heavy limb girdles, and sprawling limbs, the bones of which are relatively short and thick, the joints of which are comparatively crude. (From W. K. Gregory, 1951.)

and wedges; in some of the later labyrinthodonts these vertebrae became secondarily simplified. At an early stage in amphibian history a second large group arose from ancient labyrinthodont ancestors. This was the group of lepospondyls, with rather spool-shaped vertebrae, and also with solidly roofed skulls. The lepospondyls reached the height of their evolutionary history during the Permian period and then became extinct.

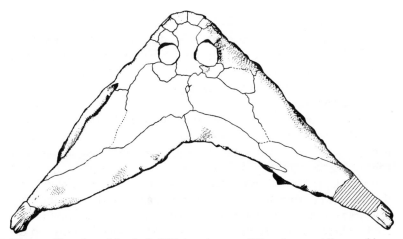

Figure 3. Top view of the skull of *Diplocaulus*, a small Permian nectridian amphibian from Texas. (From Olson, 1951.)

13

Modern frogs and toads, salamanders and tropical coecilians arose from some of these ancient amphibians, perhaps as separate lines of evolution.

The reptiles evolved much more widely and in more varied ways than did the amphibians, and their fossil remains may be classified within at least seventeen orders, most of which are now extinct. The most primitive order of reptiles is that of the cotylosaurs, derived during Carboniferous times from labyrinthodont ancestors and very much like the labyrinthodonts in many respects. These were heavy-limbed reptiles with solidly-roofed skulls and labyrinthine teeth. The

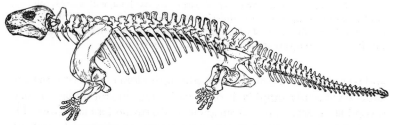

Figure 4. The skeleton of *Diadectes*, a Permian cotylosaurian reptile from Texas. In this early reptile, some six or eight feet in length, many of the primitive tetrapod features, so typical of the labyrinthodont amphibians, are still retained. Notice how the several characters listed for *Eryops* in Figure 2 generally apply to the skeleton of *Diadectes*. (From W. K. Gregory, 1951.)

turtles, which became well established during Triassic times, were seemingly directly derived from the cotylosaurs, and early became highly specialized by virtue of the protective shell and the loss of teeth in the jaws. Yet in many respects they retain various primitive cotylosaurian features:

The ichthyosaurs comprise an isolated order of reptiles ultimately derived from the cotylosaurs, of which the more immediate ancestry is as yet a mystery. These reptiles, appearing in Triassic times and continuing through the Cretaceous, were from the beginning of their history adapted for life in the oceans. The body was fish-like in form, the limbs were transformed into paddles, and the front of the skull was drawn out into a long snout, armed with numerous labyrinthine teeth. There was an opening, known as the temporal fenestra, on the top of the skull, on each side behind the eye, that allowed for bulging of strong jaw muscles. This increased the efficiency of the bite.

Another, and never a very numerous group were the protorosaurs, which were essentially Permian and Triassic reptiles that evolved in many different directions. They preceded the lizards, and perhaps

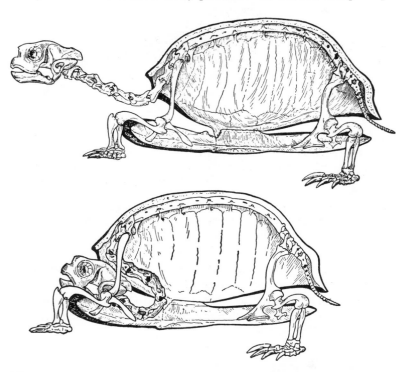

Figure 5. A turtle skeleton, showing (above) the neck extended, and (below) retracted. The articulations of the neck vertebrae are specialized to allow for extreme flexion. Notice the reduction in number of the vertebrae in the back, and the expansion of the ribs, *outside* the limb girdles, as long, flattened plates, which, joined together, help to form the carapace or upper shell (From W. K. Gregory, 1951.)

occupied the ecological niches in their days that the lizards were to fill later on. These were generally small and slender reptiles. They, too, had a single upper opening (different in origin from that of the ichthyosaurs) on each side of the skull behind the eye, as an accommodation for the jaw muscles.

From terrestrial protorosaurian ancestors the marine sauropterygians arose. These were the nothosaurs and placodonts of Triassic age, and the plesiosaurs which ranged through much of Mesozoic time. The limbs were large paddles, used to row the animal along the surface of the water. The neck was often long and sinuous, the skull

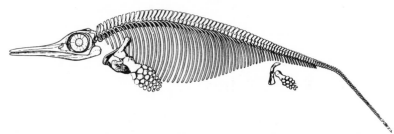

Figure 6. Jurassic ichthyosaur from Europe. Here we see extreme specialization for life in the open ocean, in a ten-foot long reptile that is nicely streamlined, as is a fish or a porpoise, for fast swimming. The jaws are elongated and set with many teeth for catching fish. The eye is very large, for seeing in the dim light beneath the waves. The limbs are balancing and control paddles, while the flexible backbone, the posterior part of which is turned down to support the lower lobe of the tail, was, in association with powerful muscles, the principal propulsive mechanism of this reptile. (From Andrews, 1910.)

either elongated or quite small. In these reptiles, as in their ancestors, there were upper openings in the skull.

During the Permian period there appeared some small reptiles, the eosuchians, in which the skull was rather deep, and was characterized

Figure 7. The Triassic protorosaur, *Trilophosaurus*, from Texas. This reptile, six or eight feet in length, probably occupied a position in the ecology of its environment similar to that now taken by the very large lizards. (From J. T. Gregory, 1945.)

by two openings on each side behind the eye, one on the top of the skull, one on the side. From this ancestry various orders of two-arched or diapsid reptiles with two temporal openings in the skull arose, to dominate the Mesozoic scene. The rhynchocephalians, represented today by the tuatera of New Zealand, appeared during the Triassic period, as did the first lizards. The lizards, belonging to the order Squamata, were the ancestors of the snakes, also belonging to this same order. Another reptilian order that arose during the Triassic period was the thecodonts, the first of a group of related reptilian

Figure 8. The Jurassic plesiosaur, *Muraenosaurus*, a marine reptile about fifteen or twenty feet in length, from England. The adaptations of the plesiosaurs for life in the ocean were quite different from those of the ichthyosaurs (seen in Figure 6). The large limbs are paddles, with which the animal rowed itself along or near the surface of the water. The neck is long and flexible and the jaws bear long, sharp teeth, all in all a good fish-catching device. (From Andrews, 1910.)

orders, collectively known as the archosaurs. The thecodonts evolved as pseudosuchians, a varied group of reptiles, some large, some small, and as the phytosaurs, uniformly large, crocodilian-like animals. All thecodonts became extinct at the end of the Triassic period.

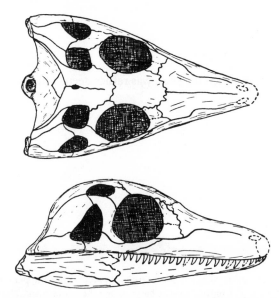

Figure 9. The skull of *Youngoides*, a very small Permian diapsid reptile from South Africa. Note the superior and lateral temporal openings behind the eye, to allow for the bulging and increased power and efficiency of the jaw muscles. Top view above, side view below. (From Olson and Broom, 1937.)

17

Figure 10. *Staganolepis*, a Triassic thecodont, from England. This is one of the early archosaurian reptiles, a member of the large assemblage of two-arched reptiles that dominated the Mesozoic continents. The body of this reptile, about nine feet long, was protected by heavy bony plates (not shown here) these in life being covered with thick, horny skin. Armor is characteristic of the thecodont reptiles. (From Walker, 1961.)

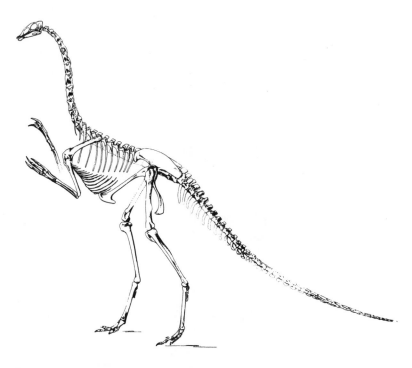

Figure 11. The saurischian dinosaur, *Ornithomimus*, from the upper Cretaceous of North America. The bipedal pose is basic among the saurischians. Note the pelvis, with the pubic bone extending forward, a diagnostic character for these dinosaurs. The slender, well-articulated bones and the long hind limbs indicate that this was an active, fast-running reptile. The skeleton is about fifteen feet in length. (From Osborn, 1917.)

But from certain small, hollow-boned pseudosuchian thecodonts, reptiles which walked on strong hind legs, and in which the small front legs were used like arms and hands, there arose in late Triassic time the saurischian dinosaurs. These dinosaurs, characterized by

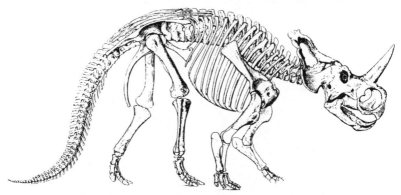

Figure 12. The North American ornithischian dinosaur, *Monoclonius*, of Cretaceous age. Note the pelvis, with the pubis (the shaft here greatly reduced) running back parallel with the ischium, which is diagnostic for the ornithischians. The front part of the pubis is much enlarged, and extends forward. The quadrupedal pose is secondary. A ponderous reptile, some eighteen feet long. (From Brown, 1917.)

the forwardly pointed, often rod-like pubic bone in the pelvis, evolved during the Mesozoic as the numerous theropod or meat-eating dinosaurs, retaining the ancestral bipedal pose, and as the gigantic, swamp-dwelling sauropods, secondarily quadrupedal. The ornithis-

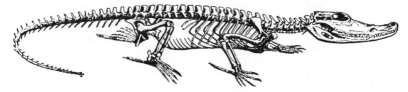

Figure 13. The skeleton of a modern alligator, one member of the order Crocodilia, the closest living relatives of the dinosaurs. (From Reese, 1915.)

chian dinosaurs, in which the rod-like pubic bone of the pelvis had rotated backwardly to run parallel to the ischium, also a rod-like element, were, like their saurischian cousins, of late Triassic origin. These dinosaurs radiated along several lines of evolution – as the bipedal camptosaurs, iguanodonts and hadrosaurs, or ornithopods, as the plated stegosaurs, as the armored ankylosaurs and as the horned ceratopsians, these last-named groups again secondarily quadrupedal.

Another order of archosaurs, the crocodilians, appeared during the transition from Triassic to Jurassic time and have continued successfully to the present day. These familiar reptiles need no further description here.

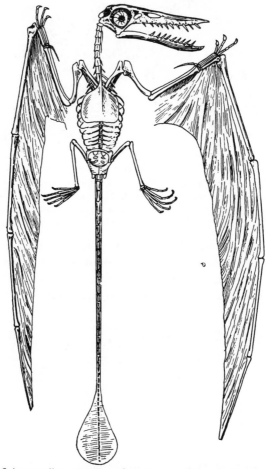

Figure 14. A flying reptile or pterosaur from Europe, *Rhamphorhynchus*, of Jurassic age. The greatly elongated fourth finger of the hand was the support in life for a wing membrane. Note the weak hind limbs – the pterosaurs, like modern bats, were probably rather helpless on the ground. About eighteen inches long. (From W. K. Gregory, 1951.)

Finally, among the archosaurs there were the pterosaurs or flying reptiles, appearing at the beginning of the Jurassic, and continuing through the Cretaceous period[*]. These were lightly built, hollow-boned reptiles, in which the front limbs were modified as wings.

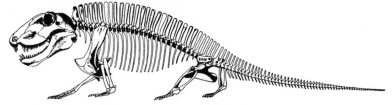

Figure 15. A Permian pelycosaur, *Sphenacodon*, from New Mexico, the skeleton of which is some ten feet in length. This is an early member of the evolutionary line that was to lead eventually to the mammals. Even at this stage we see some beginnings of differentiation in the dentition. Note the elongation of the spines of the vertebrae, a specialization that reached extremes in some of the other pelycosaurs. (From Romer and Price, 1940.)

One other group of reptilian orders of great evolutionary importance was characterized by deep skulls with a single temporal opening on each side behind the eye. Of these the pelycosaurs appeared in the

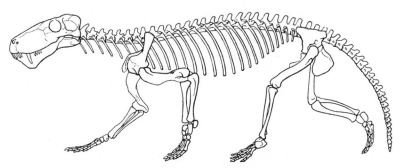

Figure 16. A mammal-like reptile, *Lycaenops*, about the size of a large dog, from the Permian of South Africa. The trend toward the mammals is clearly shown by the enlarged temporal opening on the side of the skull, by the differentiation of the teeth as incisors, a canine and post-canines, and by the pulling in of the limbs, so that the feet are close to the midline, beneath the body. (From Colbert, 1948.)

Carboniferous and continued through much of Permian history, along varied lines of evolution. From the pelycosaurs there arose the therapsids or mammal-like reptiles, living in Permian and Triassic times. In some of these reptiles a close approach was made in many

21

[*]See 'Page Corrections and Emendations' in Addendum.

aspects of the anatomy to the mammals, of which the therapsids were the ancestors. It seems probable that the advanced therapsids may have attained a certain degree of endothermy or warm-bloodedness, and that they may have had other mammalian attributes, such as hair and external ears.

Within the therapsids there arose the most mammal-like of the reptiles, the ictidosaurs. These reptiles, of Triassic age, all of them small, were very close indeed to the mammalian threshold.

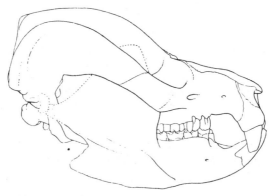

Figure 17. The skull of *Bienotherium*, a tritylodont reptile from the Triassic of western China, that shows many advanced mammal-like characters. The development of the skull, showing coalescence and reduction of bones, a large temporal opening confluent with the eye opening, a single opening for the external nostrils, the dominance of the dentary bone of the lower jaw, and the extreme reduction of the old reptilian jaw hinge, composed of the quadrate and articular bones, along with other features, indicate very clearly the close approach of *Bienotherium* to the mammalian threshhold. Perhaps this animal was warm blooded and had hair. Perhaps it had external ears, as do the mammals. (From Young, 1947.)

The first bird, of Jurassic age, was essentially a reptile, probably of thecodont ancestry, with feathers. And in a sense all modern birds are feathered reptiles, as is quite evident from the structure of the skeleton. Evolution in the birds was a matter of specializations in some parts of the skeleton beyond the reptilian condition, the loss of teeth, the perfection of the feathers, and of course various high specializations in physiology and behavior.

Among the advanced therapsid reptiles there was strong differentiation of the teeth, so that instead of being all more or less alike, as is common among reptiles, they were specialized into nipping incisors, piercing canines, and crushing or biting cheek teeth. The differentiation of the teeth is nicely shown in the earliest mammals of Jurassic and Cretaceous age. Indeed, the fossils of these archaic mammals,

Figure 18. The skeleton of *Archaeopteryx*, the first bird, of Jurassic age, with the skeleton of a pigeon, to which it is comparable in size. Although *Archaeopteryx* was a bird, as is indicated by the imprints of feathers found with the skeletons in the Solnhofen limestone of southern Germany, it retained various archosaurian characters, such as teeth in the jaws, and a long, bony tail. It is an almost ideal intermediate form between two great classes of vertebrates. (From Heilmann, 1927.)

23

which lived during the days when dinosaurs were dominant, consist for the most part of tiny jaws and teeth, and, as is shown by these fossils, the lines of mammalian evolution were diverse. The middle and late Mesozoic years were, one might say, a time of experimentation in the evolution of the mammals.

Among the orders of Mesozoic mammals were the multituberculates, in which some of the cheek teeth were long, with many rows of cusps, perhaps for grinding or cutting food, rodent-fashion. There were the triconodonts, in which each cheek tooth was composed of a central pointed cusp, with a small cusp in front and one behind it, all on a line. There were also the symmetrodonts, in which the cheek

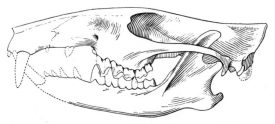

Figure 19. The skull of a Cretaceous placental mammal, *Zalambdalestes*, from Mongolia. This tiny mammal, contemporaneous with the great dinosaurs, is related to the modern shrews and Old World hedgehogs. (From Simpson, 1928.)

teeth were tricuspid, the cusps being arranged in triangles which opposed each other in upper and lower jaws. In the pantotheres there were not only high triangles of cusps in each cheek tooth, but a strong inner extension of each upper tooth, and a sort of basin behind the triangle in each lower tooth, to receive the inner cusp of the upper tooth – a sort of mortar and pestle arrangement. The pantotheres were obviously ancestral to the opossum-like mammals, the marsupials, and to the most primitive placental mammals, ancestral shrews and hedgehogs, or insectivores, all appearing in Cretaceous sediments. There is no record in the Mesozoic of monotremes, represented today in Australia and New Guinea by the platypus and the echidnas, but it seems very likely that these mammals also were then living. They are exceedingly primitive mammals, possessed of numerous reptilian features.

These are some of the general characters of the animals with which we will be concerned, and from this broad base of characterizations we will follow the reptiles and contemporaneous tetrapods through the long years of late Paleozoic and Mesozoic time, to see them evolve along very particular lines, producing in the process a tremendous range of specializations in the skull, teeth and skeleton, and, as interpreted from these hard parts, in musculature, physiology and habits.

The interrelationships of the various tetrapod orders and their subordinate higher groups that have been briefly described in the preceding paragraphs will perhaps be more readily understood if they are brought together in a simple outline classification. In this way the grades in the hierarchy of tetrapod classification are set down contiguous to each other and may thus be compared. Moreover, such a tabulation should serve as a handy reference for the reader who may occasionally find himself lost among the battalions, companies and platoons of ancient tetrapods that will parade through subsequent pages of this book.

PHYLUM Chordata: animals with an internal support along the back.
SUBPHYLUM Vertebrata: support formed by vertebrae.
CLASS Amphibia: tetrapods showing metamorphosis during development.
SUBCLASS Apsidospondyli: vertebrae preformed in cartilage.
SUPERORDER Labyrinthodontia: solid-skulled amphibians.
ORDER Ichthyostegalia: ancestral labyrinthodonts, Devonian and Carboniferous.
ORDER Rhachitomi: the dominant labyrinthodonts, Carboniferous and Permian.
ORDER Embolomeri: evolving toward reptiles, Carboniferous and Permian.
ORDER Stereospondyli: last of the labyrinthodonts, Triassic.
SUPERORDER Salientia: frogs, toads, and their ancestors.
ORDER Eoanura: the beginning of salientian evolution, Carboniferous.
ORDER Proanura: possible ancestors of the frogs and toads, Triassic.
ORDER Anura: frogs and toads, Jurassic to Recent.
SUBCLASS Lepospondyli: vertebrae not preformed in cartilage.
ORDER Aistopoda: limbless lepospondyls, Carboniferous.
ORDER Nectridia: varied lepospondyls, Carboniferous and Permian.

ORDER Microsauria: small lepospondyls, Carboniferous and Permian.

ORDER Urodela: salamanders and newts, Cretaceous to Recent.

ORDER Apoda: tropical limbless amphibians, Recent.

CLASS Reptilia: tetrapods in which development is direct.

SUBCLASS Anapsida: reptiles with solid skull roofs.

ORDER Cotylosauria: stem reptiles, Carboniferous through Triassic.

ORDER Chelonia: turtles and their ancestors, Permian to Recent.

Of uncertain relationships

ORDER Mesosauria: ancient aquatic reptiles, Permian.

SUBCLASS Parapsida: marine reptiles, with upper openings in the skull behind the eyes.

ORDER Ichthyosauria: fish-like reptiles, Triassic through Cretaceous.

SUBCLASS Euryapsida: mostly marine reptiles, with upper openings in the skull (different from the parapsids) behind the eyes.

ORDER Protorosauria: varied, land-living types, Permian and Triassic.

ORDER Sauropterygia: the marine placodonts, nothosaurs and plesiosaurs, Triassic through Cretaceous.

SUBCLASS Diapsida: the ruling reptiles of the Mesozoic with both upper and lateral openings in the skull, behind the eyes.

SUPERORDER Lepidosauria: Primitive diapsids and their descendants.

ORDER Eosuchia: ancestral diapsids, Permian and Triassic.

ORDER Rhynchocephalia: the rhynchocephalians, Triassic to Recent.

ORDER Squamata: lizards and snakes, Triassic to Recent.

SUPERORDER Archosauria: advanced diapsids.

ORDER Thecodontia: ancestral archosaurians, Triassic.

ORDER Crocodilia: crocodilians, Triassic to Recent.

ORDER Pterosauria: flying reptiles, Jurassic and Cretaceous.

ORDER Saurischia: saurischian dinosaurs, Triassic through Cretaceous.

ORDER Ornithischia: ornithischian dinosaurs, Triassic through Cretaceous.

SUBCLASS Synapsida: the mammal-like reptiles, with lateral openings in the skull behind the eyes.

ORDER Pelycosauria: early mammal-like reptiles, Carboniferous and Permian.

ORDER Therapsida: advanced mammal-like reptiles, Permian and Triassic.

CLASS Aves: feathered tetrapods.

SUBCLASS Archaeornithes: primitive, toothed birds.

ORDER Archaeopteryges: *Archaeopteryx*, Jurassic.

SUBCLASS Neornithes: advanced, fully adapted birds.

ORDER Hesperornithes: ancient aquatic birds, Cretaceous.

ORDER Ichthyornithes: early flying birds, Cretaceous.

(The remaining orders of birds are of post-Cretaceous age, and do not concern us.)

CLASS Mammalia: tetrapods with hair, that suckle their young.

SUBCLASS Allotheria: early, specialized mammals.

ORDER Multituberculata: with multicuspidate cheek teeth, Jurassic through Paleocene.

SUBCLASS uncertain.

ORDER Triconodonta: triconodonts, Jurassic.

SUBCLASS Theria: most of the mammals.

INFRACLASS Pantotheria: early therians.

ORDER Pantotheria: ancestors of the marsupials and placentals, Jurassic.

ORDER Symmetrondonta: symmetrodonts, Jurassic.

INFRACLASS Metatheria: the marsupials.

ORDER Marsupialia: the pouched mammals, Cretaceous to Recent.

INFRACLASS Eutheria: the placental mammals.

ORDER Insectivora: the most primitive placental mammals, Cretaceous to Recent.

(Most of the remaining orders of mammals are of post-Cretaceous age, and do not concern us.)

The words 'hard parts' are of particular significance in what has been written on page 25, because it is from the fossils that we get our

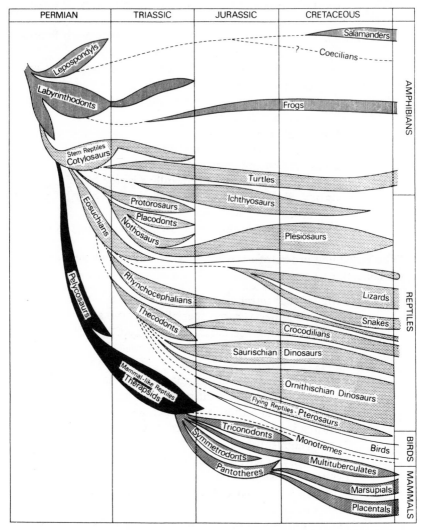

Figure 20. A phylogeny of the late Paleozoic and Mesozoic tetrapods[*].

information about life in the past. Fossils are the remains or indications of extinct life on the earth. They commonly occur through the deposition of minerals from infiltrating ground waters in the minute

[*]See 'Tables and Diagrams' in Addendum.

pores of bones, shells, wood and other such relatively hard structures that have been buried in marls, muds and sands accumulated in the bottoms of seas, lakes, ponds, streams, rivers and occasionally even in dunes. In time such organic remains become very hard as a result of the accretion of mineral matter, and thus are petrified. They are then preserved through vast millennia in the sedimentary rocks of the earth, the limestones, shales and sandstones that have hardened from the original marls, muds and sands.

But fossils are not necessarily formed in this way. They may be the original bone, and occasionally may consist of skin, hair and soft internal organs. We need not here be concerned with such fossils, for these are commonly the remains of animals frozen in the ice in far northern latitudes, and are only a few thousand years in age. Some fossils may be thin films of carbon, left when the more volatile organic compounds have disappeared. Fossil leaves are commonly preserved in this fashion. Other fossils may be natural molds in the rock, left after the original fossil bone or shell or wood has been destroyed. Or they may be natural casts – the filling of such molds with mud or other material that eventually is hardened into stone.

Fossils are the indications, as well as the remains of former life on the earth, so they may be in the form of footprints, or fossilized eggs, or even pieces of fossilized dung, known as coprolites. They may be structures manufactured by ancient animals, nests and burrows, and such. The paleontologist is indeed confronted by an interesting variety of objects.

The sedimentary rocks which enclose fossils in such variety are found all over the world as sheets of limestone, shale and sandstone of diverse extent and thickness. Originally these were, of course, deposited as horizontal or nearly horizontal beds, by the waters of oceans and lakes, by river and stream currents, by wind, and even by glaciers. During the long history of the earth such sheets of sediments, eventually hardened into layers of rock, are commonly tilted, broken and distorted by immense earth forces – the forces that are usually manifested to us as earthquakes. Moreover, sedimentary rocks are frequently cut by volcanoes and long dikes of volcanic rock that push through them from below. Many sedimentary rocks are removed from the area which they formerly occupied by erosion. Consequently the interpretation of the sediments in which the fossils are contained is a complex and exacting discipline. But such

29

interpretation is of importance if the sequence of the fossils and the consequent evolutionary conclusions as based on this sequence are to be correctly understood. This is the study of stratigraphy, and it involves the correlation of sediments in different parts of a continent and in different parts of the world. Correlation depends primarily upon the restriction of particular fossils to particular sediments. The occurrence of similar or closely related fossils in sediments at two separated localities generally implies a similar or nearly similar age for the beds. By comparing back and forth, by making allowances for distortions of beds or the absence of beds and so on, the stratigrapher builds up a comprehensive picture of the succession of sediments the world over, and the succession of life contained within these sediments.

What has been said is, in a way, circular reasoning. The ages of sediments are determined by the fossils they contain. The evolutionary sequence of life as revealed by the fossils is determined by the succession of these fossils in the sediments. Think of it as a long accretion of knowledge. In the early years of geology, during the first part of the nineteenth century, students of earth history were concerned with establishing the proper sequence of rocks of the earth's crust. The succession of sediments could be observed in one particular locality, and the fossils characteristic of these sediments could be studied. It was all rather empirical, without any particular thought of an evolutionary sequence. Once the succession of sediments as identified by the contained fossils had been established in one part of the world this knowledge could be applied in another part of the world, the beds in the new area being compared and correlated so far as possible with those in the original region.

As the last century approached its middle years, and particularly as a result of the impact of Charles Darwin, the theory of evolution became established in the minds of men, and it was then apparent that the sequence of fossils in the sediments showed very clearly the way in which life has evolved through the immense span of geologic time. The fossil record forms cogent proof that evolution actually occurred in past ages.

Each sedimentary unit – a well-defined bed of limestone or sandstone or shale, or a combination of such beds which clearly comprise one cycle of deposition – is generally designated as a 'formation'. Each formation has a distinctive name, very commonly based upon the locality at which it was first delineated and described. Many

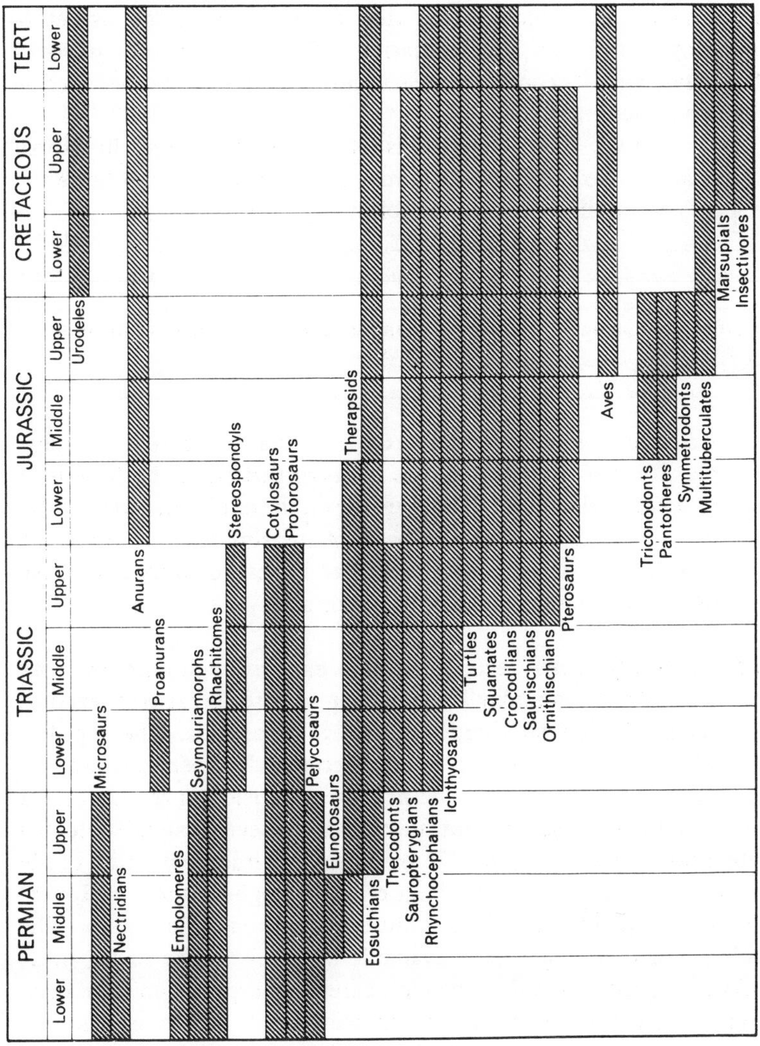

Figure 21. The duration through time of the orders of tetrapods that lived through the Age of Reptiles. The arrangement is not according to the relationships of the orders, but rather from left to right according to their first appearances in the geologic record.*

*See 'Tables and Diagrams' in Addendum.

formations, one following another, make up the rock record that defines a period of earth history. Thus the story is put together.

Of course, formations in different parts of the world will have different names, even though they may be of the same age, as determined by their fossils. The formation is the local expression of rocks of a certain age; its contained fossils correlate it with another formation in another region.

For example, three formations of late Jurassic age, in North America, Europe and East Africa may be correlated, in part upon the basis of certain dinosaurs, in the following manner.

NORTH AMERICA	EUROPE	AFRICA
Morrison formation *Apatosaurus* *Brachiosaurus*	Kimmeridge formation *Apatosaurus*	Tendaguru formation *Brachiosaurus*

The comparison is much more extensive than is apparent from this example. What is intended here is to show that since the Morrison may be correlated with the Kimmeridge on the one hand and with the Tendaguru on the other on the basis of the similarity of dinosaurs found in these sediments, it is therefore logical to think that these formations are of approximately the same age.

In summary, the fossil record that goes back through more than six hundred million years may be divided into three great eras, each of these being further subdivided into several periods. The reptiles, derived from amphibian ancestors, became dominant on land at the end of the Paleozoic era, the first great division in the history of life, and this dominance continued and was even extended to the water and the air during the Mesozoic era, the middle division of life history. They thus enjoyed a long reign throughout the world, persisting through a time span of about two hundred million years. The evidence of this long rule is available as fossils in the rocks, these rocks being sediments that through careful interpretation have been arranged and correlated on a world-wide basis. These are the elements from which our story is composed.

Chapter 2

Beginning of the Age of Reptiles

PICTURE, if you will, a tropical world in which the continents were rather low, and occupied by many sluggish rivers and broad swamps, with gentle rolling hills forming uplands which in some regions occupied the flanks of mountains – a world of vast green jungles of primitive plants, stretching mile after mile across the earth, from far northern latitudes to the southern tips of the antipodean land masses, and in which there was for the most part very little change from season to season as the earth swung around the sun in its annual orbit. This was the world of Carboniferous times, the habitat of the first land-living vertebrates or backboned animals. It was a world far removed from us in time because it existed some two hundred million years and more in the past, and it was a world far removed from us in appearance because it was filled with plants and animals most of which were quite different from any organisms living today.

Let us look at this Carboniferous world in a little more detail.

Perhaps the most enduring impression to be gained from such a view back through time would be of the richness of the vegetation, of the dense jungles and strange plants that would have been seen in all directions. This was the first great age of land plants, an age when trees quite unlike the trees of today's forests carried their branched and tufted crowns on the tops of straight, scaled trunks. These were the plants known as *Lepidodendron, Sigillaria, Cordaites* and *Calamites*, many of them growing to great size, some of them being one hundred feet or more in height. Among these large trees were giant tree ferns, adding to the variety of the ancient forest, and beneath was a heavy growth of ferns, mosses, hepaticas, lycopodes and other primitive plants. The scene was lush and verdant.

All of which was in great contrast to the preceding geological age, the Devonian period, when plants were very simple indeed, and formed but a sparse cover over the ancient lands of that distant time.

The evolution of plant life had been greatly accelerated in those last years preceding the advent of Carboniferous history; the relatively empty Devonian lands had offered wide opportunities for colonization by the various plants that were appearing for the first time, so that the vegetation spread and burgeoned accordingly. Thus the Carboniferous was a time of almost unprecedented vegetable luxuriance, a time when countless trees grew and died, when countless trunks and leaves were buried in wide swamps, gradually to be converted into the coal that we mine and burn today. For our modern culture depends very much on Carboniferous fossil fuels. The coal deposits, that occur in both hemispheres east and west and both hemispheres north and south, are perhaps an index of the extensive tropical climates so characteristic of middle Paleozoic history. They are a carbonaceous record of the spread of jungles that embraced wide ranges of latitude, all around the globe.

Evidently there was little of the marked zonation of climates extending on either side of the equator with which we are so familiar today. Consequently it must have been on the whole a rather uniform world, lacking those extremes of temperatures from the middle of the globe to the poles, which we accept as the normal condition. Actually strongly zoned climates with polar ice caps crowning the ends of the earth's axis are the exception rather than the rule in the long record of earth history, a point that will perhaps become evident during this account of the Age of Reptiles. Indeed, we are living in an atypical time so far as earth's climates are concerned.

And yet in spite of the great mass of geological evidence attesting the generally tropical environments of the Carboniferous world, there are glacially striated rocks and tillites – heterogeneous, unsorted deposits of glacial origin – in Africa, and likewise in peninsular India, Australia and South America, all indicating an interlude of very extensive glaciation (with, of course, accompanying frigid temperatures) in the southern hemisphere during this part of the Paleozoic era. The southern hemisphere glaciation, which had its inception during the Carboniferous period and which in some areas even extended into Permian times, was the last great glacial age before the Pleistocene ice age of the past million years, and its significance is a matter of much debate. By many geologists it is thought to be evidence of the former presence of these southern land masses near the South Pole, a matter that may be explained with facility if one invokes the principle of continental drift, which supposes that the continents at one time wandered from far distant positions to their present locations. Another explanation for this, the result of recent studies of magnetism in ancient rocks, is found in the growing feeling among some geologists that perhaps the poles themselves wandered widely during past geologic ages.

Although the southern continents evidently experienced glacial conditions for a time during the Carboniferous and early Permian periods, these effects evidently did not reach into northern lands, because the fossils of that age in North America and Eurasia seem to bespeak environments of tropical warmth. Even in the southern hemisphere the effects of glaciation were transitory, so that much of the Permian–Carboniferous record is likewise one of warm climates, tropical vegetation and cold-blooded vertebrates on the land.

One other aspect of the Carboniferous environment should be emphasized, namely that this was generally a time of low lands. Mention has been made of forests and swamps universally distributed during much of Carboniferous history, and it would appear as if these tangled and wet jungles were for the most part not much above sea level. This seemingly was not a time of extensive mountains, and although there undoubtedly were many hills and low ranges and even mountain uplifts in the central portions of the North American and European continents, very likely there were no elongated mountain chains extending for thousands of miles, such as the Andes or the Himalayas.

But let us proceed from this attempt to recreate the environments in which the Carboniferous animals lived to a consideration of the animals themselves.

The emergence of the backboned animals from their ancestral watery habitat to a life on the dry land took place, as we have seen, immediately before the beginning of Carboniferous times. In the final days of the Devonian period some very advanced, air-breathing fishes approached the threshold between fish and amphibian, and shortly and imperceptibly, almost, they were fishes no more. The paired fins were transformed into legs; the deep tail, though retaining something of its fish-like form, lost its primary function as a propelling organ; the skeleton in general became adapted for supporting the animal against the constant downward pull of gravity. The first amphibians had appeared.

These most ancient amphibians were the stem labyrinthodonts, clumsy and slow, but none the less very successful because they were the sole vertebrate pioneers on the land. From them, at an early stage in Carboniferous history, other amphibians arose, as well as the first cotylosaurian reptiles, these latter very much like their amphibian ancestors in many respects, but different in one crucial way – the method of reproduction. For a time there was close competition between Carboniferous amphibians and contemporaneous cotylosaurian reptiles, but in the end, and that end geologically speaking was

Figure 22. The tetrapod-like fish, *Eusthenopteron*, from eastern Canada, and the primitive amphibian, *Ichthyostega*, from Greenland, both of Devonian age. The beginning of the tetrapods.

not long in coming, the amphibians lost their position of dominance on the land.

At what time the amniote egg with its protective shell first appeared in the geologic record we do not know, and probably we never shall. But certainly we can be sure that the earliest reptiles, as they may be defined from the characters of their bones, were the producers of these specialized eggs.

Here was a great step forward in the evolutionary development of the backboned animals. From this point on the tetrapods were completely independent of the water; they were free to roam far and wide across the continents, and to them countless new environmental opportunities were opened.

Naturally, this one fact gave the early reptiles, which belong to the archaic cotylosaurs, a great advantage over the amphibians, even though structurally they were not so very different from the primitive labyrinthodonts. Consequently the amphibians soon lost their position as the only land-living vertebrates; they even lost their position as the dominant tetrapods. The reptiles had appeared to challenge this dominance well before the end of Carboniferous times.

As Carboniferous history reached its final stages the world was inhabited by three great classes of backboned animals – the fishes in the seas and in the rivers and lakes of the continents, the amphibians in and out of the continental waters, and the reptiles ranging widely across the continents. The stage had been set for the transition to Permian times – for the beginning of the Age of Reptiles.

The beginning of reptilian dominance, insofar as a beginning can be specified within a continuous sequence of evolutionary events, may be placed at about the beginning of the Permian period of earth history. During Carboniferous times, so briefly reviewed in the past few pages, the reptiles which were newcomers on the land, had to struggle against the well-established amphibians in order that they might find room to live. But as the days of the Carboniferous period ran to their end the balance, as has been said, began to change in favor of the reptiles, so that with the advent of Permian history we find these tetrapods clearly dominant on the land, even though there still remained many large and powerful amphibians.

The Permian period, named from the old district of Perm in northern Russia, where rocks of this age were first defined by the English geologist, Roderick Impey Murchison, was a time of considerable variety in topography and climates as compared with the Carboniferous. Of course, at its beginning it was little different from the end of the preceding geologic age – the one merged into the other. But as the years wore on land areas became greater in extent and more rugged than they had been, and climates trended away from the tropical uniformity that had been so characteristic of many Carboniferous environments. There were seasonal differences and latitudinal differences. The glacial climates that seemed to have prevailed in some parts of the southern hemisphere during a part of late Carboniferous history continued into the early days of the Permian period. There were inland deserts in some regions. All of these factors were favorable to the diverse evolution of the reptiles.

This is amply verified by the variety of reptiles to be found in Permian deposits throughout the world. Except to one who is a specialist in this field of paleontology, the reptiles of the Carboniferous look very much alike, being for the most part small, primitive types, with heavy skulls, short necks, thick bodies and sprawling limbs. But with the advent of Permian times the reptiles had entered upon a kaleidoscopic pattern of development that resulted in greatly divergent forms, the differences between which are striking even to the most casual eye. These varied reptiles occur in Permian deposits at numerous localities throughout the world. Some of the oldest of the fossils are contained within a series of successive red-colored formations of early Permian, and even of late Carboniferous age, in north central Texas. Here in a continuous sequence of a dozen or more horizons one can follow the evolutionary progress in North America of the early Permian reptiles, and of the amphibians that lived with them. Similar reptiles and amphibians are to be found in other parts of the continent – to the west in New Mexico, to the north-east in Pennsylvania and Ohio, and even farther in this direction on Prince Edward Island. This same association of early amphibians and reptiles is found in the lower Permian or Rothliegende beds of Europe, particularly in southern France and central Europe.

Reptiles and amphibians of middle* Permian age – the division that in central Europe is designated as the Kupferschiefer – have been excavated from a sequential series of formations in northern Russia, where, as in the lower Permian of Texas, there is a rather complex succession of sediments one above the other, carrying faunas in which the evolutionary stories of various amphibians and reptiles may be traced. Reptiles of this age are also found in England. Middle Permian reptiles are additionally found in the Karroo series of South Africa, where they occur profusely in beds that initiate an abundantly fossiliferous sequence. This is perhaps one of the most remarkable of all such sequences in the world, carrying the record on through the Permian and continuing through the Triassic period.

Finally, upper Permian or Zechstein reptiles and amphibians are known from various parts of Europe as well as South Africa, although they are absent from the western hemisphere, where there is a dearth of middle and upper Permian continental deposits. Furthermore, tetrapods of this age are found in the peninsular part of India, and in Australia.

The age relationships of these various Permian horizons in which fossil reptiles and amphibians are found, and also the remains of freshwater fishes, may be represented in a correlation table (Table 2).

---

* The manner of subdividing the Permian varies among the authorities who have studied the rocks and fossils of this age. Some authors use a threefold division of the Permian, others recognize only lower and upper, or early and late Permian. Still others, especially American students, favor a fourfold division of Permian rocks and events. In this book Permian rocks will be classified as lower, middle and upper, Permian history as early, middle and late.

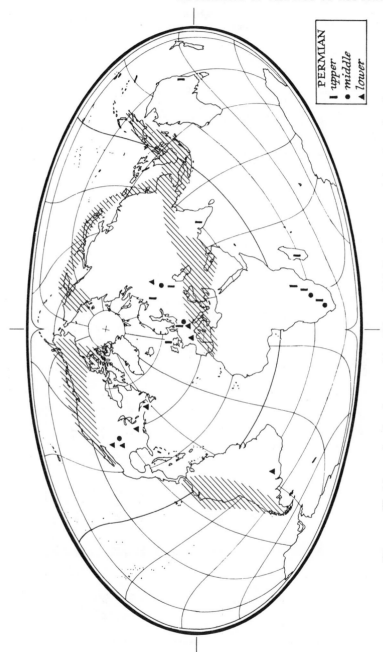

Figure 23. World map showing the general localities at which Permian tetrapods have been found. The shaded areas represent regions of major submergence.

PERMIAN
| upper
• middle
▲ lower

Table 2. Correlation of Permo-Carboniferous vertebrate horizons *

	Carboniferous	Lower Permian	Middle Permian	Upper Permian
SOUTH AMERICA		Itararé (Brazil)		
NORTH AMERICA	Joggins, Linton-Mazon Creek, Conemaugh, Monongahela	Wichita, Clear Fork, Dunkard, Abo-Cutler, Hennessey	Pease River	
ASIA		Mhum Mu (Kashmir)		Bijori (India)
EUROPE	English Coal Fields, Kounova, Nýřany	Autun (France), Rothliegende	Kupferschiefer	Zechstein, Cuttie's Hillock (Scotland)
RUSSIA		Zone 0	Zone I, Zone II	Zone III, Zone IV
AFRICA		Dwyka	Ecca, Tapinocephalus Zone	Lower Beaufort — Endothiodon Zone, Cistecephalus Zone [Ruhuhu, Tanga (E. Africa), Chiweta (Nyasaland)]
AUSTRALIA				Upper Newcastle

40

*See 'Tables and Diagrams' in Addendum.

Note that in Russia the Permian beds have been subdivided into numbered zones. Likewise the sediments are zoned in South Africa, but here the zones are designated by the names of characteristic reptilian genera.

This allocation of fossiliferous horizons, of formations and groups of formations, to different sections of the Permian period, is the result of long years of study by numerous paleontologists throughout the world. It is the result of many comparisons, between individual fossils and between the species and genera to which they belong, between groups of fossils that occur together – the record in the rocks of ancient faunas – and between successions of faunas that once lived on various continents. Thus the body of knowledge has been built up a little at a time, so that after many years devoted to careful collecting and careful study the large picture begins to emerge. In this day, a hundred years and more after the tentative beginnings of the first scientific studies of Permian fossils, the picture has become reasonably clear, even though there are fuzzy spots here and there, areas that can be sharpened only by future evidence as yet undiscovered.

The reptiles of Permian age and the animals that lived with them probably can best be understood by looking at them in sequence, from the oldest to the youngest, and the logical place to begin such a review is with the lower Permian faunas of the Texas red beds. Here is revealed the association of early reptiles that shared the earth with numerous amphibians of varied size and form, the record of an age when the newly established dominance of the reptiles was to some degree still being challenged by a host of varied amphibians.

It is a record that extends through a series of a dozen or more formations, as has already been mentioned, occurring in sequence as shown on p. 42, with as usual the oldest bed at the bottom and the youngest at the top.

In early Permian times, when these sediments were being laid down, that portion of North America which is now north-central Texas was a low, tropical delta, receiving its accumulation of sands and muds from a vast land area to the north and east and bordered by a shallow sea to the south and west. Streams and rivers flowed across this delta, many of them leading into ponds and lakes. The land was blanketed by primitive plants, and across this land lived the numerous amphibians and reptiles of that distant age. Here we see indicated for the first time associations of tetrapods showing strongly differing specializations for different modes of life. Here were faunas the members of which displayed striking contrasts in size and shape, in the development of their bodies and their legs, their heads and their teeth. Here were large amphibians and reptiles, and small ones.

GROUP	FORMATION
Pease River	Dog Creek Blaine Flowerpot San Angelo
Clear Fork	Choza Vale Arroyo Leuders Clyde
Wichita	Belle Plains Admiral Putnam Moran Pueblo

Here were plant-eaters and flesh-eaters, dwellers in the ponds and streams, frequenters of the pond and stream margins, and wanderers that ranged across the 'uplands' – a term used to indicate low hills and raised ground between the water courses, for it must be kept in mind that this was a low land, without much topographic relief. Yet in spite of what was probably a rather flat land surface and what would seem to us as a rather uniform climate, the environment was

Figure 24. The North American lower Permian amphibian, *Eryops*, from the red beds of Texas. This amphibian lived in streams and ponds, where it preyed upon fishes. It was about five or six feet in length.

sufficiently varied to support animals adapted for quite different ways of making their separate ways through an ancient world.

In that ancient world there were large, clumsy, plant-eating cotylosaurs, exemplified by the genus *Diadectes**, with solid skulls, short necks, heavy bodies and stout, sprawling legs, that fed upon plants. These herbivores had broad, rather flat teeth, well adjusted for crushing plant food, not at all like the simple, conical teeth of their primitive ancestors. With them were other plant-eaters in this early Permian scene, particularly certain pelycosaurs, members of an order

Figure 25. *Diadectes*, an herbivorous cotylosaurian reptile from the lower Permian red beds of Texas. About six or eight feet long.

of reptiles that had appeared early in the history of tetrapod evolution – in Carboniferous times.

The pelycosaurs show definite advances over the primitive cotylosaurs from which they and all other reptiles had descended, particularly in the more slender bones of the skeleton and the improved articulations between these bones, so that they were quite obviously better suited for getting over the ground efficiently than their clumsier cotylosaurian neighbors. In addition, as previously mentioned,

43

*See 'Page Corrections and Emendations' in Addendum.

they show definite advances over the cotylosaurs in the structure of the skull, notably in the development of a large temporal opening on either side behind the eye tq allow for a bulging of the jaw muscles.

Some of the pelycosaurs were plant-eaters, rather heavily built reptiles with extraordinarily small heads. Among these certain edaphosaurs were particularly strange-looking, with long bodies and slender limbs, and a great 'sail' running down the middle of the back. This sail, a membrane supported by elongated spines of the vertebrae, these in turn decorated along their sides with bony knobs and projections, has been a puzzling structure to paleontologists for the better part of a century. In an edaphosaur ten feet long (these were sizeable reptiles) the sail may extend four feet or so above the back. Explanations for this queer adaptation have been numerous and sometimes naïve (such as the picturesque idea that the membrane was a sail, with which the pelycosaurs were wafted across Permian lakes by Permian breezes). Modern opinion is inclined to regard the membrane as some sort of temperature regulating device, a large surface for absorbing the heat from sunlight to warm the animal, and to radiate heat away from the body when it was desirable for the animal to cool off. But the meaning of the knobs and the cross bars on the edaphosaur spines has so far defied any very good explanation. These reptiles have many small teeth on the palate which might have been used for crushing rather hard plants growing in the water, perhaps even for breaking mollusc shells. The sediments in which edaphosaurs are frequently found would seem to indicate that these reptiles lived along the edges of water courses and ponds.

In the ponds there lived numerous amphibians of varied sizes and shapes, feeding for the most part on fishes. Some of them, such as *Eryops*, were large, others, such as *Trimerorhachis*, were small. Perhaps some of the smaller dominantly aquatic amphibians caught insects, as did the small land-living amphibians and reptiles, these latter being for the most part cotylosaurs. There were, among the land-living reptiles of this Permian scene, some very slender protorosaurs which also probably lived upon insects and other small game, as do lizards today. These protorosaurs, along with some of the small cotylosaurs, certainly must have filled the niches in the economy of Nature that lizards do today.

So far we have peopled the scene with various amphibians, plant-eating reptiles and some of the smaller predators, these latter feeding for the most part upon insects and other small forms. At the top of this complex association of animals were the large reptilian predators that fed upon large fishes, upon amphibians, and upon other reptiles. These were all large and active pelycosaurs, long of body and swift of limb. The ophiacodonts, which were fish-eaters, had elongated jaws set with many sharp teeth that made excellent fish traps. The

Figure 26. The North American carnivorous pelycosaur, *Dimetrodon*, from the lower Permian red beds of Texas, a dominant animal in its environment. The large sail on the back possibly was a temperature regulating device. Large specimens are ten feet in length.

dimetrodonts were fin-backed reptiles, with unusually elongated, smooth vertebral spines to support the sail. These reptiles, ten or twelve feet in length, had deep skulls and jaws with long, saber-like teeth, obviously weapons for striking down large victims, and were the dominant animals of their environment.

Perhaps the entire range of these lower Permian amphibians and reptiles may be looked at in the manner shown by plate 3.

It was remarked in a preceding paragraph that the delta on which the Permian deposits of Texas accumulated was bordered to the south and west by the ocean. This was an early Permian seaway reaching northward, through what is now western Texas, up into the Great Plains to form an effective temporary barrier separating the land-living animals of the Texas region from those of the area now comprised by New Mexico and adjacent states. This is not to say that the broad saltwater strait completely isolated Texas from New Mexico during all of lower Permian time, because the numerous resemblances between the western and eastern faunas are proof enough that there was communication between the two areas, probably at the very beginning of the Permian period. Many reptiles typical of the Wichita sediments of Texas are found in the Abo sediments of New Mexico, but there are differences. In New Mexico amphibians are rare, which may mean much or little. Of particular interest is the lack of any specimens of the sail-backed *Dimetrodon* in New Mexico. Instead, the ecological position of this very characteristic Texas predator was taken in New Mexico by *Sphenacodon*, a reptile closely related and similar to *Dimetrodon* in all respects except that it lacks the sail. The spines of the vertebrae are somewhat elongated, but only to the extent that they might have provided attachments for very strong back muscles.

This raises some interesting speculations about reptilian adaptations. If the sail was an important functional structure in *Dimetrodon*, presumably a temperature regulating device that increased the efficiency of this reptile as a predator, why was it not necessary in *Sphenacodon* ? What were the differences in life and in environments during early Permian times between Texas and New Mexico ? Perhaps the differences were those of evolutionary history more than anything else. *Dimetrodon* and *Sphenacodon* arose from a common ancestry, but early in their separate evolutionary histories became isolated from each other by the Permian seaway that invaded the middle of the land. As a result of natural selection acting on certain mutations the sail developed at a precocious rate in *Dimetrodon*. In contrast, the elongation of the spines of the vertebrae was slow in *Sphenacodon*. Perhaps we see in this latter reptile an animal that was on the verge, so to speak, of developing a large sail.

In this respect a parallel may be seen in the evolution of modern seals and sea-lions. Both seals and sea-lions live much the same sort of life, but seals are considerably more specialized for this way of living than are sea-lions. Nevertheless they may live side by side, and the more generalized animal manages very well indeed when compared with its more specialized cousin.

Lower Permian tetrapods very much like those of the Texas red beds evidently lived far and wide across North America, as is shown by their fossils in various scattered localities. Various reptiles have been found in Oklahoma, while farther afield a rather rich fauna of very early Permian amphibians and reptiles once occupied the Tri-state area, where Pennsylvania, Ohio and West Virginia come together. A few fragments have been found to the north, on Prince Edward Island.

The presence of lower Permian amphibians and reptiles at these several localities shows that the entire North American continent as it then existed was very probably inhabited by the strange and interesting array of tetrapods which have come briefly under our scrutiny. That these ancient animals ranged even more widely across the earth is indicated by lower Permian fossils from a number of localities in western Europe. Indeed, the European faunas of this age are readily comparable with the American ones, for in both regions there are closely related and even generically identical forms. Perhaps the greatest difference between the lower Permian tetrapods of Europe and those of North America is the preponderance of amphibians and the rarity of reptiles in the European assemblages, as contrasted with the more balanced proportions of amphibians and reptiles in the western hemisphere faunas. This suggests an abundance of pond and stream environments in the European region during early Permian time.

During the transition from the early to the late Permian the fossil records of several interesting lines of tetrapod evolution come to an end. Did the large and small amphibians, the clumsy diadectids and the strange, sail-backed pelycosaurs continue through the subsequent years of Permian history in North America? The answer to this question cannot now be given, because the record of later Permian land life in North America is missing; the sediments, if ever present, that would contain a sequence of fossil vertebrates, have seemingly

Figure 27. A gigantic pelycosaur, *Cotylorhynchus*, from the middle Permian Hennessy formation of Oklahoma. This massive reptile, eight or ten feet in length, was the North American ecological equivalent of the gigantic Permian pareiasaurs and dinocephalians of South Africa and Russia.

been long since swept away by the forces of erosion. They are lost pages in the textbook of the rocks.

Only a glimpse of the beginning of middle Permian faunas in North America is to be had, showing that in the San Angelo and Flower Pot formations of Texas there are some interesting, and in many respects some rather tantalizing fossils. These include a large cotylosaur, the teeth obviously adapted to a vegetable diet, and a varied series of unusually large and heavy pelycosaurs, some of them carnivores, some of them plant-eaters. One of the carnivores, *Steppesaurus*, would seem to be a veritable giant among Permian reptiles, with a skeleton perhaps eighteen feet or so in length, while one of the herbivores, *Cotylorhynchus*, first appearing in the Hennessey formation of Oklahoma, is a massive herbivore, as big as an ox, with a barrel-like body, heavy limbs and broad feet, and an amazingly small skull. Fossils of amphibians in these beds are very fragmentary.

Two outstanding facts are apparent from these last brief remarks. One is the almost complete lack of amphibian material; the other is the general large size of the reptiles in the middle Permian sediments. And these two facts epitomize very nicely the trends of amphibian and reptilian evolution from middle Permian time through the remainder of this period, and on through the Mesozoic era. The amphibians had passed their zenith, and from this point onwards theirs was a history of contracting evolutionary lines, with none the less marked success to be attained in future geologic periods by the frogs and toads, and the salamanders. The reptiles were ever on the increase, and from this point until the end of the Mesozoic theirs was a history in which giants were dominant.

Chapter 3

Early Reptilian Rulers of the Land

TO TRACE the development of the tetrapods that lived during middle and late Permian times it is now necessary to leave North America and to examine the fossil vertebrates that have been found in the Permian beds of two Old World regions, South Africa and northern Russia. Of course, middle and upper Permian vertebrates are found in other places, too, but the succession of deposits in northern Russia and in South Africa give so graphic a representation of tetrapod evolution during the long time with which we are concerned that attention will be centered upon them.

In the Lower Beaufort beds of the Karroo basin in South Africa is an unsurpassed record of middle and upper Permian fossil reptiles, based upon thousands of specimens – a truly gigantic array of forms. This magnificent accumulation of fossils not only represents the latter part of Permian time in Africa, it continues uninterruptedly through much of the Triassic period. For the moment our concern is with the Permian sequence, the succession of beds in the Lower Beaufort series that have been named, from bottom to top, the *Tapinocephalus*, *Endothiodon* and *Cistecephalus* zones.

An analysis of the sediments, and of the fossils within them, indicates that the reptiles living during Lower Beaufort times inhabited a rolling upland plain, a region not unlike the Great Plains of North America in topography and general appearance. Of course, the vegetation of this plain was of ancient aspect and of tropical and subtropical affinities. Rivers and streams crossed the landscape and there were many little ponds. But on the whole it was a fairly dry environment.

It is not surprising that amphibians should be sparse in such a landscape, and in fact only a very few labyrinthodont genera make up the amphibian record of the Beaufort series. But aside from the upland nature of the country in which amphibians would be at something of a disadvantage, the scanty record of Beaufort amphibians is also very probably a result in considerable degree of the diminishing fortunes of this class of vertebrates. It is all part of an integrated series of happenings through time. Environments favored reptiles, and reptiles waxed while amphibians waned.

In addition to the scarcity of amphibians there is another outstanding feature of the Lower Beaufort faunas, and this is the overwhelming dominance of therapsid or mammal-like reptiles, related to and very probably derived from the pelycosaurs. As in the pelycosaurs, the therapsids possess a skull in which the temporal region behind the eye is opened by a large fenestra to allow for the bulging of jaw muscles. But in the therapsids, especially the more advanced ones, this temporal opening is much enlarged, and often confluent with the opening for the eye, a character seen also in primitive mammals. These reptiles show resemblances to mammals in other respects, too. There is often a bony secondary palate, to separate the nasal passage from the mouth, there is an approach toward the mammalian type of jaw articulation, and the teeth show progressive degrees of specialization and differentiation. The upshot of this last character is that in the most advanced mammal-like reptiles there are small incisor teeth, enlarged canines, and post-canine teeth of varying stages of complexity – teeth that show trends toward the crushing or cutting premolars and molars of mammals. In the skeleton there is generally considerable differentiation of the vertebral column, and the legs are pulled in beneath the body, so that these reptiles in life walked with the belly raised well above the ground. They were evidently very active animals, and they approach so gradually the mammalian condition that where the line of separation between mammal and reptile is to be drawn becomes an academic question.

There are different degrees of 'mammalness' among the mammal-like reptiles of the Beaufort beds, so that they form a sort of graded series with various side branches, from types that are only a bit more advanced than the pelycosaurs to types that are quite literally at the very edge of being out-and-out mammals. In broad terms there are three large groups of these therapsid reptiles, which may be designated as the anomodonts, the theriodonts and the ictidosaurs. The anomodonts may be further subdivided into the tapinocephalians, which are large, massive, heavy-boned therapsids, generally adapted as herbivores, and into the dicynodonts, which are very specialized plant-eating therapsids, having the body surmounted by a beaked skull of open structure. The fossil remains of dicynodonts, which incidentally range from very small individuals to very large ones, occur in great profusion within some parts of the Beaufort series, so that skulls may be found by the hundreds, scattered over the surface of the ground. These were indeed extraordinarily successful reptiles, not only as indicated by the great numbers of them in the South

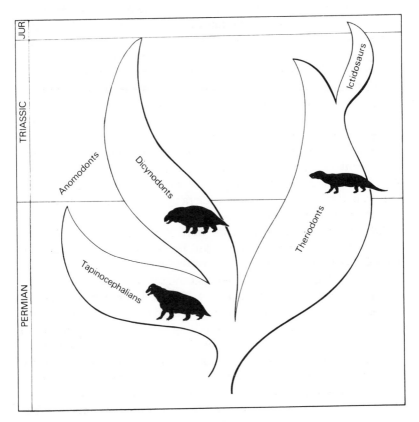

Figure 28. The evolution of the therapsid reptiles.

African deposits, but also because of their long-ranging migrations over all the continents during Permian–Triassic times[*].

While the anomodonts were evolving in their own specialized ways, the theriodonts were developing along lines that led by various paths to the mammals. These are the mammal-like reptiles that look like mammals. They commonly have rather dog-like or wolf-like skulls,

[*]See 'Page Corrections and Emendations' in Addendum.

with long canine teeth for slashing their adversaries and diversely developed cheek teeth, often complex, and obviously adapted for cutting food into small, quickly assimilated pieces. The significance of this adaptation is important; it shows that these were active animals with a high rate of metabolism, requiring frequent and quick energy replacement. Not for them was the usual reptilian feeding pattern of a big meal, swallowed whole, followed by long hours of torpidity.

Finally, the ictidosaurs, the most mammal-like of the therapsids, carried specializations of structure and presumably of physiology and behavior to the threshold of mammalian organization.

The overwhelming dominance of the therapsids in the middle and upper Permian faunas of Africa is indicated by the fact that approximately ninety per cent of the genera of Beaufort reptiles belong to this one order. The remainder of the reptiles are contained within a few scattered groups, of which the cotylosaurs are the most numerous. At first glance these may look like unbalanced faunas from the standpoint of animal classification, but if one analyzes the South African Permian reptiles upon the basis of their ecological roles it is readily apparent that they show wide ranges of adaptations to various modes of life. The important point is that during Permian times in South Africa the different niches were almost all of them filled by therapsids: other reptiles seem for the most part to have been crowded out.

Let us look in a little more detail at the sequence of reptiles in the Permian sediments of South Africa. At the beginning of Beaufort times, when the fossils now contained within the *Tapinocephalus* zone were the living inhabitants of the rolling plains of an ancient South Africa, the land was well populated by various reptiles, and seemingly a few amphibians. Among the reptiles were numerous large cotylosaurs known as pareiasaurs; heavy, ungainly animals with capacious bodies, strong limbs and broad feet, and thick solid skulls, the fossilized jaws of which are set with numerous small, rather blade-like teeth. Here we see a group of large herbivores, occupying in Africa a niche similar to the one that had been filled in North America by the diadectids and the massive herbivorous pelycosaurs during early Permian times. It should be said that the pareiasaurs, of which the *Tapinocephalus* zone genus *Bradysaurus* is typical, are generally much larger than the diadectids of North America – more like the pelycosaur *Cotylorhynchus* in this respect. These large plant-eaters, many of them probably weighing five hundred pounds and more, roamed the Beaufort plains in great numbers, to be preyed upon by a varied host of predators.

The pareiasaurs were not the only vegetarians of that day. They had to contend for food with tapinocephalids and dicynodonts, the

Figure 29. The middle Permian pareiasaur, *Bradysaurus*, from the Lower Beaufort beds of South Africa. This was a large herbivore – the skeleton is about eight feet long.

two therapsid types briefly described above. The tapinocephalids, of which *Tapinocephalus* and *Moschops* are characteristic, were equally as large, and one might say equally as clumsy as the pareiasaurs. They rival the pareiasaurs in the heaviness and thickness of the skull, a skull in which the temporal opening behind the eye is much reduced and the bones are exceedingly thick. In these reptiles the pineal organ, a light-receptor on top of the head, was housed in a raised, volcano-like eminence, as if it had some very important function in the economy of the animal. This is a matter for some speculation. Even though the tapinocephalids may have been direct competitors with the pareiasaurs for food, as for example are zebras and antelopes on the plains of modern Africa, there was food for all, and, probably, as among modern herbivores, the competition was of a friendly sort.

Just what the beaked dicynodonts ate and how they ate it is something of a puzzle to paleontologists who have to interpret the fossil remains of animals that lived two hundred million years ago. Very likely the dicynodonts, too, were plant-eaters, perhaps browsing on low vegetation. And if the fossils are any indication of numbers, they must have covered the plains of ancient Africa in prodigious herds.

In any good sample of Karroo reptiles, for example, about eighty per cent of all specimens are dicynodonts.

It is no surprise that with the plains of Permian Africa the feeding ground for vast numbers of pareiasaurs, tapinocephalids and dicynodonts, there should have evolved various carnivores to prey upon

Figure 30. The role of the herbivores during Permian times in South Africa was shared by the cotylosaurs and the therapsids, of which latter *Moschops*, shown here, is an example. *Moschops* is a dinocephalian, standing some five feet in height at the shoulders.

them. These were the carnivorous therapsids, represented in the *Tapinocephalus* zone by titanosuchids, gorgonopsians and therocephalians.

The titanosuchids were gigantic, heavy-skulled predators, with large canine teeth. They could not have been very agile or fast, so it is to be presumed that they preyed upon the largest and clumsiest of the vegetarians. Titanosuchids are not particularly numerous as fossils, so it may be that they had a limited role in the ecology of the *Tapinocephalus* zone life.

The other carnivores, the gorgonopsians and the therocephalians, can best be described as refined in structure when compared with the titanosuchids. They have supple bodies, slender limbs, well-integrated and efficient feet, well-formed necks, and elongated, dog-like skulls. There can be no doubting that the gorgonopsians and therocephalians were quick and agile, quite able to cut down their victims by the speed and impact of their attack. These carnivores were of assorted sizes, from very small types that evidently lived upon very small game, to large animals, the hunters of the abundant herbivores that populated the plains.

The gorgonopsians were established at a very early stage in their evolutionary history in a trend toward the exaggerated enlargement of the upper canine teeth. These were 'saber-toothed' reptiles anticipating by millions of years the saber-toothed cats, so abundant during the Age of Mammals. It seems obvious that the gorgonopsians

Figure 31. *Endothiodon*, a small, beaked anomodont, two feet in length, is one of the common therapsids in the uppermost portions of the South African Permian Beaufort beds. It was probably a herbivore.

struck their victims hard, killing them with deep thrusts of their great daggers. Many of the therocephalians showed a somewhat parallel development, except that in these reptiles it is common for two upper teeth on each side to be enlarged into long 'canines'.

Other reptiles of the *Tapinocephalus* zone are of little importance. There is a small protorosaur and a few small pelycosaurs.

As one passes up through the Beaufort into the overlying *Endothiodon* zone, it is possible to see the fauna continuing through time, with, of course, certain changes. Labyrinthodonts hold on, as do the pareiasaurs, there being in this higher zone, among others, *Pareiasaurus* itself. The dicynodonts and their relatives carry on the line of therapsid herbivores, one of them being the zone marker, *Endothiodon*, the genus especially characteristic of this subdivision of the Beaufort sequence. But the tapinocephalids have disappeared. Likewise, the large, clumsy carnivorous titanosuchids drop out – perhaps as a result of the extinction of the tapinocephalids.

The other carnivorous therapsids, the gorgonopsians and therocephalians, continue to evolve. Of the former, *Lycaenops* is particularly well known.

Proceeding upward through the sediments, we come to the *Ciste-cephalus* zone, named from an anomodont characteristic of this level, the final Permian subdivision in the Karroo. Generally speaking, there is a continuation of the animals that lived in earlier Beaufort time. The labyrinthodont amphibians are still represented, and pareiasaurs and dicynodonts are numerous, as are the carnivorous gorgonopsians and therocephalians that preyed upon them. Indeed, these last two groups of therapsids show a considerable expansion in the *Cistecephalus* zone, being considerably more numerous (at least as indicated by the fossils) than in preceding ages. In addition there appear for the first time the cynodonts, very highly developed

Figure 32. The most numerous and varied of the predators during late Permian time in South Africa were the gorgonopsians, of which one, *Lycaenops*, is shown here. These are saber-toothed carnivores, in which the canine teeth are very long, evidently for stabbing their prey. *Lycaenops* is about the size of a large dog – many gorgonopsians are larger, and some attain the size of lions.

mammal-like reptiles, predators that were to enjoy great success in subsequent Triassic times.

Other new and advanced reptiles also appear in the *Cistecephalus* zone, to adumbrate the life of the Mesozoic era. Particular mention should be made of the eosuchians, reptiles close to the ancestry of the lizards, and perhaps not far removed from the stem of the archosaurs, which were the dominant reptiles of Mesozoic times. Also in the *Cistecephalus* zone is a primitive rhynchocephalian, the forerunner of another group that was shortly to become prominent.

Such is the parade of Beaufort tetrapods through middle and late Permian times; a parade of an ever-developing faunal complex through long years, a parade marked, as usually are all parades, by some of its members dropping along the wayside, while new members join its ranks. It is, all in all, one of the best of the many parades that compose the fossil record, and it extends on into the Triassic, as we shall see in a later chapter.

The sequence of middle and upper Permian continental sediments in South Africa, the successive faunas of which give such a graphic picture of reptilian evolution during the final stages of Paleozoic times, is augmented by related deposits in other parts of this great continent. Characteristic Beaufort reptiles are found in the Luangwa valley of southern Rhodesia. At Ruhuhu, in east Africa, is an horizon, the Lower Bone Bed, that may be equated in a general way with the *Endothiodon* zone of the Karroo area, while fossils of this same age are found in the Chiweta beds in Malawi and the Mangwa beds in northern Rhodesia. Likewise at Tanga, near the eastern coast in Tanganyika, are fossils of late Permian age, and not so very far away, on Madagascar, are sediments that contain Permian fossils, perhaps of about *Cistecephalus* zone age.

But let us turn from Africa to northern Europe, particularly to the northern portion of European Russia, for a look at the middle and upper Permian tetrapods of that region – a region not far removed from the type Permian, where Murchison worked early in the last century. Here fossils are found due east of Moscow and north of the Caspian sea, and from that area north to the Dvina and Mesen rivers which flow into the White Sea. Great quantities of material have been excavated and studied for many years by Russian paleontologists, so that large assemblages of fossils are now at hand from many localities.

The interpretation of fossils from this region is not easy. The specimens come from many localities, which may be grouped according to their ages in several 'complexes'. But these complexes overlap in age, and in part they may represent different environmental conditions, sometimes reflected by the differences in their constituent fossils. The problem of trying to solve this paleontological puzzle is difficult, and will take much time, and require the attentions of numerous students.

It would appear that the Russian deposits were accumulated to a large degree on deltas and other low sites. Consequently the faunas of this region differ from those of the Karroo by reason of the presence of numerous persistent amphibians, and there is afforded the opportunity to bridge the gap between these middle and upper Permian assemblages and those of lower Permian affinities, in which amphibians are so prominently represented. The interpretation of the transition from early into middle Permian times is further facilitated in Russia because of the discovery in recent years of some lower Permian fossiliferous horizons that allow direct comparisons with the lower Permian amphibians and reptiles of North America and Europe.

The successive middle and upper Permian faunas of northern Russia have been grouped into a series of zones, originally numbered I, II, III and IV. As a result of the discovery in recent years of lower Permian deposits, zone 0 has been added to the base of the series.

What do these zones show? To begin with zone 0: here are found various rather conservative labyrinthodont amphibians. These amphibians naturally frequented streams and ponds. Along the pond margins were primitive cotylosaurs, while on the higher ground were other cotylosaurs of diadectid type. And with them were pelycosaurs. So the scene is not very different from Texas at the same time, an indication that lower Permian amphibians and reptiles, well exemplified in the Texas sequence, were widely distributed across the globe.

Then comes a break in the quality of life, especially of reptilian life, nicely indicated by the differences between the fossils of zone 0 and those of zones I and II. It is, above all, the break between the pelycosaurs, characteristic of early Permian times, and the therapsids, dominant during middle and late Permian times; essentially the replacement of pelycosaurs by their therapsid descendants.

A few pelycosaurs continue into zones I and II, and amphibians likewise persist. But the notable change that occurs with the advent of late Permian faunas is, as in Africa, the overwhelming influx of varied therapsids. This is shown in zone II of the Russian series. Here were heavy-bodied tapinocephalids, very similar to those of the southern hemisphere, and always on their trail the large titanosuchids. The more advanced and the more active predators were gorgonopsians and therocephalians, again as was the case in Africa. Yet there were still varied amphibians, relatives of the lower Permian amphibians which were so numerous and widely adapted across the northern hemisphere, living with small rather primitive cotylosaurs that inhabited stream banks and undergrowth, with large, ungainly pareiasaurs, and with a few surviving pelycosaurs. Such was the association of amphibians and reptiles living in the far north, between latitudes fifty degrees and sixty-five degrees toward the end of

Permian time. This faunal assemblage continued in a general way to the close of the period, as shown by the fossils of zone IV.

Zone III is a transitional zone, not represented at the present time by a definite fauna. In zone IV, which may be equated with the *Cistecephalus* zone of Africa, the amphibians continued, as did the primitive cotylosaurs, these latter represented by *Kotlassia*, an interesting regressive type that evidently had become secondarily adapted for an almost total aquatic existence. The large herbivores are represented at this stage by dicynodonts. *Inostrancevia* is a gigantic saber-toothed gorgonopsian that certainly must have been a predator on the various large plant-eaters. Other predators at the end of Permian times in the Russian area are the therocephalians and the cynodonts, these latter marking the appearance of very advanced therapsids in the far north.

From this survey it can be seen that the evolution of middle and upper Permian land-living vertebrates in Russia ran parallel to that of related animals in South Africa, so that the northern faunas have much the same complexion as the southern ones. In both Russia and South Africa there were varied massive herbivores, these being cotylosaurs and herbivorous therapsids. In both areas there were large carnivores that preyed upon these clumsy plant-eaters, the almost equally clumsy titanosuchids, and the more agile gorgonopsians, therocephalians and cynodonts. And in both areas there were smaller tetrapods, in Russia these being various amphibians, and small cotylosaurs. In addition, a few pelycosaurs inhabited the northern region. Some of these latter forms give us a clue as to the derivation of many middle and late Permian reptiles from their early Permian progenitors. They show also the connections of Russia with western Europe and perhaps North America, as well as with Africa.

A comparison of the parallel successions of fossiliferous zones in Africa and Russia, running through the Permian sequence and into the Triassic, is made in Table 3.

Western Europe has been mentioned. In northern Scotland are dicynodonts and a small pareiasaur, *Elginia*, with a spiked skull, that indicate a sort of extension of the zone IV assemblage of Russia. In India, in the Bijori beds of the peninsular area, are fossiliferous beds of late Permian age. Continuing to the southeast, a late Permian dicynodont is found in former Indochina. Beds of this age, the Upper Newcastle Coals, occur in Australia.

What bearing do the analyses and comparisons of Permian land-living animals, presented here and in the preceding chapter, have on the physical world of that distant age – on the relationships of continents to each other and to climates and environments? These are important considerations. As for the connections between ancient

*Table 3. *Comparison of the Permio–Triassic zones of Russia and South Africa*

	RUSSIA	SOUTH AFRICA	
Upper Triassic		Stormberg	Cave Sandstone
			Red Beds
			Molteno
Middle Triassic	Zone VII		
Lower Triassic	Zone VI	Upper Beaufort	*Cynognathus* zone
	Zone V		(*Procolophon* zone)
			Lystrosaurus zone
Upper Permian	Zone IV	Lower Beaufort	*Cistecephalus* zone
	Zone III		*Endothiodon* zone
Middle Permian	Zone II		*Tapinocephalus* zone
	Zone I	Ecca	
Lower Permian	Zone 0	Dwyka	

continents, there are essentially three schools of geological thought: first, that the continents were very much as they are today, linked by isthmian land bridges; second, that the southern continents – Africa, South America, India and Australia – were parts of a great transverse land mass, Gondwanaland, which subsequently broke up as parts of it foundered into the oceanic deeps; and third, that the lands of the earth were in those days connected into a single large mass that· later broke into fragments, these separate continental components

*See 'Tables and Diagrams' in Addendum.

drifting away from each other to the positions they now occupy. The proponents of these widely divergent theories are equally vigorous and sincere in the defense of their ideas.

The evidence of the land-living vertebrates certainly shows that North America, western Europe and northern Russia were in some way connected during early Permian times[*]. The similarities of their faunas have been mentioned. Perhaps closely related early Permian amphibians and reptiles were even more widely dispersed than is indicated by the evidence of these regional faunas, but as is so often the case in paleontology, our record is far from being complete. That there were connections between northern Europe, Africa and southeastern Asia during middle and late Permian times is clearly shown by the resemblances of faunas in which large pareiasaurs and widely adapted therapsids are so very prominent. But here again the fossil record is deficient for many great areas of the earth's surface, notably for North America. Furthermore, it is an unfortunate fact that we have very little evidence of the land-living vertebrates of South America throughout almost the entire span of Permian times. Yet in spite of these deficiencies, the distribution of Permian amphibians and reptiles may be reviewed and some conclusions reached.

Having said what has been said, it must be admitted that nothing is definitely conclusive. The interpretation of events that took place two hundred million years and more in the past upon the basis of the rocks and the fossils is an exercise involving many uncertain factors. It may be argued that the resemblances between the lower Permian fossils of North America and Europe indicate that these areas were contiguous regions of a single continent. Likewise, the same argument may be applied to the resemblances between middle and upper Permian fossils in Russia and Africa. Yet it may be argued with equal validity that such resemblances indicate no more than the fact that there were once open avenues of migration between areas quite far apart. For example, in the modern world the mountain lion has spread from Canada almost to the tip of South America, making its way between the two continental masses from north to south across a narrow isthmian link. Other characteristic North American mammals, such as raccoons, foxes, deer and rabbits made this same isthmian crossing. Conversely, we know that porcupines and armadillos traveled north along the isthmus, from South to North America, in comparatively recent geological history. Moreover, such long movements between widely distant regions, although often involving

61

---

[*] See 'Page Corrections and Emendations' in Addendum.

changes along the way, are not necessarily marked by any significant differences between the animals at each end of the route. The mountain lion is a single species from north to south, over a distance of seven thousand miles.

If there were isthmian links in Permian times connecting continents located about as they are today, is it possible that there were some connections in addition to the ones obvious from present-day geography? Is it possible that there was a land bridge across the North Atlantic, in the general vicinity of Greenland and Iceland, which might account for the close resemblances between the lower Permian reptiles of North America and northern Eurasia? Is it possible that there was an isthmus or an archipelago across the South Atlantic, from western Africa to Brazil, rather than a broad Gondwanaland connection, which might account for the presence of *Mesosaurus*, a little freshwater reptile of early Permian age in these two regions? These are questions that cannot be certainly answered upon the basis of our present knowledge.

Let us digress for a moment on the subject of *Mesosaurus*, which has been widely cited as proof of an ancient Gondwanaland or of the separation of South America from Africa by continental drift. (*Mesosaurus* was not mentioned in our review of the South African faunas because it occurs below the Beaufort beds.) But the presence of *Mesosaurus* in the lower Permian sediments of South Africa and Brazil does not necessarily imply close contiguity of these two regions, or their connection as parts of a broad east to west southern land mass. *Mesosaurus* might very well have made its way from the one area to the other along a narrow isthmus, or even along a chain of islands. The evidence of *Mesosaurus* to prove any particular theory of ancient continental relationships is thin evidence indeed.

In short, the distributions of Permian amphibians and reptiles in themselves do not solve our problem. The breaking apart of an ancient continent, with the drift of its component parts away from each other, the presence of a great east to west Gondwanaland in the southern hemisphere, the presence of isthmian links across the North and the South Atlantic, may all be invoked to account for the presence of Permian land-living vertebrates in various parts of the world. Conversely none of these explanations is essential to explain the patterns of amphibian and reptilian distributions during Permian times, because those animals might have made the crossings from the Old World into North and South America the long way around – by way of trans-Bering and Panamanian bridges. Thus any explanation depends largely on personal bias, which is not a very satisfactory statement with which to end a discussion.

What about climates ? The distributions of Permian amphibians and reptiles around the world, as far north as Spitzbergen and as far south as the tips of the southern land masses, would seem to show that climates then were generally tropical and subtropical*, even though there were the many local differences already mentioned in preceding pages of this chapter. It is hard to believe that the amphibians and reptiles of Permian times could have thrived in climates much more rigorous than those which today typify the tropics, and subtropical areas such as Florida, Paraná in Brazil, the Indian peninsula and northern Australia. The early Permian land-living animals of Texas and of northern Europe would indicate such climates in the northern hemisphere at the outset of Permian history, even though there may have been cold climates and glaciers in the southern hemisphere. With the advent of middle Permian times mild and tropical climates extended far and wide over the globe, as is attested by the spread of pareiasaurs and therapsids from southern Africa to northern Russia, and from western Europe through eastern Asia. And there is good reason to think that if only we had the record of middle and upper Permian amphibians and reptiles in the New World, we would see similar broad distributions of these animals over wide ranges of latitude.

We have looked at and speculated about the world and its land-living animals at the close of the Paleozoic era. We now come to the opening of the Mesozoic era – to the advent of the Triassic period, a time of transition in the evolutionary history of the amphibians and reptiles.

*See 'Page Corrections and Emendations' in Addendum.

Chapter 4

The Transition

THE ADVENT OF the Triassic period is on the whole clearly marked in the record of the rocks, for in most parts of the world there are breaks in sedimentation between the uppermost Permian beds and those of lowermost Triassic age. And in most parts of the world there are distinct differences in the fossils, particularly marine fossils, which are contained within these youngest of Permian and oldest of Triassic sediments*. The break is generally clear and profound, the expression in the fossil record of world-wide exterminations of numerous marine invertebrates at the close of Permian time. For this reason it has long been recognized as the line of differentiation between two of the great eras of earth history. Yet we know in our minds that there are no breaks in time or in life. Days and years and centuries succeed each other with steady regularity as the earth wheels around the sun through the ages, while in spite of extinctions many plants and animals continue to beget their successors in the great drama of life. The breaks which we use to divide the stream of earth history into eras and periods and lesser units of time and of rock associations are based in part upon the blanks in the record, which point in some degree to our lack of complete knowledge concerning the earth's past.

Luckily for us, however, there are a few places on the earth's surface where it is possible to see the almost continuous transition from Permian to Triassic history preserved in sequences of sandstones and shales that represent deposits formed on the bottoms of rivers or streams or ponds, and in fossil sequences of faunas that lived through this crucial time. These places are preserved for us particularly in South Africa and to some degree in northern Russia. We need not examine in detail just now the manner in which Triassic tetrapods succeeded Permian ones in South Africa or in Russia; these interesting examples of faunal parades, the beginnings of which we have

*See 'Page Corrections and Emendations' in Addendum.

already seen, will be considered farther on. But perhaps it may be of some interest to review in a general way the Permian–Triassic transition, so far as it affected the amphibians and reptiles of two hundred million years ago.

One of the great contrasts between late Paleozoic and early Mesozoic life is to be seen in the development of the amphibians. The Permian period, notably in its early stages, was the time when the amphibians attained the zenith of their success, the time when in some regions of the world these numerous and often large animals were active and direct disputants with the early reptiles for living space on the land. Yet the amphibians during the later phases of Permian history had entered into a decline, so it would seem as if in the final days of the Paleozoic (even discounting the bias of preserved fossil environments) the amphibians were far outnumbered and very much dominated by the reptiles. Consequently the Triassic period opened with a depleted array of amphibians, as compared with those that had inhabited Permian lands.

Yet in spite of the increasing dominance of the reptiles one group of labyrinthodont amphibians did continue through the Triassic period in a final outburst of evolutionary diversity. These labyrinthodonts were the stereospondyls, many of them the giants of the amphibian world, all of them obviously constant dwellers in streams and ponds*. They were able to continue through this period when reptiles ruled the world mainly because they were confined to a habitat in which there was a certain degree of protection from their reptilian enemies. They populated the world from east to west and far to the north and to the south, forming a somewhat archaic element within the varied assemblages of progressive reptiles that so characterized the Triassic period.

The stereospondyl amphibians were the last of a long line of amphibian evolution, a line that had its beginning far back in time. Other amphibians that had enjoyed long successes during the last part of the Paleozoic era were now extinct; new amphibians were beginning to appear. The Triassic period was in truth a crucial interlude in the history of the amphibians, a time during which there was a complete replacement of the ancient lineages by new ones, a time when the long-established labyrinthodonts, successful through a hundred million years and more of evolutionary history, continued their success through this final phase of their development while the amphibians of the modern world, so familiar to us, came upon the

*See 'Page Corrections and Emendations' in Addendum.

scene. It was the period in which the first frogs, seemingly insignificant in comparison with their giant stereospondyl cousins, made their appearance. As for the other modern amphibians, the salamanders and their relatives, and the tropical coecilians, the fossil record tells us nothing. But it is not improbable that these amphibians, too, arose at about this stage of earth history.

During the Triassic period there was, one might say, an explosion of progressive and active reptiles of diverse types, yet there also were various reptilian holdovers from the late Paleozoic scene. For example, the cotylosaurs, the earliest and most primitive of the reptiles, continued into and through the Triassic, just as did the labyrinthodont amphibians. These cotylosaurs, known as procolophonids, were

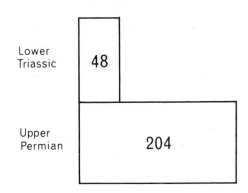

Figure 33. A comparison of the number of tetrapod genera from upper Permian sediments with those known from the lower Triassic. The figures give some measure as to the amount of extinction that occurred during the transition from Permian to Triassic times[*].

Lower Triassic 48

Upper Permian 204

restricted and specialized in their mode of life, being small, stubby-bodied reptiles, often with spikes on the skull, probably frequenting undergrowth in search of food. In a general way they played the role in Triassic faunas that lizards do today, and may be compared with such modern lizards as the 'horned toads' of Texas and adjacent states, or analogous Old World types.

Other reptiles successfully passing through the difficult time of transition from a Permian into a Triassic world were of more advanced types. Among these were the lizard-like protorosaurs, reptiles of varied form that, like the procolophonids, may have occupied niches which today are filled by certain lizards. The same applies to the eosuchians[†], very much like lizards in external appearance and perhaps in their habits, but of strategic importance in reptilian history since they are structurally the group from which the great group

[*]See 'Tables and Diagrams' in Addendum.
[†]See 'Page Corrections and Emendations' in Addendum.

of archosaurs – the thecodonts and crocodilians, the flying reptiles and the dinosaurs – had their origin.

Finally, some of the mammal-like reptiles which so strikingly dominated late Permian continents continued through the Triassic period with marked success, even though a great wave of extinction swept through the therapsids during the transition from Permian to Triassic time. The tusked dicynodonts, though reduced in variety, became especially ubiquitous during the course of Triassic history, migrating from one continent to another, until they were universally distributed throughout the world. The advanced mammal-like reptiles, especially the therocephalians and the cynodonts, are very important in Triassic faunas, and by studying the progression of mammal-like reptiles through successively later Triassic sediments we can almost see these particular reptiles being transformed, throughout the extent of their anatomy, into mammals. Indeed, some of the Triassic ictidosaurs, which are the most advanced of the mammal-like reptiles, are so close to the lower borders of mammalian organization that it is almost an academic question whether they are to be labeled reptiles or mammals.

So we see the Triassic period as an interval in earth history during which, in spite of extinctions, many groups of land-living vertebrates continued as the heirs of long evolutionary lineages extending back into Paleozoic history. At the same time the Triassic was a period when many new lines of reptilian evolution made their first appearance.

Among the reptilian newcomers on the Triassic scene were the turtles. These have been extraordinarily successful animals, continuing essentially in their present form through almost two hundred million years of earth history, seeing many families of animals, great and small, appear and disappear, surviving through the rise and fall of numerous evolutionary dynasties, all the while continuing their slow but steady way of life. The ancient fable of the tortoise and the hare may very appropriately be applied in an evolutionary context to the history of turtles. It should be said here that the turtles, which seemingly arose suddenly in Triassic times, are very probably the descendants of the eunotosaurian reptiles[*], at the present time known from rare and incomplete fossils found in the Permian *Endothiodon* zone of the Karroo beds.

One of the far-reaching events in vertebrate history that took place during the days of the Triassic was the invasion of the oceans by the

[*] See 'Page Corrections and Emendations' in Addendum.

THE AGE OF REPTILES

reptiles. This was indeed something new – the return of land-living vertebrates to a life in the sea. It marks in a sense a reversal in the trend of tetrapod evolution, which up until this time had been increasingly oriented to life on dry land. Now many reptiles abandoned the land and became largely aquatic, in some cases completely aquatic, inhabitants of the environment of their distant ancestors.

Several groups of reptiles made their separate excursions into the seas during Triassic times. The ichthyosaurs, the most highly adapted of all reptiles for marine life, suddenly appear in beds of middle Triassic age. These reptiles, fish-like or porpoise-like in form, with the body streamlined, with the tail specialized into a propulsive fin, with the legs flattened into paddles for balancing, with a fleshy dorsal fin on the back to prevent the animal from rolling, with the jaws elongated and furnished with many teeth for fish-catching, and with enormous eyes for scanning the dimly lit water, swim into the Triassic world from some mysterious past. The first ichthyosaurs are highly specialized and there is no fossil evidence to show what their ancestors may have been like. It has recently been suggested that the ichthyosaurs, and the turtles as well, may have originated from a common ancestor – perhaps a Permian reptile related to the little procolophonids, those lizard-like cotylosaurs that became so widely distributed in Triassic times[*].

The first nothosaurs were early Triassic newcomers, adapted to life in the ocean. These elongated reptiles, with large paddles used for swimming, and long sinuous necks, with small skulls, the jaws of which are armed with long, fish-catching teeth, show clear adaptations for a mode of life quite different from that of the ichthyosaurs. The nothosaurs were evidently dwellers of the ocean margin, living perhaps like modern sea-lions or seals, pursuing fishes in the shallow waters near the shore, perhaps scrambling out on the rocks to sun themselves. The nothosaurs, continuing through Triassic history, are interesting not only in their own right, but also because they were the ancestors of the plesiosaurs. The plesiosaurs were essentially nothosaurs modified and grown to gigantic proportions, inhabitants of the surfaces of the oceans throughout the world during Jurassic and Cretaceous times. The first plesiosaurs are found in middle Triassic beds.

Another group of Triassic marine reptiles, the placodonts, were cousins of the nothosaurs. These reptiles, which made their appearance during late Triassic times, were in effect the 'marine turtles' of

[*]See 'Page Corrections and Emendations' in Addendum.

those distant days. It must not be thought, in using this statement, that the placodonts are in any way related to the turtles (beyond the fact, of course, that they are reptiles) but rather it must be recognized that they must have been in appearance and adaptations strikingly similar to the great sea turtles of our present-day oceans. They have round or flat bodies, covered with armor, flipper-like limbs, and a strangely specialized skull, deep, and rather pointed in some forms, flat and truncated in others. The jaws are furnished with a few huge, flattened teeth, quite obviously used for crushing molluscs. So the placodonts, though like the modern marine turtles in form, were probably somewhat different in habits. They may have lived more like modern walruses, swimming down to the bottom of shallow waters to dig up shelled invertebrates.

On preceding pages it has been said that some Triassic reptiles, members of groups holding over from Permian times, were probably lizard-like in their life habits. Recent fossil evidence would seem to indicate that the true lizards arose during the final stages of Triassic history, and as this proves to be correct these reptiles also may be listed among the progressive newcomers in the Triassic world.

Rhynchocephalians, today represented by the lone tuatera of New Zealand, were particularly characteristic of Triassic times, when they spread throughout the world. They are of special interest because of their close relationships to the archosaurian reptiles, the rulers of the Mesozoic era.

The first archosaurians to appear during early Triassic history were the thecodonts, occupying a significant and central position in the story of the Age of Reptiles*. They were numerous and successful during the Triassic, and then at the end of this period became extinct, but before they disappeared into limbo they gave rise to the dinosaurian rulers of the Age of Reptiles, animals that were destined to dominate all of the continents through a span of a hundred million years.

The first and most primitive thecodonts were the pseudosuchians, the stem members being small, lightly built reptiles, in which the body was held in a partially upright position and pivoted at the hips. The bird-like hind limbs are very strong, and it is evident that these reptiles relied almost entirely upon them for locomotion, running across the ground like long-legged birds. The fore limbs are short and the hands were in life evidently used as grasping organs. The tail is long, in part a counterbalance to the weight of the body. The

69

skull is lightly constructed, narrow and deep, the jaws set with many sharp teeth. Evidently these were active and agile reptiles, able to pursue and catch small game.

From these stem pseudosuchians evolved larger pseudosuchians, including heavy, armored types that walked on all four feet, and also in late Triassic times the crocodile-like phytosaurs, which anticipated almost exactly the crocodiles in structure and obviously in habits, too. But the phytosaurs were not able to survive beyond the end of Triassic time and were replaced by their imitators, the crocodiles, also descended from primitive, pseudosuchian ancestors.

Late in Triassic history there arose the first dinosaurs, the ancestral saurischians and ornithischians, early representatives of the two orders of dinosaurs. The first saurischians were essentially enlargements of primitive pseudosuchians, although even so they are not very big. In them the pose is bipedal, the hind limbs are bird like, the fore limbs are small, the tail is long, the skull is narrow and deep and the jaws are set with many blade-like teeth. The same description applies in a very general way to the first ornithischians, too, with the exception that these dinosaurs show, even at this early stage of their development, the specialized pelvis, the characteristic limbs, the beaked skull and the blade-like, cutting teeth, so typical of all ornithischian evolution. These early dinosaurs, between six and ten feet in length, were secondary members of the hierarchy of late Triassic reptiles; certainly they were no match in direct competition with the huge, aggressive, crocodile-like phytosaurs. But they were the progenitors of Jurassic and Cretaceous reptilian giants, some of which were to be the largest animals ever to walk upon the earth.

This has been a review of tetrapod life at the beginning of the age of dinosaurs. An attempt has been made to show that at that time, almost two hundred million years ago, tetrapod life was in a stage of transition so that the world was inhabited in part by amphibians and reptiles belonging to groups which had dominated the Permian scene, and in part by amphibians and reptiles which were progressive newcomers – animals destined to give to the years of the dinosaurs a very special look. Perhaps the coming together in Triassic times of these two groups of tetrapods, the older forms, some of them archaic – some of them not so archaic, and the newer forms, some of them progressive – some of them not so progressive but none the less well adapted to the world around them, can be graphically summarized in two parallel lists.

HOLDOVERS FROM PERMIAN TIMES	NEW GROUPS, ARISING IN TRIASSIC TIMES
Labyrinthodont amphibians	Frogs
Cotylosaurs ⎫ Protorosaurs ⎬ role of lizards in Triassic Eosuchians ⎭	True lizards
Dicynodonts: ancient herbivores	
Therocephalians ⎫ mammal-like Cynodonts ⎭ reptiles	Ictidosaurs: final step toward mammals
	Turtles
	Ichthyosaurs ⎫ Nothosaurs ⎬ marine reptiles Plesiosaurs ⎪ Placodonts ⎭
	Rhynchocephalians
	Thecodonts
	Crododilians: appear at end of the Triassic
	Saurischian dinosaurs
	Ornithischian dinosaurs

The transition among land-living vertebrates that took place during Triassic times may be correlated with the environmental changes that set the beginning of the Mesozoic era apart from the final stages of Paleozoic history. Thus if we look at the Triassic period as a time of new opportunities for land-living animals, a time when, more than ever before in the history of the earth the advantages were with those animals that had the strength and the agility to move forcefully and quickly across the land, the evolution of Triassic reptiles fits logically into the pattern of global evolution.

This was a time of variety, as is shown not only by the evidence of the fossils, but also by that of the rocks within which the fossils are enclosed or near which the fossils are entombed. It was a time when lands were high – higher than they had been during the preceding Permian period, when inland seas, which are always present through time in one place or another, were limited in extent, even more limited than they had been in Permian times, and when climates were varied, even more varied than were the climates that had made the Permian period a time of climatic differences. But although there were many differences in climates from one part of the earth to another, these differences probably did not result in great extremes of temperature. Once again as in preceding geologic periods the earth was largely tropical and subtropical over much of its extent, so that large amphibians and reptiles, obviously limited to rather benign climates, if the physiological evidence from their modern relatives has any meaning in interpreting the past, lived far and wide. Climatic variability in Triassic times was probably expressed in some succession of seasons, in alternations of wet and dry periods, and in the simultaneous presence of jungles, of wide plains and even of deserts. There was much volcanic activity, so that cones and lava fields added to the variety of Triassic landscapes. In general the seas were warm. Perhaps at the close of Triassic history climates were somewhat cooler and moister than they had been through much of Triassic time, but the change in this direction was moderate. All of which was favorable to animals that were quick on their feet, and to animals that swam in the oceans.

The evidence for what has been said about the transitions among land-living vertebrates as they may be correlated with the development of climates and environments during Triassic times is, of course, derived from the study of Triassic rocks and fossils around the world. This study began in central Europe, particularly in Germany, where rocks of this age can be divided into three great groups, these being, from bottom to top, the Buntsandstein or Bunter, the Muschelkalk and the Keuper. These three divisions, which also may be thought of as Lower, Middle and Upper, the triad that constitutes the first great period of Mesozoic history, were established in 1834 by the German geologist, H. von Alberti. The concept of a threefold division for the rocks of early Mesozoic age was quickly and universally adopted by geologists – and Triassic, or Trias, it has been, ever since.

The Bunter and the Keuper in Europe are sediments deposited in streams and ponds, in rivers and lakes, in which sandstones are predominant. They are commonly of a dark red color. The Muschelkalk is an intercalated limestone, obviously the record of an invasion of the land by a shallow sea. In England, however, there is no Muschelkalk, possibly an indication that this part of the world was dry land during the extent of Triassic history.

We may now return to the subject, hitherto deferred, of the transition from the Permian into the Triassic period, as seen in the more

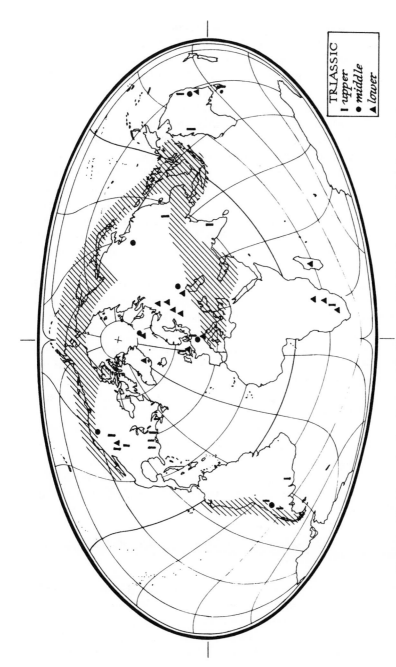

Figure 34. World map showing the general localities at which Triassic tetrapods have been found. The shaded areas represent regions of major submergence.

TRIASSIC
| upper
• middle
▲ lower

or less continuous sequences of sediments in South Africa and in northern Russia. In Russia the fifth zone of the succession, introduced in our discussion of Permian history, follows the fourth zone to represent the beginning of the Triassic in that part of the world. The sixth zone, which follows the fifth zone without any significant lapse, is also of early Triassic age. Finally, the seventh zone, the last of the Russian succession, is seemingly to be placed at the top of the middle Triassic, perhaps even at the bottom of the upper Triassic.

In the parallel South African series, the lower Triassic is represented by the Upper Beaufort beds, which in turn may be subdivided from bottom to top into the *Lystrosaurus* and the *Cynognathus* zones. The so-called *Procolophon* zone, long considered as a distinct horizon between the *Lystrosaurus* and *Cynognathus* zones, is now thought to consist of locally deposited pockets within the *Lystrosaurus* beds. Above the Beaufort beds are the Molteno beds of basal upper Triassic age, which sediments have as yet yielded few fossil bones, although at one locality, at least, some interesting and very diagnostic reptilian trackways are to be seen. Finally, above the Molteno are the fossiliferous Red Beds and Cave Sandstones, these together with the Molteno constituting the Stormberg series.

The evolution of amphibians and reptiles may be traced elsewhere in lower Triassic sediments in western North America, in the Moenkopi beds, in India in the Panchet and Yerrapalli beds, in China by some scattered fossils found in Sinkiang, and in the Narrabeen sediments of Australia.

The record of middle Triassic tetrapods is not particularly extensive. The classic European Muschelkalk contains marine fossils, and in the Alpine region, especially, are beautifully preserved protorosaurs, nothosaurs and other reptiles. In western North America are middle Triassic sediments containing primitive ichthyosaurs, while in the southwest the Moenkopi formation, already mentioned, may extend beyond the lower into the middle part of the Triassic sequence. Middle Triassic vertebrates are also found in Shansi, China, and in the Hawkesbury beds of Australia.

By contrast, upper Triassic fossil vertebrates are abundantly represented in many localities throughout the world. There might be mentioned, first of all, the Santa Maria beds of southern Brazil, in which there is a remarkably rich fossil record, and the correlative Ischigualasto beds of northern Argentina, some eight hundred miles or so west of the Santa Maria exposures, these Argentinian sediments containing fantastically large numbers of fossil reptiles. There is a sharp division of opinion among interested authorities at present on whether the South American beds and their contained fossils are of upper middle or lower upper Triassic relationships. Such arguments, which are often carried on with great vigor year after year, may seem a bit esoteric, or perhaps a little unreal, to the outsider looking in. What matter whether these particular fossil reptiles of South America mark the close of middle Triassic or the opening of late Triassic history? In one sense, it is of no great import; in another it is quite significant. On such arguments, of the seemingly minute splitting of hairs, is built up our knowledge of evolutionary history. The age of Triassic reptiles in South America may have some bearing on the age of Triassic reptiles in other parts of the world, or conversely it may be significant in trying to determine the relationships of the South American continent to other continents at this period of earth history. It may be important in attempting to reconstruct the ancient movements of land-living animals from one part of the world to another. It may figure to some degree in visualizing the evolutionary radiation of certain groups of extinct reptiles. Moreover, it adds a fillip of spice to the lives of some paleontologists.

What has been said about the Triassic beds of South America applies in much the same way to correlative sediments in Africa. In East Africa the Manda beds may be equated with the Triassic sediments of South America, and thus may be of uppermost middle or lowermost upper Triassic affinities, according to the bias of the student. In this part of the world also are the upper Ruhuhu beds, possibly of middle, possibly of upper, Triassic relationships.

The classic upper Triassic is, of course, the Keuper of Europe. In the sediments of this division are found many fossil remains of amphibians and reptiles. Here we see the entrance of the first dinosaurs on the Mesozoic scene, and with them are huge labyrinthodont amphibians and phytosaurs. This triumvirate of primitive dinosaurs, phytosaurs and large amphibians (the last of the labyrinthodonts) is characteristic of upper Triassic sediments throughout the northern hemisphere. Interestingly enough the combination is not found in southern hemisphere sediments.

In the Newark sediments of eastern North America, the Chinle beds of Arizona and New Mexico, the Dockum beds of Texas and the Popo Agie beds of Wyoming are found the fossils of land-living vertebrates, among which dinosaurs, phytosaurs and large amphibians are prominent, that tie these localities very closely to the European exposures, indicating that there was in late Triassic times an open lane of communication between North America and western Europe. The same faunal complex is found in the Maleri beds of India. And finally, in the Lufeng beds of China, are found upper Triassic dinosaurs that are very closely related indeed to some of the Keuper dinosaurs of Europe and the dinosaurs from the Red Beds of the South African Stormberg series. But in Africa there have not been found the accompanying phytosaurs and amphibians, so characteristic of the European–Indian–North American associations.

In Europe there are sediments above the Keuper beds, known as the Rhaetic. These may be regarded as representing the very end of the Triassic record: the final chapter in the story of Triassic life, immediately preceding the advent of Jurassic history.

The age relationships of these Triassic horizons may be represented in a correlation chart (Table 4).

Such are some of the general aspects of this transitory phase in the history of reptilian evolution. Let us now look at a few details.

On the Island of Spitzbergen, far above the Arctic Circle and not so far below the North Pole, and in East Greenland, at a latitude above seventy degrees, are sediments of early Triassic or Bunter age, containing the fossils of some rather long-snouted amphibians known as trematosaurs. These trematosaurs, labyrinthodonts descended from some of the amphibians so abundant during Permian times, were evidently fish-eaters that hunted in shallow waters for their food. And their occurrence in such very high latitudes must mean that bland climates extended over almost all of the surface of the globe at the beginning of the Triassic period. Lands that today are covered with ice and snow were, some two hundred million years ago, warm and moist, the habitat of animals quite incapable of surviving rigorous winters.

In the Bunter beds of northern Europe there are also trematosaurs, and it may be that there were connections between Europe and other northern lands allowing these amphibians to move back and forth across the top of the world. There are other amphibians, too, in the Bunter sediments of northern Europe, of which *Capitosaurus* is especially well known. This large amphibian is a long-headed animal with a remarkably flat skull, and a skeleton in which the legs are comparatively small and weak. *Capitosaurus* and the other Bunter

Table 4. *Correlation of Triassic vertebrate horizons* *

Lower Triassic		Middle Triassic	Upper Triassic			
			Ischigualasto (Argentina)			SOUTH AMERICA
			Santa Maria (Brazil)			
Moenkopi			Chinle		Wingate / Moenave / Kayenta	NORTH AMERICA
			Dockum			
			Alcova			
Red Peak			Crow Mt.	Popo Agie		
			Newark			
Panchet (India)	Yerrapalli (India)	Shansi (China)	Maleri (India)	Lufeng (China)		ASIA
Bunter		Muschelkalk	Keuper			EUROPE
			Lettenkohle	Gyps-Keuper	Rhaetic	
Zone V	Zone VI	Zone VII				RUSSIA
Upper Beaufort			Stormberg			AFRICA
Sakamena Madagascar / *Lystrosaurus* *(Procolophon)* Zone	*Cynognathus* Zone		Molteno	Red Beds	Cave Sandstone	
Narrabeen		Hawkesbury	Wianamatta			AUSTRALIA

77

*See 'Tables and Diagrams' in Addendum.

amphibians which had evolved along more or less similar lines were inhabitants of streams and ponds, where, reasonably safe from the reptiles of those days, they preyed upon clumsy, heavily scaled fishes. By reason of their specializations and their habits, these amphibians were numerous and successful in an age when the reptiles were becoming increasingly dominant on the land.

Large and aggressive reptiles undoubtedly wandered across what is now the European continent during Bunter times, but if so their fossils are strangely lacking. The record of reptiles in the lower Triassic of central Europe is indeed sparse so far as bones are concerned, much of what we know about the inhabitants of the land at this stage of earth history being based upon footprints. It would seem that the conditions of climate and environment were such when the Bunter sandstones were being deposited that bones and skeletons were rarely preserved, even though footprints made by the animals were. This is a condition encountered time and again in the fossil record, as we shall see, and it adds many difficulties and a considerable amount of frustration to the life of the paleontologist.

There are fortunately a few skeletons or partial skeletons of the Bunter reptiles of Europe at hand, mainly of small animals. The restricted fossil record gives us an impression of various lizard-like reptiles lurking in the undergrowth to feed upon insects and other small game, perhaps to eat plants as well. The little procolophonids were inhabitants of this land – probably in great numbers. There may be mentioned among them *Koiloskiosaurus* and *Anomoiodon*, small reptiles with rather flattened, triangular skulls, enormous openings to accommodate the eyes, and limited ranges of chisel-like teeth around the margins of the jaws. These rather stocky procolophonids must have fed on some very special diet, to judge by the specialized teeth, but we can only guess what their food might have been – perhaps they ate some sort of plant food that needed to be chopped into fragments by the blades of the chisel-shaped teeth.

Fortunately, we get in addition to this very fragmentary glimpse of life on the land a supplementary glimpse of life in Bunter seas, based on the fossil remains of *Nothosaurus*. This little reptile, three feet or so in length, and one of the first of the reptiles to migrate into the sea in Triassic times, was in a sense a leader of the evolutionary trend that was to become so widely established along several separate lines as the years of the Triassic flowed through time, as life on the land became ever more competitive for the reptiles.

A much more satisfactory look at the northern hemisphere amphibians and reptiles of Bunter times is to be had from the fossil deposits of zones V and VI of north Russia, the former exposed in a wide band to the north and east of Moscow, almost to the White Sea, the latter in a rather restricted area to the north of the Caspian. Here

Figure 35. *Nothosaurus* (above) and *Placodus* (below), Triassic reptiles from Europe. *Nothosaurus*, four or five feet in length, probably lived along shorelines, where it pursued fishes. *Placodus*, eight feet or more in length, frequented shallow sea floors, where it ate hard-shelled molluscs, crushing them with its broad teeth. Both of these reptiles may have been capable of climbing out on rocks and beaches, like modern seals and walruses.

is a continuation of the record that we saw so nicely developed for upper Permian vertebrates. It may be recalled that in zone IV of late Permian age, there are numerous labyrinthodont amphibians, cotylosaurian reptiles, a host of mammal-like reptiles, together with a few other reptilian groups, thus giving some variety to the assemblage. In zone V, the very base of the Triassic, there are also varied labyrinthodonts, some cotylosaurs, and several groups of reptiles, yet in spite of these general similarities between the lower Triassic vertebrates and those of the upper Permian in this region, the later faunas are rather different from the earlier ones.

The amphibians of zone V, for example, are the specialized descendants from certain Permian labyrinthodonts. There are long-snouted amphibians, the benthosuchids, paralleling the trematosaurs and, like the trematosaurs, they were probably aquatic, fish-catching animals. A number of well-known genera have been described: *Benthosuchus*, *Wetlugasaurus*, *Thoosuchus* and *Volgosuchus*. Capitosaurs are present, and carry on into the next zone, where *Capitosaurus* is associated with *Trematosaurus*. Also in zone V there is a very short-headed stereospondyl with a strange skull, wider than it is long. Amphibians of this type became very widely distributed over the world during Triassic times, and here we probably see the beginning of a successful evolutionary line.

Turning now to the reptiles, we can see a great change taking place between late Permian and early Triassic times in this part of the world. The mammal-like reptiles, which had flourished in such abundance during the final years of the Permian period, suffered a great reduction during the transition from Permian to Triassic times, the seeming sole survivors being some tusked dicynodonts and (in zone VI) some of the very mammal-like theriodonts. In place of the mammal-like reptiles there are representatives of other groups, some holdovers from the Permian, some newcomers. Among the holdovers are procolophonids and also a small protorosaur, *Microcnemus*. Among the newcomers is a small rhynchocephalian and a pseudosuchian, *Chasmatosuchus*. There are also some other archosaurian reptiles.

The general complexion of the lowest Triassic tetrapod fauna of Russia, especially the presence in it of small reptiles, gives to the assemblage a cast that relates zone V with the Bunter fauna of Europe, such as we know it. It shows that in this part of the world there was essentially a single fauna or, if you will, a series of related faunas, composed of animals wandering freely throughout lands of northern latitudes and eastern longitudes. But there were broader faunal connections as well, and as in late Permian sediments the early Triassic faunas of northern Russia show relationships with correlative faunas in South Africa.

In the southern continent the lower Triassic land-living vertebrates show a course of development rather different from that followed by those of the northern hemisphere. Here, in the *Lystrosaurus* zone of the Beaufort beds, there is no replacement of mammal-like reptiles by other groups, as in Russia, but rather a limited continuation of the evolutionary development of these progressive reptiles, with a small leavening of other reptilian groups. On the other hand there are, as in the north, numerous stereospondyls – something of a contrast with the paucity of amphibians in the Permian record of South Africa.

These amphibians are of several types. Some of them are rather large, others are quite small. Their presence in the *Lystrosaurus* zone, this being the lowest zone of Triassic sediments in the South African Upper Beaufort group, would seem to show that by early Triassic times environments in South Africa were somewhat different from those of the late Permian. In short, South Africa at the beginning of Triassic history was very possibly less of a rolling upland than it had been during the closing phases of Permian history, with perhaps more ponds and streams than in the preceding period.

Yet even though the environment may have been somewhat different, the dominance of the mammal-like therapsids continued. It was nevertheless a reduced dominance – an indication that the mammal-like reptiles were approaching the end of their long and complex history. As reptiles they were almost through, and those that continued into the later stages of Triassic history were able to persist largely because they were becoming mammals. They were able to compete and hold their own because most of them lived like mammals rather than like reptiles, because their habits and their behavior were mammalian, or perhaps one should say proto-mammalian, which took them out of direct competition with the archosaurs and the other reptiles then inheriting the Triassic world.

Figure 36. The lower Triassic reptile *Lystrosaurus* of Africa and Asia. *Lystrosaurus* seemingly was aquatic, as indicated by the elevated nostrils and other features – a sort of small, reptilian 'hippopotamus', two feet and perhaps as much as four feet long. Fossils of this reptile are found in prodigious numbers in the *Lystrosaurus* zone of the Upper Beaufort beds in South Africa.

Thus in the *Lystrosaurus* zone there are only two genera of dicynodonts, whereas in the immediately preceding Permian *Cistecephalus* zone there are twenty-four genera of these therapsids. One of these is *Lystrosaurus*, a reptile found in great numbers at this horizon, and consequently the one for which the zone is named. *Lystrosaurus* has a peculiarly shaped skull, with the nostrils high on the skull, between the elevated eyes. This almost surely indicates aquatic habits, and one may imagine this dicynodont as a sort of small reptilian hippopotamus, completely at home in rivers and lakes, perhaps feeding upon aquatic vegetation. The widespread occurrences of *Lystrosaurus* give some indication of the prevalence of waterways in the South African scene during early Triassic times.

In the late Permian of South Africa there is a host of gorgonopsians, the active, 'saber-tooth' therapsids; in the early Triassic there are none. The therocephalians drop from thirty-five genera to one known genus during the transition from the Permian to the Triassic, and only the cynodonts survive in some strength, there being fourteen upper Permian genera and eight lower Triassic forms, these latter being very near to the mammalian threshold. One of them, *Thrinaxodon*, may be mentioned. Recently the fossil remains of an adult, presumably a female, and a baby were found together, a tempting suggestion that perhaps we see here a mother and her young preserved as an example of parental care, so typical of the mammals and so unusual in the reptiles.

Other *Lystrosaurus* zone reptiles of South Africa are some small eosuchians and some pseudosuchians. *Prolacerta*, one of the eosuchians, is an almost ideal ancestor for the lizards, and it may very well be the base from which the lizards arose*.

The essential features of reptilian and amphibian evolution which had become established at the beginning of Triassic times in Africa was continued in that part of the world with some variations through the remainder of early Triassic history. In short, the dominance of therapsid reptiles, so typical of the *Lystrosaurus* zone fauna, is still apparent in the *Cynognathus* zone fauna, the fossil assemblage representing those land-living vertebrates that lived at the close of early Triassic times. The differences are mainly those of details, as might be expected during the time passage from the beginning to the end of early Triassic time, a span of some millions of years. (The *Procolophon* zone, commonly placed between the *Lystrosaurus* and *Cynognathus* zones, is here being purposely omitted because the fossil

82

*See 'Page Corrections and Emendations' in Addendum.

evidence from this supposed level is so scanty as to be of little use in a general discussion. Indeed, there are some who would doubt the existence of a *Procolophon* zone, regarding the sediments containing *Procolophon* as pockets eroded into the *Lystrosaurus* zone.)

It would appear that the highly progressive mammal-like reptiles, the theriodonts that approached the very threshold of mammalian anatomy and physiology, reached the climax of their development when the animals of the *Cynognathus* fauna were alive, during the

Figure 37. The theriodont reptile, *Cynognathus*, from the Lower Triassic Beaufort beds of South Africa. This predator, about as large as a wolf, is one of the very advanced mammal-like reptiles, which in life may possibly have been clothed with hair, rather than scales. Perhaps it had external ears. Perhaps it had a more or less constant body temperature. In short, this animal may have had, internally as well as externally, many of the attributes of mammals.

closing years of early Triassic time. Thus there are known a score and more genera representing these advanced mammal-like reptiles. *Cynognathus*, for which the zone is named, is characteristic – a medium to rather large, wolf-like reptile, with dagger-like canines, cheek teeth differentiated and specialized for cutting food, and with strong limbs drawn in beneath the body, thus allowing this active and aggressive predator to move about efficiently and probably with a considerable show of speed. The bauriamorphs, representing an evolutionary line distinct from and parallel to that typified by *Cynognathus*, are likewise very advanced types. So, too, are the diademodontids, named from the genus *Diademodon*, in which the cheek teeth are broad, obviously for crushing and grinding food, an indication that these reptiles were not simple meat-eaters, but rather must have subsisted on specialized diets. Incidentally, these are the only cynodont reptiles to persist beyond the limits of early Triassic time[*], their fossils are found in higher Triassic beds in South America.

And along with these advanced mammal-like therapsids in the *Cynognathus* zone is an even more mammal-like ictidosaurian reptile, *Karroomys*. The fauna is indeed a progressive one.

As for other reptiles, there is a single dicynodont known, a few pseudosuchians and rhynchocephalians and perhaps some procolophonids, these last being, as we have seen, small, Triassic cotylosaurs which in their mode of life must have been very much like the lizards that eventually were to supplant them.

Stereospondyl amphibians are also present in the *Cynognathus* zone, including *Wetlugasauras*, which it may be remembered was living in Russia at this same time.

With this brief survey of the lower Triassic amphibians and reptiles of South Africa we come to the end of a long succession of late Paleozoic and early Mesozoic faunas, a succession that shows the evolution of land-living vertebrates in Africa through a vast span of time. The *Cynognathus* zone fauna is the last among a series of assemblages marking the evolution of amphibian and reptilian life through the Lower and the Upper Beaufort groups. In the sequence of zones, *Tapinocephalus–Endothiodon–Cistecephalus–Lystrosaurus–(Procolophon)–Cynognathus*, we are afforded a magnificent and unexcelled demonstration of early tetrapod evolution, of origins, climaxes, extinctions and replacements, at one locale on the earth: Within the framework of this book it has been necessary to treat the Beaufort faunas separately, according to the context of their age relationships, but it is hoped that the reader will keep in mind the fact that here is a remarkable evolutionary succession transcending the man-made divisions of time.

The fossil remains of lower Triassic reptiles and amphibians are scattered and generally fragmentary in other parts of the world. The South African complex, especially of the *Lystrosaurus* zone which has been described, is indicated in India, where *Lystrosaurus* and a short-headed amphibian occur, and in Sinkiang, China, where again there has been found *Lystrosaurus*, associated with *Dicynodon* and a pseudosuchian. Recent discoveries in India have revealed a horizon containing a dicynodont very close to *Kannemeyeria* of the South African *Cynognathus* zone, while in Shansi, China, the dicynodont

[*]See 'Page Corrections and Emendations' in Addendum.

Sinokannemeyeria gives still more evidence of the close relationships between Africa and Asia during early Mesozoic history. Evidently, if the fossil record were adequate, we would be able to trace very nicely the early Triassic amphibians and reptiles of South Africa eastwardly across much of Asia.

In the southwestern part of the United States, in the Moenkopi formation, are found some amphibians and some fragments of reptiles, these latter too incomplete for good identification. Among the amphibians are a short-headed type and some rather large stereospondyls. The Moenkopi formation, an horizon that may extend from the lower into the middle Triassic, is a difficult formation in which to collect fossils. They are exceedingly rare and hard to come by, but perhaps future work will yield new materials which will help to solve the age and relationships of the Moenkopi fauna.

The end of early Triassic history is marked by a break in the evolutionary sequence of reptilian faunas throughout much of the world. It is the break between the Moenkopi formation of southwestern North America and the complex of upper Triassic formations – a break in the record involving many years of geologic time. It is the break in Africa between the Beaufort series, which had extended in unbroken continuity through much of the Permian and on through early Triassic time, and the overlying Stormberg series. It is the break in Europe between the continental Bunter and the marine Muschelkalk. It is a break that is perhaps bridged in one region, northern Russia, where the seventh zone of the Permian–Triassic sequence has been distinguished as following immediately the sixth zone. It is a break that gives us a chance to shift our attention from the reptiles living in early Triassic times to those inhabiting the world during the later stages of Triassic history. In short, it is a break that makes a good separation between this chapter and the next one.

Chapter 5

Supremacy of the Reptiles

BY THE END OF lower Triassic times the reptiles filled and ruled the continents almost completely. There were very few habitats on the land not occupied, hardly a niche that was not filled by a reptile adapted to a special kind of life enabling it to live successfully in its own particular fashion. There were large reptiles and small ones, plant-eating types and meat-eaters that fed upon the herbivores. Some reptiles lived on high ground, some along the rivers, some in trees. The competition among them for a place in which to live, in which to feed and perpetuate their own kind, must have been very intense. And so it was that with the advent of the middle Triassic many reptiles went to sea.

The record of this reptilian invasion of the oceans is especially well preserved in the middle Triassic Muschelkalk of Europe. Here are limestones and other sediments that accumulated in the bottom of a warm, shallow sea which through time advanced across Europe. It was an encroachment across the land comparable with the occupation today of the Mediterranean Basin by oceanic waters coming in through the Straits of Gibraltar, or the flooding of northern Canada by Hudson's Bay. And it is in the Muschelkalk deposits, as well as in other marine beds of this age, that the ichthyosaurs appear with dramatic suddenness. As has been remarked above, there are no solid clues to what the ancestors of the ichthyosaurs may have been like; the first ichthyosaurs are complete ichthyosaurs, streamlined and of piscine form. The only respects in which these ichthyosaurs are more primitive than their descendants are in certain details of the skull and in the fact that the tail fin is not quite as highly developed for swimming as in the ichthyosaurs of Jurassic and Cretaceous age. *Mixosaurus*, from Europe and Spitzbergen, and *Cymbospondylus*, from Europe and North America, are ichthyosaurs of this type. Incidentally, the presence of ichthyosaurs in so northern a locality as

Spitzbergen is a telling indication of the great spread of tropical seas at this stage of earth history.

At this time, and in these same seas, there were numerous nothosaurs, typified by *Nothosaurus* itself, which had survived from lower Triassic time, and by other genera as well. They were all elongated, supple animals of rather small size, with sinuous necks and small skulls, these latter furnished with long, sharp teeth for catching fishes, and with four large paddles for swimming in the shallow waters near the shore. Some of the nothosaurs have rather long skulls, others have short skulls, but on the whole they are all cut pretty much to a single pattern, a good pattern for living in Triassic seas, so that the nothosaurs, which had appeared at the beginning of this period of geologic history, continued throughout the extent of Triassic time.

Pistosaurus, the first plesiosaur, also makes its appearance in the Muschelkalk sediments, a neighbor of the nothosaurs whose grandparents were its own progenitor. The middle Triassic ichthyosaurs and nothosaurs, and the single plesiosaur, *Pistosaurus*, were all active fish-catchers that pursued their prey through the surface waters of the open ocean or near the shore. The placodonts were more sluggish marine reptiles that fed upon molluscs, crushing the shells of their victims between huge, expanded teeth. There may very well be a direct correlation between the development of such extremely heavy teeth in the middle Triassic placodonts and the fact that within the Muschelkalk sediments are molluscs with particularly heavy, hard shells.

Along the shores of the Muschelkalk sea and back in the low hills and the swamps away from the strand, there lived various amphibians and reptiles, of which we have a partial record in the rocks. The amphibians are seemingly for the most part very large stereospondyls – *Capitosaurus* and *Cyclotosaurus*, which were also inhabitants of early Triassic landscapes, and the gigantic *Mastodonsaurus*, with a broad, extraordinarily flat skull three or four feet long. The land-living reptiles of this stage of earth history in this part of the world, are, so far as we know them, rather small types – lizard-like procolophonids and protorosaurs, and small rhynchocephalians. There must have been many large reptiles living on land during Muschelkalk times, just as there were in the preceding Bunter and the following Keuper times, but the fossil record is largely blank on this score. This strange absence of large middle Triassic land-living reptiles is a nice illustration of the peculiarities of the accidents of preservation, with which the paleontologist often must cope.

Every now and then the paleontologist encounters a fossil that baffles him thoroughly, a specimen that defies all attempts to explain how it lived. The characters of the skeleton are so grotesque that one is hard pressed to guess what they mean in terms of adaptations to environment. Such a fossil is *Tanystrophaeus* from the middle Triassic of Europe. This reptile, that may be as much as ten feet in length,

Figure 38. One of the strangest of all Mesozoic reptiles is *Tanystrophaeus*, from the middle Triassic marine sediments of Europe. Much of the six to ten foot length of this reptile is taken up by the giraffe-like neck, the adaptive significance of which is not easy to fathom.

has a reasonably normal body, limbs and tail, all of these parts of the skeleton being 'lizard-like', to use a much over-worked term, but the neck is out of all proportion to the rest of the animal, for it is as long as the body and tail combined. It is like the neck of a giraffe, in that it is composed of comparatively few vertebrae, twelve to be exact, of which nine are extraordinarily long. And on the end of this boom-like neck is a small, elongated skull, the jaws of which are furnished with sharp teeth.

How did this strange reptile live ? It was probably an inhabitant of ponds and streams, or at least it may have lived along the edges of waterways. But what were its habits ? What could have been the purpose of such a long, and rather clumsy neck, a neck that because of the length of each individual vertebra could not have been flexible as a nothosaurian neck was flexible. These are questions that await answers.

There were various reptiles in Europe during middle Triassic times that can be described as 'lizard-like'. Some rhynchocephalians complete the roster of Muschelkalk reptiles.

Elsewhere in the world the middle Triassic record of fossil vertebrates is very spotty, to put it mildly. In Africa and South America are some reptile-bearing deposits that may have accumulated at the very end of middle Triassic times, or perhaps at the beginning of late Triassic time. In this book they will be discussed in connection with the upper Triassic, not because that age is unequivocally proven, but rather because the faunas are readily compared with upper Triassic faunas in other parts of the world.

In north Russia is the uppermost of the Triassic zones, with some large amphibians, gigantic dicynodont reptiles, and footprints in the sandstones that represent reptiles of unknown relationships. There is left one other record to mention, of a labyrinthodont, *Bothriceps*, from the middle Triassic Hawkesbury beds of Australia.

With the close of middle Triassic times the Muschelkalk sea retreated from central Europe, as this region was elevated into a broad, continental platform. Everywhere all over the earth lands became higher than they had been – there began a phase of earth history during which continents were extensive, in which landscapes were rather varied, and in which climates were anything but monotonous, even though tropical and warm temperatures prevailed over most of the surface of the globe. The transition of life on the land, which had begun with the advent of the Triassic period, reached its climax, and reptiles, to judge by the fossil record, were numerous and varied to a degree never previously attained in their evolutionary history.

Abundant remains of upper Triassic fossils greet the delighted paleontologist at numerous localities throughout the world, and he frequently finds himself digging in richly fossiliferous quarries where every day brings new adventures of discovery. But in this world of man no joy is completely unalloyed, and one of the less happy aspects of collecting upper Triassic fossils is the fact that in many areas these specimens occur in difficult matrices of very hard sandstone, often impregnated with iron, so that the rock is much harder than the fossil bones enclosed within it. The job of collecting and preparing fossils found in such refractory rocks is difficult and time-consuming, to put it mildly. At the other extreme, some Triassic fossils are found in clays so soft and friable that the attention of collector and preparator must be concentrated on delicate techniques aimed at preventing the fossils from crumbling into tiny fragments, completely beyond recovery. Yet in spite of these problems of technique which frequently but not invariably go along with the study of upper Triassic reptiles and amphibians, large collections have been accumulated in many museums to give us a broad and fascinating picture of the tetrapods of that age.

The classic upper Triassic fossil assemblage is that of the Keuper beds of Europe. It is the standard of comparison for students interested in upper Triassic life. What were Keuper tetrapods like ? Keuper labyrinthodonts are represented far and wide by large, flat-headed creatures that lived in shallow ponds and rivers and fed upon bony, heavy-scaled fishes. The most characteristic of these in Europe is *Metoposaurus*, an animal some five or six feet in length, with an inordinately large, flat skull, with the skeleton behind the skull weak, the vertebrae poorly articulated with each other, and the legs and feet ridiculously small. It seems quite obvious that such amphibians were permanent inhabitants of the streams. And sharing the streams and ponds with *Metoposaurus* were some medium-sized labyrinthodonts known as plagiosaurs. These animals are also flat-headed, but the skull is very broad and short, giving a wide, side to side gape of the mouth. In spite of what seems to us a very weird appearance these were extraordinarily successful amphibians, to judge by their broad distribution in upper Triassic sediments.

The stereospondyl amphibians, although numerous as individuals, are limited in variety; they make up a small fraction of the list of Keuper tetrapods. The variety in this fauna is rather to be found among the reptiles, which are of many kinds, adapted to different modes of life. To them we may now turn our attention.

One might expect with good reason to find the bones of procolophonids at various localities in the Keuper sediments, but to date the only indication of their presence in the upper Triassic beds of Europe is furnished by a little skeleton, the skull of which is decorated with spikes, from Scotland. This is *Leptopleuron*. The paucity of procolophonids may very well be a result of the accidents of preservation and of discovery, owing to the small size and delicate nature of the fossils. Be that as it may, there are the fossil remains of the first very primitive turtles in the Keuper deposits. *Proganochelys* and *Triassochelys* are full-fledged turtles, with well-developed shells, beaked skulls and heavy limbs. About the only large difference between these ancient turtles and their modern descendants is the fact that the Triassic turtles were not able to pull the neck and the legs into the shell in so complete and neat a fashion as can turtles of the present day. Also, these turtle progenitors have a few small teeth on the palate, a leftover character inherited from cotylosaurian ancestors.

Figure 39. One of the earliest turtles, *Triassochelys*, from the upper Triassic of Europe.

The reptiles that had taken to the sea during earlier phases of Triassic history continued into late Triassic times, and ancient turtles on the beaches might have seen ichthyosaurs, nothosaurs, plesiosaurs and placodonts in the waters beyond the strand. The turtles on the land (they did not venture into the sea in late Triassic times) and the placodonts in the oceans make an interesting combination, because the placodonts of the late Triassic evolved along lines that made them uncannily similar to the marine turtles of later ages. In these placodonts, represented by such genera as *Placochelys* and *Henodus*, there is a heavy bony armor over the back, which in form and function imitates very nicely the shell of a turtle.

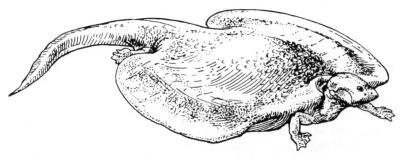

Figure 40. *Henodus*, the last of the placodonts, is known from several complete skeletons recovered from the upper Triassic beds of southern Germany. Here we see an interesting parallelism with the turtles. The 'shell' of *Henodus* is about four feet in length.

Whether or not the procolophonids were common inhabitants of the Keuper scene, it does seem probable from recent discoveries in England that the first true lizards had appeared at this time. They are very small, comparable in size with small lizards found throughout the world today. Of particular interest is the fact that some of the first lizards, exemplified by *Kuehneosaurus*, discovered in Triassic fissure deposits near Bristol, England, show remarkable specializations for aerial locomotion. The ribs are greatly elongated, obviously to support a membrane with which the animal could glide from tree to tree, just as does the modern gliding lizard, *Draco*, of the East Indies. It is surprising, to say the least, to find this extreme specialization appearing at the very beginning of the evolutionary history of the lizards.

Reptiles that were numerous and very characteristic of late Triassic times were the rhynchosaurs, related to the modern tuatera, medium-sized and even rather large reptiles[*]. The body is compact, the legs strong, and it is evident that these animals were active walkers. The skull is peculiar, and highly specialized for some particular mode of life – just what we cannot say. It is very broad in the back and tapers to a point in the front, where are located two large tusks, side by side, like the teeth of a big rodent. The very strange thing about these tusks is that they are not teeth at all, but pointed premaxillary bones that have imitated in form and function the teeth that might be expected to occupy this position in the skull. Likewise, the bony front of the lower jaw is pointed, to function as a set of lower 'teeth' opposing the upper 'tusks'. Then, in the sides of the jaws, above and below, are large plates, carrying longitudinal rows of small, button-like teeth.

What is the meaning of such strange adaptations in these reptiles ? It has been suggested that the rhynchosaurs may have lived along shores, where they fed upon molluscs, or perhaps, as seems more probable, that they may have lived in jungles, where they ate heavy-husked fruits of some sort. They offer the paleontologist some tantalizing exercises in deduction.

Dominating all of these Keuper reptiles are the archosaurs, the thecodonts represented by pseudosuchians and phytosaurs, and the first saurischian dinosaurs represented by theropods and prosauropods. Here we see structural ancestors and descendants living side by side, because the primitive thecodonts were the progenitors of more advanced thecodonts and of the first dinosaurs as well. And

[*]See 'Page Corrections and Emendations' in Addendum.

primitive thecodonts are continued into late Triassic times by such genera as *Saltoposuchus* in Europe and *Hesperosuchus** in North America.

Hesperosuchus (we digress briefly from the type Keuper fauna) is a small and lightly built reptile, a few feet in length. The skeleton shows that this was a very active animal, running about on strong,

Figure 41. The large, heavy rhynchocephalian, *Scaphonyx*, from the Triassic Santa Maria beds of Brazil. This rhynchosaur, member of a group that was widely distributed throughout the world during late Triassic time, stood some three feet in height and in life weighed many hundreds of pounds. The strange dentition of the rhynchosaurs may have been adapted for eating husked fruits.

bird-like hind limbs, the body being pivoted at the hips. There is a long tail which in life served as a counter-balance to the body. The fore limbs are small, and the hands were used for grasping, as an aid in feeding, rather than for locomotion. The skull, at the end of a strong neck, is narrow and deep, with a large eye, and with two large openings on each side behind the eye, one on the top of the skull and one on the side of the skull, these being the two temporal openings, so very characteristic of all of the archosaurians. In front of the eye is yet another opening on each side. So the skull is lightly constructed, but at the same time it is strong. Along the edges of the jaws are sharp, blade-like teeth.

Hesperosuchus was a small agile hunter, that pursued small game; seemingly a rather insignificant inhabitant of the late Triassic scene. But from such a structural type (but one of earlier age) evolved not only the varied pseudosuchians of late Triassic times and likewise the crocodile-like phytosaurs, all of these being thecodonts, but also the crocodiles themselves, the flying reptiles, and the two great

93

*See 'Page Corrections and Emendations' in Addendum.

orders of dinosaurs. There is no doubting the fact that primitive types of thecodonts, such as *Hesperosuchus*, occupy a very strategic position in the Age of Reptiles.

The several groups of thecodonts that were descended from *Hesperosuchus*-like ancestors tended to get down off their hind legs, and walk on all four feet. Among the upper Triassic pseudosuchians this return to quadrupedalism probably went along with the development of heavy armor, for these animals were indeed very thoroughly protected by an enclosing cuirass of overlapping bony plates, covered in life with horny plates, making of them reptilian 'armadillos' of various sizes and forms. The aetosaurs, typified by *Aetosaurus*, are small pseudosuchians of this type in the European Keuper – reptiles three or four feet in length, slender of body and limb, evidently active, and looking very much like armor-plated lizards. The stagonolepids are rather large members of this particular line of reptilian evolution, *Stagonolepis*, with a pig-like snout, perhaps for rooting food out of the ground, being the Keuper representative. The armored pseudosuchians as a group have small, leaf-shaped teeth, and it would appear that in life they were inoffensive reptiles, very likely feeding upon plants.

Cause and effect go together in the world of the past as in the world of today, and the proliferation of heavy armor among the late Triassic pseudosuchians may very probably be correlated with the rather sudden appearance and the wide spread of the phytosaurs during this time. These reptiles appear in upper Triassic sediments, at which horizon they become very characteristic of the faunas in the northern hemisphere. These are uncannily crocodilian-like reptiles, which to the casual glance would appear to be large, heavily built crocodilians, with armor plates on the back. They have almost all of the crocodilian attributes – long jaws with sharp teeth, cylindrical body, short legs and a long, deep tail obviously used for sculling through the water. For these reasons the phytosaurs were considered by early workers in paleontology to be the ancestors of the crocodiles, but careful study has shown that this is not so. Instead of being the grandfathers of the crocodiles they are the grand-uncles. This is a striking case of parallelism in evolution, of animals with a common ancestry (for the crocodiles were descended from primitive thecodonts, too) developing along similar lines. The phytosaurs would seem to have been very nicely fitted for the life they lived during Triassic times. In some ways they were more efficiently adapted for living in streams and lakes than the crocodiles that succeeded them, because the phytosaurs, for example, have the nostrils placed high up on the skull, between the eyes, like a snorkel, and this is a very good device for breathing among aquatic tetrapods. But it and the other adaptations of the phytosaurs evidently were not good enough, and these reptiles were replaced by the crocodiles, which imitated them almost exactly. Nevertheless the phytosaurs enjoyed a brief period of success, and during the years of late Triassic times they were aggressive and dominant, the scourge of their world.

They were even probably dominant over most of the dinosaurs of that day. *Phytosaurus* in the Keuper environment of Europe had little to fear from the early saurischian dinosaurs, such as *Halticosaurus* and *Saltopus*, which were essentially enlargements of such ancestral pseudosuchians as *Hesperosuchus* and *Saltoposuchus*, with certain refinements. These small, agile, lightly built dinosaurs, belonging to the group known as coelurosaurs, evidently pursued their prey in the undergrowth of late Triassic times – keeping well out of reach of the large phytosaurs that frequented the edges of streams and lakes. There were larger Keuper dinosaurs, however. *Teratosaurus*, a large carnivore, is one of them[*]. This dinosaur is of considerable size, perhaps twenty feet in length, with a very large skull (thus giving a big bite, necessary to a hunter of large game) armed with enlarged, dagger-like teeth. Yet *Teratosaurus*, in spite of its size, retains the primitive bipedal pose, and for good reason; it could get over the ground rapidly – like a gigantic ostrich.

One other group of dinosaurs is very characteristic of the European Keuper – that of the prosauropods. These are perhaps the largest of Triassic dinosaurs, with skeletons that may run to more than twenty feet in length, and as their name indicates they are near the direct line of evolution that was to lead in the following Jurassic period to the immense sauropod dinosaurs, the giants of the Mesozoic world. Abundant fossil remains of *Plateosaurus*, perhaps the best known of the prosauropods, were excavated in southern Germany some decades ago, so that this dinosaur is known from a series of complete skeletons. This rather massive reptile still retains the primitive bipedal pose, but the fore-limbs are enlarged and heavy, and it is quite evident that *Plateosaurus* could get down and walk on all fours if necessary. The neck is elongated and flexible, the head quite small in comparison with the size of the animal, the jaws being furnished with flattened, leaf-shaped teeth. Consequently we can

95

[*]See 'Page Corrections and Emendations' in Addendum.

picture *Plateosaurus* as the big herbivore of late Triassic times in Europe.

We have now had a glance at tetrapod life of the European Keuper; we have seen an ancient tropical world inhabited by large, flatheaded amphibians, primitive turtles, rhynchosaurs and early lizards, thecodonts of various types, including lightly built and heavily-armored pseudosuchians and phytosaurs, small and large bipedal dinosaurs, and, in the oceans, ichthyosaurs, nothosaurs, plesiosaurs and placodonts. The fauna that has passed before our view is particularly characteristic of late Triassic life across the northern continents. Consequently the same general assemblage of amphibians

Figure 42. The large Triassic dinosaur, *Plateosaurus*, from southern Germany. This herbivorous reptile was one of the first dinosaurs to attain some degree of gigantism, reaching a length of twenty feet or more.

and reptiles is to be seen in the upper Triassic rocks of North America. These are found in the Newark beds of eastern North America, and the equivalent Chinle, Dockum and Popo Agie beds of the western states.

The large amphibians are represented by *Eupelor**, so very close in structure to *Metoposaurus* of Europe that the differences between them are significant only to the trained paleontologist. Close similarities between European and North American tetrapods are continued among the archosaurian reptiles. *Saltoposuchus* of Europe finds its counterpart in *Hesperosuchus* of the Chinle beds of Arizona. The armored pseudosuchians are represented on the American scene by

*See 'Page Corrections and Emendations' in Addendum.

Desmatosuchus with a pair of large, curved spikes projecting to each side from the shoulders, and *Typothorax* in which the neck and back are covered with very broad armor plates, these terminating along the sides of the body in heavy points or spikes. The phytosaurs, represented by several genera in North America, are of the same general type as those of Europe, and one genus, *Phytosaurus*, would seem to have extended across the two continental areas through a wide range of longitude. Some of the phytosaurs in North America attained the status of giants, with skulls four feet and more in length. Finally, the upper Triassic dinosaurs of North America are closely comparable with those of Europe. Of particular importance is the genus *Coelophysus*, a lightly built reptile, perhaps eight or ten feet in length. This dinosaur is now known from beautifully complete skeletons found in the Chinle formation of New Mexico, affording a detailed picture of a hollow-boned predatory dinosaur not far removed in time from the ancestral stem of the saurischians.

Occasionally in the search for fossils it is the good fortune of the paleontologist to find a large series of excellent fossils, such as the complete skeletons of *Coelophysis*. And where fossil bones are found in profusion, there are seldom any footprints to go along with them. As against this, footprints may occur at some places in incredible abundance, with never or hardly ever a bone to supplement them.

In the Newark beds of the Connecticut Valley, running north from the southern shore of Connecticut, through the state and on into the northern part of Massachusetts, are thousands of reptilian footprints preserved in the rocks. A large proportion of these are obviously the bird-like tracks made by primitive dinosaurs, and some of these, especially those that have been called *Grallator*, may very well represent the footprints of *Coelophysis*. Other Connecticut Valley tracks indicate other types of Triassic dinosaurs, and contemporary reptiles as well. The disadvantage of footprints found in this way is that only by making very broad assumptions can one correlate them with the fossil bones of known animals. The advantage is that they give us graphic impressions of how ancient animals walked about on a definite day millions of years ago; they give us a feeling of the living animal.

It used to be thought that the rhynchosaurs, so characteristic of the upper Triassic beds in other parts of the world, were absent in North America. But recent discoveries in the Newark sediments of Nova Scotia would seem to indicate that small rhynchosaurs lived in this part of the world, too. Their absence from most areas in North

America where upper Triassic beds are found may very well be an accident of preservation; it may indicate the fact that these particular reptiles were living in habitats apart from the other late Triassic tetrapods – habitats that have not been preserved in the fossil record. Or perhaps their ecological role was taken over in much of North America by *Trilophosaurus*, known from the Dockum beds, a large, deep-skulled protorosaurian, with transverse, chisel-like chopping teeth, and with the front of the jaws beak-like. Here indeed is a reptile that in life must have had a very special diet – what, we do not know.

The dicynodonts, so widely established throughout the world in Triassic times, are represented in the Chinle fauna by *Placerias*, a very large reptile of its kind, found at one locality in the eastern part of Arizona.

This review of upper Triassic amphibians and reptiles in North America has been concerned so far with animals of medium to rather large size; reptiles several feet in length, some of them twenty feet and more long. But there are various small reptiles in the upper Triassic of North America as well, these occurring especially in the eastern Newark sediments, where conditions would seem to have favored the preservation of small delicate animals. In New Jersey and in Pennsylvania there have been found the skeletons of some procolophonids, the last and most specialized of these persistent cotylosaurs. *Hypsognathus* is a reptile a foot or so in length, with a flat skull, armed on each side with an array of spikes. Quite recently a considerable series of delicate skeletons and partial skeletons have come to light immediately across the Hudson River from New York City, indicating an interesting and varied array of very small Triassic reptiles. One of these has enormously elongated ribs, a specialization parallel to the early gliding lizard of England, mentioned above, and like it quite obviously an adaptation for gliding.

Of very great significance is the discovery within recent years of completely preserved tritylodont skeletons in the Kayenta beds of Arizona, these being the remains of mammal-like reptiles on the verge of becoming mammals. These tritylodonts were associated with an ancestral crocodile, *Protosuchus*, and in the same beds was found the skeleton of a rather large theropod dinosaur.

Were the tritylodonts long-bodied, stout-limbed mammals with fur on the body, or reptiles with a naked or scaly skin? Were there external ears? Was the body temperature constantly high, or was it variable, according to the temperature of the environment ? Did they nurse the young ? Did they lay eggs ? These are questions on which we can only speculate. The tritylodont skull is rodent-like (tritylodonts have been compared with rodents in their mode of life), with a pair of large teeth in front, separated by a gap from the cheek teeth, these latter being elongated with longitudinal rows of sharp cusps. Here is an arrangement superficially not unlike that of the rhynchosaurs, and one can only wonder if the tritylodonts, too, fed upon husked fruits or nuts or seed pods.

On the other side of the world, in Yunnan, China, there are in the Lufeng beds tritylodonts extraordinarily close to those of Arizona.

Figure 43. *Bienotherium*, a late Triassic mammal-like reptile from China. The skull of this reptile, a tritylodont, is very rodent-like, and it seems likely that all of the tritylodonts, which were world-wide in distribution, had rodent-like habits. *Bienotherium*, about the size of a marmot, may have had a covering of hair.

These tritylodonts evidently lived along with a large prosauropod dinosaur, *Lufengosaurus*, which is essentially a Keuper plateosaur moved eastwardly into Asia.

In Asia, specifically in central India, are the Maleri beds, in which are found metoposaurs and phytosaurs so very similar to those of Europe and North America that one can only suppose there were open routes of migration between these regions. The metoposaurs and phytosaurs in India are associated with large, heavy rhynchosaurs.

Balanced against this array of upper Triassic localities in the northern hemisphere are three general regions where beds of similar age are to be found in the southern hemisphere – south and east Africa, the southern part of South America, and Australia.

The wonderfully fossiliferous sequence of sediments in South Africa, already given so much attention in preceding pages of this work, is continued as the Upper Triassic Stormberg beds, overlying the Beaufort series. The Stormberg series consists, from bottom to top, of the Molteno beds, the Red Beds and the Cave Sandstone. The Molteno contains plant fossils, some rare bones, and, in its upper limits, the footprints of reptiles. It has long been thought that the Molteno beds are of middle Triassic age, but the bones, and particularly the trackways, many of which are undoubted dinosaurian footprints, point to a late Triassic age for these sediments.

So we come to the Red Beds, in which are found a pseudosuchian, a large array of saurischian dinosaurs, the earliest ornithischian dinosaurs, recently discovered along the border of Basutoland, a primitive crocodilian and some very advanced mammal-like reptiles. The preponderance of dinosaurs in the Red Beds is impressive. Here are found carnivorous types and prosauropods that indicate very clearly the close relationships at that time of the African land mass with continents to the north. Among such reptiles are *Thecodontosaurus*, a prosauropod found also in Europe and North America, and *Plateosauravus*, which is certainly very close indeed to the European *Plateosaurus* and the Asiatic *Lufengosaurus*. The mammal-like reptiles of the Red Beds are among the most progressive of these animals; they are ictidosaurs, the reptiles that had all but reached the mammalian stage of development. Indeed, one of them, *Diarthrognathus*, seemingly possesses a double jaw articulation, a combination of the reptilian quadrate-articular joint with the mammalian squamosal-dentary joint, thus placing this animal on the very borderline between reptiles and mammals. Here, too, particularly in Basutoland, is found *Tritylodon*, the form from which the group of tritylodonts gets its name.

The fossils of the Cave Sandstone, similar to those of the Red Beds, carry the story to the end of the Triassic record in South Africa. Here are dinosaurs again, some of them the same as those living when the Red Beds were being deposited. Also there is a pseudosuchian reptile, a crocodilian and some ictidosaurs. The tritylodonts are not represented, but this may be the result of the accidents of preservation and of collecting, for the Cave Sandstone fauna is not very large. In this connection it should be said that the Cave Sandstone, long considered as a distinct stratigraphic unit above the Red Beds, is more probably a separate sedimentary facies, the two divisions to a certain degree grading into each other. This conclusion, based on field relationships, would seem to be borne out by the close identity of the faunas.

In East Africa, in Tanganyika, are the Manda beds, the 'upper bone-bearing series' separated by the unfossiliferous Kingori sandstone from the 'lower bone-bearing series' of this region. The lower bone beds may be equated with the upper Permian of South Africa, the upper bone beds with some part of the Stormberg series. These upper sediments have yielded some labyrinthodont material, some advanced mammal-like reptiles, several dicynodonts, a rhynchosaur, *Stenaulorhynchus*, some pseudosuchians and some dinosaurs. Just where this assemblage of holdovers from an earlier age, such as the mammal-like reptiles and the dicynodonts, and newcomers, such as the pseudosuchians and the dinosaurs, should be placed is a moot question. Certain authorities would consider the Manda fauna as of uppermost middle Triassic age. The dinosaurs, however, provide strong evidence for an upper Triassic age, because it is generally considered (although one can never be completely sure of such things) that the dinosaurs did not arise from their thecodont ancestors until about the beginning of late Triassic time.

Much the same considerations hold when we cross the south Atlantic to examine the very interesting Santa Maria fauna of southern Brazil. Here, in a band of bright red and incredibly fossiliferous sands and clays, running across the state of Rio Grande do Sul, are found abundant reptilian remains, including a procolophonid, *Candelaria*, a rhynchosaur, *Schaphonyx*, a series of large and small pseudosuchian reptiles, a small saurischian dinosaur, varied dicynodonts including some giant types such as *Stahleckeria*, and some progressive mammal-like reptiles. Opinion is at the present time divided on whether this fauna lived at the close of middle Triassic times or at the beginning of late Triassic times. The presence of the dinosaur, of the advanced pseudosuchians and of a rhynchosaur which is very close to the upper Triassic rhynchosaur of India, gives the fauna a distinct late Triassic appearance. If such is the age of the Santa Maria reptiles, then it must be the age, too, of a related fauna, containing advanced mammal-like reptiles and dinosaurs, found in the Ischigualasto beds of northern Argentina, several hundred miles west of the Santa Maria locality. Indeed, the fossils of the two regions appear to be part of a single late Triassic faunal complex that stretched across southern South America.

The presence of abundant remains of mammal-like reptiles, especially cynodonts, in Argentina and in Brazil is a point of particular interest, because of the prevalence of cynodonts in the lower Triassic *Cynognathus* zone in South Africa. Does the presence of cynodonts on the two sides of the South Atlantic indicate a land bridge or a connection linking the two continents during some part of the Triassic period*? It is easy to jump to such a conclusion. But the easy and the seemingly obvious conclusion may not necessarily be correct. Within recent years a Triassic cynodont *Sinognathus* (a name that unfortunately may all too easily be confused with the South African *Cynognathus*), has been described from China. *Sinognathus* shows certain resemblances to *Belesodon*, a cynodont from the Triassic Santa Maria beds of Brazil. Perhaps we see here the record of a group of reptiles extending themselves from South Africa to South America by the roundabout but obvious path leading through northeastern Asia, and presumably from there down through North America to Brazil.

In the upper Triassic sediments of Australia the remains of the amphibian, *Paracyclotosaurus*, have been found, an indication that this part of the world was above the sea and inhabited by land-living tetrapods identical to some of those found in Eurasia. Evidently there was a road of ingress and egress between the Australian region and lands to the northwest during late Triassic times: unfortunately the fossil record from here is at the present time very poor.

We have examined, in this chapter and the one before, some of the details in the history of the amphibians and reptiles during the great transition that took place during Triassic time. An attempt has been made to show how these animals developed and changed as the Triassic period progressed from its beginning to its end, how the holdovers from the Permian period gradually gave way to the influx of many new types, how the faunas at the end of Triassic history had a very different complexion from those of early Triassic times. This review has also attempted to show how the Triassic was the time when all of the new and highly specialized reptiles, which were to typify the years of the dinosaurs, became established on the face of the earth. It has tried to show that this was the time when the turtles and the rhynchocephalians, the various thecodonts and the dinosaurs themselves arose to inherit the land. It has further tried to show how some of the mammal-like reptiles reached the threshold of the mam-

*See 'Page Corrections and Emendations' in Addendum.

malian condition. And in addition there has been a brief attempt to show how a host of reptiles, the nothosaurs and pleisosaurs, the placodonts and the fish-like ichthyosaurs, took to the sea, where they found new opportunities for living. The story has been one of constant change.

What was the world like, during this important transition of vertebrate life from the old to the new? Do the distributions of amphibians and reptiles throw any light on climates and environments, on the relationships between continents?

Certainly, as has been seen, many of the land-living amphibians and reptiles of the Triassic lived far and wide across the surface of the earth. Lower Triassic short-faced amphibians in Spitzbergen and in southern Argentina, upper Triassic dinosaurs in North America and Eurasia, in Africa and Brazil, would seem to indicate broad lines of communication between continents during this period of earth history, and generally similar climates in these far widely separated areas.

The evidence would seem to indicate that the world was to a large degree tropical and subtropical during Triassic times, as shown by these wide distributions. This is not to say that climates were uniform, for there must have been seasonal changes and local variations. Nor is it to say that lands were uniform. Certainly there were low-lying tropical jungles during Triassic times, but there were also uplands and deserts, where conditions of life were at times and at some places harsh. All such varied conditions stimulated the development of progressive reptiles; and must be closely correlated with the transition of reptiles from the older types to the newer, progressive groups, characteristic of Triassic history. Yet in spite of these variations in land environments, the Triassic world was one of warm and temperate conditions, in which large reptiles could live in abundance over almost all of the land surfaces of the earth. And it was a time of warm, tropical oceans, where marine reptiles swam through wide degrees of latitude. But what about continental relationships? It has been argued that, during Triassic times as during antecedent Permian times, the continents of the world had different positions or relationships from those they have today. The argument for closely connected continents that later drifted apart, or for a great east to west Gondwanaland separated from a northern land mass, has been advanced vigorously for this span of earth history, as it has for Permian times.

Table 5. *Correlation of the Upper Triassic vertebrate horizons of North America* *

COLORADO	Upper Triassic; Dolores
WYOMING	Chugwater; Alcova; Crow Mountain; Popo Agie; Nugget
SOUTH-WESTERN STATES	Chinle — Shinarump, Monitor Butte, Moss Back, Petrified Forest, Church Rock, Owl Rock, Correo, Agua Zarca, Salitral, Poleo; Wingate; Moenave; Rock Point; Lukachukai; Dinosaur Canyon; Springdale; Kayenta
TEXAS	Dockum — Pierce Canyon, Santa Rosa, 'Chinle', Redonda
NEW JERSEY	Newark — Stockton, Lockatong, First Watchung, Second Watchung, Hook Mt., Brunswick
CONNECTICUT VALLEY	Newark — New Haven, Talcott, Shuttle Meadow, Holyoke, East Berlin, Hampden, Portland
EUROPE	Keuper; Lettenkohle; Gypskeuper; Rhaetic

* See 'Tables and Diagrams' in Addendum.

But as we have seen in the review of the Permian period, the distributions of land-living amphibians and reptiles do not support any extreme views concerning past continental connections[*]. These tetrapods were widely spread during the Triassic, and it is apparent that many of them could go from north to south as readily as from east to west. The distribution of the procolophonids, rhynchosaurs, dicynodonts and dinosaurs all point to this. The supposed restrictions of some groups, particularly the cynodonts, which have been used as an argument in favor of a close African–South American connection, may be more apparent than real. What we now know about the distribution of Triassic tetrapods may be in part an expression of our lack of information, of the accidents of preservation, but some of it possibly may be a true reflection of certain animal distributions in Triassic times.

In short, the spread of amphibians and reptiles over the globe during the beginning of the Mesozoic indicates that the continents could very well have been in their present positions, united for the most part at the places where they are now united. But it is quite possible that there were additional links between the continents, the evidence being strongest for a South Atlantic bridge, between Africa and Brazil. As for any other continental connections, the only one that needs serious consideration would be a North Atlantic connection. Otherwise, it would seem quite feasible for amphibians and reptiles to have crossed from east to west, and conversely, in the northern hemisphere by a trans-Bering link, and in the southern hemisphere, from Asia to Australia along a broad East Indies bridge. The movements from north to south and south to north might have taken place through the Mediterranean region in the Old World, and perhaps along a Panamanian bridge in the New World.

[*] See 'Page Corrections and Emendations' in Addendum.

Chapter 6

The First Wave of Extinction

AT THE END OF Triassic times reptiles and amphibians ruled the earth. They inhabited the continents in great numbers around the circumference of the globe and from far northern latitudes to the ultimate tips of the southern hemisphere land masses, and they swam in the wide expanses of tropical seas. Their reign over land and sea was so firmly established, it would seem, that it should have continued through millions of years into the future as it had through millions of years in the past – the past that we designate as the Triassic period. If an abundance of fossils in the rock has any meaning, the amphibians and reptiles so characteristic of late Triassic times certainly were supremely successful animals. Let us review them briefly.

Large, flat-headed amphibians peopled the streams and ponds of the northern hemisphere in prodigious numbers, predators upon the freshwater fishes of those days. With them lived the large and even gigantic crocodile-like phytosaurs, the complete masters of their environment. And on higher ground were the close cousins of the phytosaurs, the armored pseudosuchians, some of them large, some of them quite small, but all of them so remarkably well adjusted to the world in which they lived that they spread far and wide over the lands of the earth. The same was very possibly true for the little lizard-like procolophonids, although their fossil remains in rocks of late Triassic age are at the present time rather rare. Animals such as these commonly are not abundantly preserved in the rocks, in part because their small, delicate skeletons were usually destroyed before there was any opportunity for them to be fossilized, and in part because their probable secretive habits led them to live in jungle undergrowth where burial and fossilization almost never occur. Consequently their absence in the fossil record is no true indication of their abundance in life.

Similar considerations may hold for the protorosaurs, many of them very small and of delicate construction. It is notable in this connection that in those rare cases where protorosaurs are preserved in Triassic rocks, they are not infrequently fossilized as beautifully complete skeletons or as remarkably rich conglomerations of bones. In short, burial and fossilization of these little reptiles often took place only in very fine-grained sediments.

Other reptiles living at the close of Triassic times were widely distributed throughout the world, notably the early theropod dinosaurs, the rhynchocephalians in the form of rhynchosaurs and the advanced mammal-like ictidosaurs. In contrast, the gigantic tusked dicynodonts, although still numerous, very likely had suffered a decline from their earlier wide distribution, and the same is probably true for the mammal-like theriodonts, and for the eosuchian reptiles, these latter perhaps never very abundant. Again, some of the late Triassic reptiles were just making their appearance, and were as yet not common, these being the turtles, the crocodiles and the true lizards.

Finally, the oceans at the end of Triassic history were the home of many reptiles; fish-like ichthyosaurs in the open seas and shallow-water nothosaurs and placodonts along the margins of the shores.

Table 6. *Geographic distribution of amphibians and reptiles at the end of the Triassic period* *

	NORTH AMERICA	EUROPE	ASIA	AFRICA	SOUTH AMERICA	AUSTRALIA
Stereospondyls	+	+	+			+
Procolophonids	+	+			+	
Turtles		+				
Ichthyosaurs	+	+	+			
Protorosaurs	+					
Nothosaurs	+	+				
Placodonts		+				
Eosuchians	+					
Rhynchosaurs	+	+	+	+	+	
Lizards		+				
Pseudosuchians	+	+	+	+	+	
Phytosaurs	+	+	+			
Crocodiles	+				+	
Saurischian dinosaurs	+	+	+	+	+	
Ornithischian dinosaurs					+	
Dicynodonts	+				+	
Theriodonts					+	
Ictidosaurs	+	+	+	+		

* See 'Tables and Diagrams' in Addendum.

But whether they were plentiful or not (as indicated by their fossils) reptiles and amphibians were at the end of Triassic time supreme on the earth to a degree beyond any supremacy attained in previous ages. The fossil evidence for this is shown in Table 6.

And then during the transition from Triassic to Jurassic times a series of tetrapod extinctions took place throughout the world. Various large groups of these animals disappeared from the face of the earth; specifically the abundant stereospondyl amphibians, the little procolophonid diadectomorphs, the protorosaurs, the rynchosaurs, the dominant pseudosuchians and phytosaurs, the mammal-like dicynodonts and theriodonts, and the oceanic nothosaurs and placodonts. This extinction, which, as is quite apparent, wiped out a large segment of the tetrapods then inhabiting the earth, was to change very profoundly the character of vertebrate faunas through the rest of Mesozoic time. Just how extensively the nature of tetrapod faunas was changed by the extinctions at the close of Triassic

Table 7. *Major amphibian and reptile groups at the transition from the Triassic to Jurassic periods* *

	UPPER TRIASSIC	LOWER JURASSIC
Amphibians		
Stereospondyls	————	
Reptiles		
Diadectomorphs	————	
Protorosaurs	————	
Nothosaurs	————	
Placodonts	————	
Pseudosuchians	————	
Phytosaurs	————	
Dicynodonts	————	
Theriodonts	————	
Turtles	————————————	
Ichthyosaurs	————————————	
Plesiosaurs	————————————	
Eosuchians*	————————————	
Rhynchocephalians*	————————————	
Lizards*	————————————	
Crocodilians	————————————	
Theropod dinosaurs	————————————	
Ornithopod dinosaurs*	————————————	
Ictidosaurs	————————————	
Pterosaurs		————
Sauropod dinosaurs		————
Stegosaurs		————

* Fossils not known from Lower Jurassic sediments, but since these reptiles are now known from the Upper Triassic and, of course, the Upper Jurassic, it is obvious that they were present in the Lower Jurassic.

*See 'Tables and Diagrams' in Addendum.

history, can be shown by listing the major groups of these animals known from upper Triassic and lower Jurassic sediments, as in Table 7.

Of nineteen major amphibian and reptilian groups, of ordinal or subordinal rank, known to be living in late Triassic time, nine became extinct at the end of the period. Only about half of the major groups of four-footed vertebrates that had been living during the

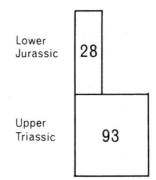

Lower
Jurassic   28

Upper
Triassic   93

Figure 44. A comparison of the number of tetrapod genera from upper Triassic sediments with those known from the lower Jurassic. This figure indicates a large amount of extinction taking place at the end of Triassic time.*

final years of the Triassic survived into the opening years of Jurassic history, to carry on the stream of tetrapod evolution.

No longer were there giant amphibians, tusked dicynodonts, armored pseudosuchians and predatory phytosaurs on the land. No longer were there procolophonids and protorosaurs in the underbrush. No longer were there nothosaurs and placodonts in the seas. The roles they had played in the Triassic scene, and had then vacated, were taken up by new animals of Jurassic age in the way illustrated in Table 8.

With the close of the Triassic there seems to have been a worldwide sinking of continents, and a correlative world-wide spread of shallow seas across these submerged lands. Land areas appear to have been restricted, which, of course, reduced the ranges and the opportunities for development among the land-living animals. Could this be a key in part to the wide extinctions of amphibians and reptiles which marked the end of Triassic time?

Perhaps this explanation may be as good as any brought forward. Certainly there were marked and wide-spread changes in environments as Triassic merged into Jurassic history, and certainly such changes must have affected profoundly the animals and plants then

*See 'Charts and Diagrams' in Addendum.

inhabiting the earth. Yet even though this explanation be accepted as the overall cause for the great wave of extinction that swept away so many Triassic reptiles, there are problems.

Extinction is a baffling phenomenon to comprehend, especially when it involves animals that disappeared from the face of the earth long before the time of man. Indeed, extinctions taking place in front of our eyes are not easy to understand. We may think we know the reasons why a species declines and disappears as we look on, but

Table 8. *Replacement of major groups at the beginning of the Jurassic period* *

TYPES UNDERGOING EXTINCTION	ENVIRONMENT	DIET	REPLACED BY
Placodonts	Shallow marine waters	Molluscs	*
Nothosaurs	Margins of the sea	Fishes	Plesiosaurs
Stereospondyls	Rivers, lakes	Fishes	Crocodilians
Phytosaurs	Rivers, lakes	Fishes, other tetrapods	Large crocodilians
Rhynchosaurs	Edges of rivers	?	
Protorosaurs	Edges of ponds, thickets, uplands	Insects, plants	(Lizards) †
Procolophonids	Thickets, rocks	Plants ?	
Small pseudo-suchians	Uplands	Insects, Tetrapods	Small theropod dinosaurs
Armored pseudo-suchians	Uplands	Plants	Plated dinosaurs
Dicynodonts	Uplands	Plants	Herbivorous dinosaurs
Theriodonts	Uplands	Animals	Theropod dinosaurs

* There was no immediate replacement of the placodonts. Marine turtles of later Mesozoic times took over, but not exactly, the role of the placodonts.
† Lizards are shown as replacing several groups of Triassic reptiles. Actually there is no fossil record of Lower Jurassic lizards, but since there are certainly ancestral lizards in the Triassic, and since lizards are well known in later Jurassic deposits, it may be safely assumed that they were established by early Jurassic times.

when we study and analyze the extinction it is to us often confused rather than comprehensible. Extinctions are complex; many subtle factors are generally involved in them. So a simple solution does not explain the event very satisfactorily.

Suppose the depression of land areas and the spread of seas during the transition from Triassic to Jurassic did bring about the disappearance of many reptiles. Why should it have caused the extinction of the nothosaurs and placodonts – these latter animals admirably suited to their own way of life ? As has been noted, the placodonts

*See 'Tables and Diagrams' in Addendum.

were not immediately replaced in the oceans during Mesozoic times; in fact they were never absolutely replaced.

Again, why under any circumstances should the phytosaurs have become extinct? They were excellently adapted for a predatory life in rivers and lakes, and to the end of their days there were no reptiles to challenge them. Yet they disappeared, and after their disappearance the crocodilians, hitherto small reptiles, grew large, and imitated the phytosaurs in a most uncanny fashion. Why should the phytosaurs have failed after a few million years, whereas their crocodilian imitators have been on the earth for more than one hundred and fifty million years? The question remains unanswered.

Again, what about the large, armored pseudosuchians? It has been suggested in Table 8 that these reptiles were replaced during Jurassic times by the plated dinosaurs. Yet pseudosuchians were rather progressive reptiles, and it seems within the bounds of probability that they might have continued successfully through a long interval of time after the close of the Triassic period. They did not; the fossil record is quite clear about this.

Some mention has just been made of 'progressive' reptiles. It is not always easy to define a progressive animal or plant as contrasted with a conservative one. Generally speaking we may think of the progressive types as those which have departed to a considerable degree from the condition of their ancestors; of the conservative types as those which retain ancestral traits. Of course, such a definition is open to various objections. How, for example, does one draw the line of difference between a progressive animal and an aberrant one? How can one say that a conservative animal is not progressive, if it manages to change just enough during time to remain well adjusted to the environments in which it lives? Such questions reveal the subjectivity of words, and the difficulty of their use. But with these qualifications in mind, suppose we recognize the general condition of progressiveness and conservatism in evolving animals, as being marked respectively by great or by small changes of structure and function. With such powers of deduction as we may apply to things that took place so long ago, can we perhaps understand why some of the Triassic amphibians and reptiles gave way to progressive Jurassic forms? What are the possibilities?

It is easy to say that the large stereospondyl amphibians became extinct because they had 'reached the end of their rope'. The idea that groups of animals and plants have evolutionary life histories just as an individual animal or plant has its own limited existence on the earth, is common in discussions of the fossil record. But this does not explain anything; it does not offer any solution to the problem of why some groups of organisms persist over vast expanses of geologic time whereas others have very short spans. As for the stereospondyls, last of the great labyrinthodont amphibians, it seems likely that they finally disappeared because they were competing directly with progressive reptiles. During the Permian period there were no large reptiles living in ponds and streams that seriously threatened the

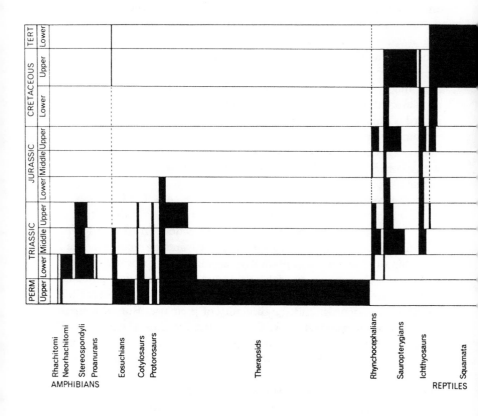

Figure 45. The range and abundance of tetrapods that lived during the age of reptiles. The arrangement is by first appearances in the geologic record, rather than by taxonomic relationships. The widths of the bars are proportional to the number of known genera at each geologic stage.*

*See 'Charts and Diagrams' in Addendum.

labyrinthodont amphibians, and the same seemingly was true through much of Triassic time. In the later years of Triassic history, however, the aggressive phytosaurs took up their abode in the waters of the northern continents, and one would think that they might have pushed the stereospondyl amphibians into the shades of extinction, perhaps in part by preying upon them, perhaps in part by crowding them out of their feeding grounds. It is quite obvious that this did not take place. But in the long run the big amphibians did give way to reptiles that were becoming ever better suited to the environments

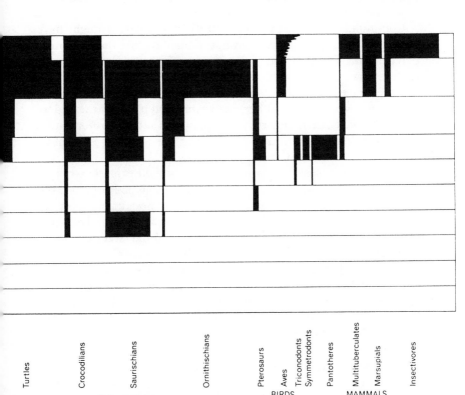

Turtles Crocodilians Saurischians Ornithischians Pterosaurs Aves Triconodonts Symmetrodonts Pantotheres Multituberculates Marsupials Insectivores

BIRDS MAMMALS

of the Mesozoic world. They passed into limbo, and from that day until now the amphibians have been small but none the less successful animals of stream and pond – the frogs and toads, the salamanders and the tropical coecilians.

As for the nothosaurs, it is probable that they were unable to hold on in the face of competition from their plesiosaurian descendants. In short, the plesiosaurs were improvements on the nothosaurian pattern, more efficiently adapted for life in the surface waters of the oceans. So they prevailed. It is like the replacement of old automobiles on the road by newer models.

Continuing, it is not difficult to see why the lizards might have taken over the roles of various groups of small reptiles that had prospered during Permian and Triassic times. The lizards were active reptiles, that by reason of the structure of skull and skeleton and the accompanying arrangements of muscles and soft parts, were better able to prey upon insects, other small game, and plants of the underbrush and rocks, than were the procolophonids and the protorosaurs. One can think of the lizards as elbowing these earlier established reptiles out of their habitats.

The dinosaurs were from the beginning of their evolutionary history very specialized reptiles, well adapted for an active life on the land. Consequently the small, early theropod dinosaurs probably replaced the small pseudosuchians from which they had evolved, just as the plesiosaurs replaced the nothosaurs, and the larger dinosaurs may have replaced various other large Triassic reptiles.

As for the disappearance of the dicynodonts, this may very probably be attributed to the rigidity of their anatomical pattern, which had persisted without appreciable change since middle Permian time. These animals in late Triassic time were not progressive, but rather aberrant. The structure of the skull is especially bizarre, and with its long arches, its lack of teeth and its beaked jaws, was quite obviously highly specialized for some very particular type of feeding. The world changed and the dicynodonts did not change; they died out.

This argument, seemingly so logical and satisfying when applied to the dicynodonts, breaks down completely if it is applied to the turtles. The turtles have been as bizarre and as rigidly fixed in structure since Jurassic time as the dicynodonts were during the Permian and Triassic periods, yet the unchanging turtles have done very well in a changing world. This thought is inserted here merely to emphasize once again the difficulties of trying to discuss extinctions.

The theriodonts had almost died out before the Triassic period came to a close. These very advanced mammal-like reptiles were evolving into mammals at this time, so their disappearance may be attributed to progressive evolutionary development rather than to extinction. And those theriodonts not on direct lines to the mammals may have been forced out of their habitats by the small and extraordinarily agile carnivorous dinosaurs.

Having said all of this, we come in a full circle to the beginning of our discussion. If we grant that some extinctions at the end of Triassic times are explainable, why did others occur? Why did the placodonts die out? Why did the phytosaurs give way to the crocodilians? And why did the large, armored pseudosuchians disappear, subsequently to be replaced by large plated dinosaurs? In these latter instances the replacing animals seem at this distance to be no more suited for the niches they occupied than the reptiles that disappeared before them.

To return to the facts without the explanations, there is no doubt that a remarkable number of extinctions among amphibians and reptiles accompanied the close of Triassic history. This was a crucial time in the evolutionary development of the tetrapods; it was a time when the old gave way to the new, a time of replacement when the reptile assemblages that were to dominate one hundred million years of middle and late Mesozoic history took on their characteristic features. It was the beginning of a new age within the Age of Reptiles – namely the age of dinosaurian dominance.

Chapter 7

New Ruling Reptiles

IT WAS A watery world in which the early Jurassic animals lived, a world of low continents and widely spread seas, a world of restricted land surfaces*. Not for many millions of years had the oceans encroached so extensively upon the lands, not for long geologic ages had land-living animals and plants been so limited as to habitats. A long, finger-like sea stretched along the west coast of North America, and a similar and parallel seaway covered the western mountain region of the continent. The Gulf Coast and the West Indies were likewise under water, as was the western coastal region of South America. The European continent all but disappeared, the land areas in this region being limited to islands and archipelagos, set in a broad, shimmering ocean. Central and eastern Asia formed an island continent, bounded all around by waters which extended southeastwardly to flood the Indies. A great, narrow east to west sea channel (Tethys) cut across northern India, to separate the Peninsula from the Asiatic island continent, and this arm of the sea extended westwardly into the present Mediterranean region†. The northern and eastern borders of Africa were also inundated, as were various parts of Australia and New Zealand.

So it is that the sedimentary record of Jurassic rocks is largely a marine record, not only because of the great extent of Jurassic oceans, but also because there is a strange paucity of continental deposits, perhaps the result of extensive erosion, to give us clues to the world of land-living organisms. Most of what we know about the reptiles of early and even of middle Jurassic times is based upon

---

* See 'Page Corrections and Emendations' in Addendum.

† The recent discovery (as yet unpublished) of a large deposit of lower Jurassic sauropod bones in central India raises problems about the continuity of a Mesozoic Tethys sea. The same may be said with regard to Triassic and Cretaceous tetrapods in the Indian peninsula. Obviously there were open routes for the movement of land animals into and out of central India during the extent of Mesozoic time.

fossils found in Europe – a region where the land-living animals of that far-off time were never far from the seashore, and where the marine animals swam in great numbers near the strand.

The record may be simply listed as follows.

Table 9. *Early Jurassic reptiles and their geographic distribution* [*]

	NORTH AMERICA	EUROPE	ASIA	AFRICA	SOUTH AMERICA	AUSTRALIA
Turtles		+				
Ichthyosaurs		+				
Plesiosaurs		+				
Crocodilians		+				
Pterosaurs		+				
Theropod dinosaurs	+	+				
Sauropod dinosaurs			+		+	+
Stegosaurian dinosaurs		+				
Ictidosaurs		+				

Not only is it plainly a European record, but also it is for the most part a rather thin one. If we knew more about the land-living vertebrates on other continents at the beginning of Jurassic time, we would have a much clearer picture than is now available of the changes that took place among the amphibians and reptiles during the transition from the Triassic to the Jurassic. Unfortunately the record is lacking.

The spread of oceanic waters over the continents in the initial days of Jurassic history probably was accompanied by cool, moist climates, quite in contrast to the varied climates of late Triassic times. Extensive muds and carbonaceous beds were deposited during the early Jurassic interval of coolness and moisture, so that among the deposits of this age black shales are frequently predominant. In Germany, where the Jurassic (named from the Jura Mountains) was first studied a century and a half ago, these lower beds were dubbed the Black Jura. In England at about the same time they were designated as the Lias.

But as early Jurassic history merged into that of the middle Jurassic, there was a warming of climates over the world, and tropical conditions became widely prevalent. Coral seas covered many regions that are now parts of our modern continents, and in these warm seas

[*] See 'Tables and Diagrams' in Addendum.

there were extensive reefs and other limy deposits. This trend continued into late Jurassic times. Consequently the rocks of middle and late Jurassic age became progressively lighter in color, those of the middle Jurassic being the Brown Jura of Germany, those of the upper Jurassic being the White Jura. In England these same rocks have long been called the Dogger and the Malm, respectively.

Thus the rocks in which fossils of Jurassic reptiles have been found in Europe are:

UPPER	Malm	White Jura
MIDDLE	Dogger	Brown Jura
LOWER	Lias	Black Jura

Lower Jurassic, or Liassic, rocks are extensively exposed along the Channel Coast of England, particularly in Dorset, and here for more than a century there have been excavated the skeletons of marine reptiles; ichthyosaurs and plesiosaurs, as well as occasional land-dwellers that were buried and fossilized at the edge of the shore. Similar deposits are to be seen across the Channel, as might be expected, especially in the vicinity of Caen, France. And farther inland, in the Black Jura of southern Germany, are the famous slate quarries at Holzmaden, Württemberg, where spectacular skeletons of ichthyosaurs have come to light, associated with plesiosaurs, marine crocodiles and other denizens of a shallow sea.

Elsewhere in the world lower Jurassic vertebrate-bearing deposits are very scattered. In the southwestern United States is the Navajo sandstone, a strikingly impressive formation of white dune sands, in which fossils are almost non-existent. Some continental deposits of lower Jurassic age are found in eastern Australia.

The Jurassic record is continued into middle Jurassic times in England as the Stonesfield slate, the Forest Marble and the Oolites, these deposits being found in the southern part of the country. The Stonesfield beds contain a few land-living reptiles, turtles, dinosaurs and pterosaurs, and some classic fossil remains of archaic mammals. In Morocco there have been discovered in recent years the fossil remains of middle Jurassic crocodiles and dinosaurs, and similar fossils are found in the Jurassic deposits of Madagascar.

Such is the evidence of the rocks. Their age relationships, and in addition the relationships of pertinent Upper Jurassic sediments, may be plotted in the manner of Table 10.

Table 10. *Correlation of Jurassic vertebrate horizons**

Lower Jurassic	Middle Jurassic	Upper Jurassic	
Navajo		Morrison	NORTH AMERICA
Kota (India)		Weiyan Kuangyuan (China)	ASIA
Lias	Dogger	Malm	EUROPE
L. Lias / M. Lias / U. Lias	Stonefield slates / Forest marble	Oxford / Kimmeridge / Portland / Purbeck	
Holzmaden		Solnhofen	
Morocco	Morocco Madagascar	Tendaguru	AFRICA
Talbraggar / Lower Walloon / Durham Downs			AUSTRALIA

It is a pleasant, one might say an exhilarating, experience to walk along the Dorset coast from Lyme Regis to Charmouth on a sunny summer day, the black cliffs on the left, the pounding waves on the right, glinting in the sunshine. Among the blocks of weathered rock on the beach, that have been torn from the cliffs by storm-lashed waves and by the gentler erosive action of the rain, are found numerous fossil sea shells, especially large coiled ammonites related to the pearly *Nautilus* of modern seas. And occasionally, but only very occasionally, there will be found among the detritus, or protruding from the cliffs, the fossil bones of an ichthyosaur or perhaps a plesiosaur. Here some of the first of these ancient marine reptiles known to science were discovered and removed in the early days of the nineteenth century by Mary Anning, a remarkable young woman who made a career of fossil hunting.

Ichthyosaurs and plesiosaurs were the dominant reptiles of the shallow seas near the ancient Liassic coast, where they lived in abundance and in considerable variety, too. Many of the ichthyosaurs are small or medium sized animals, comparable in this respect to modern dolphins or porpoises, but some very large ones have been found, thirty feet or more in length. These animals undoubtedly lived about the same kind of life that porpoises and small whales do today, pursuing fishes through the restless waves. The long-necked plesiosaurs rowed themselves along on the surface with their long, powerful paddles, to snap up any fishes that may have been unwary enough to drift into close range.

Long-snouted crocodilians, the mystriosaurs, were here, too, probably spending most of their time in the streams that emptied into the sea, but not improbably venturing beyond the coastline. Various modern crocodiles do not hesitate to swim out into salt water; the Liassic crocodilians might have had similar habits.

Most of the Liassic vertebrate fossils of the Channel coast represent marine reptiles, but we do get rare and tantalizing glimpses of the land-dwellers from the fossils of reptiles that got washed into the ocean and were buried near the shore. One such glimpse is given us by the skeleton of *Scelidosaurus*, the earliest known armored dinosaur, found near Charmouth. This rather specialized ornithischian dinosaur, in which the back is well protected by bony plates, and which has a skeleton twelve feet or more in length, shows many departures from what might be regarded as a primitive condition. It indicates quite clearly that there was obviously a time between the last days of the Triassic period and the early days of the Jurassic period when these reptiles rapidly evolved from small, primitive ancestors into sizable, specialized types. The skeleton of *Scelidosaurus* is, in short, a

Figure 46. An ichthyosaur of Jurassic age. These reptiles, highly adapted to a marine environment, ranged up to thirty feet or more in length; more commonly they were eight or ten feet long.

nice testimonial to what we do not know about the history of the dinosaurs during this portion of geologic time.

What other dinosaurs lived on the land during Liassic times ? For the most part we can only guess the answer to this question, as we will on a later page, basing such guesses upon what we know of late Triassic dinosaurs and of late Jurassic dinosaurs – interpolating in between. But there is one other record* of a lower Jurassic dinosaur from Europe – *Sarcosaurus*, a theropod, again from the Liassic, of southern England. Only fragments of skeletons have been found.

121

*See 'Page Corrections and Emendations' in Addendum.

There were undoubtedly many other reptiles living with *Scelido-saurus* and *Sarcosaurus*, on the uplands, and along the shores that ran down to the Liassic sea, but for the most part they disappeared into the mists of time without leaving any traces of their long sojourn on the earth. The record is almost blank. Almost, that is, except for the fossils of some small and delicate pterosaurs or flying reptiles, and

Figure 47. The plated dinosaur, *Scelidosaurus*, from the lower Jurassic beds of southern England. This reptile was about fifteen feet in length.

ictidosaurs or mammal-like reptiles. One of the earliest flying reptiles, *Dimorphodon*, is known from the lower Jurassic shales at Lyme Regis, a small, queer-looking reptile, with a relatively enormous head, a long tail, and with the fourth finger of each hand greatly elongated to support a wing membrane. This was one of the earliest backboned animals to attempt true flight. It is, in spite of its somewhat clumsy appearance, a highly specialized animal, that bespeaks a most inter-esting evolutionary history bridging the gap from ground-living or tree-dwelling reptiles to fully fledged flying types, a history of which there is not the slightest trace to be found in the rocks.

As for ictidosaurs, numerous bones of a little tritylodont reptile known as *Oligokyphus* are known from fissure fillings in old lime-stones in southern England. Evidently these little mammal-like rep-tiles lived in small caves or crevices back in the hills away from the seashore, from which lairs they ventured out to prey upon small animals, or perhaps to feed upon fruits of some sort.

Such is a very imperfect picture of reptilian life along the English coast, when that coast bordered a great sea covering most of Europe.

The picture is repeated in central Europe, at Holzmaden in southern Germany, where in black Jurassic shales are found ichthyosaurs and plesiosaurs that during their lifetimes may have ranged as far as the English coast. With them also there have been found the bones of a flying reptile, *Dorygnathus*, related to *Dimorphodon* of England. In this region, too, are found mystriosaurs or long-snouted crocodilians,

Figure 48. *Dimorphodon*, an early Jurassic flying reptile, or pterosaur, from Europe. About three feet long.

and ancient turtles, additional slight evidence of the reptiles that once lived on islands set in a great northern sea.

By way of contrast to this picture of life in the ocean and on oceanic islands, the partial skeleton of a small theropod dinosaur, *Segisaurus*, from the Navajo sandstone of Arizona, is the only indication to date of the reptiles, and they must have been of various kinds, which in lower Jurassic times wandered across the desert sands of a North American continent*.

That land-living reptiles were abundant during early Jurassic

* Some years ago the skeleton of a carnivorous dinosaur from the Kayenta formation of Arizona was described as *Megalosaurus wetherelli*, and was indicated as of lower Jurassic relationships. In this present work the Kayenta sandstone is regarded as of upper Triassic relationships (see pages 77, 104). See also 'Page Corrections and Emendations' in Addendum.

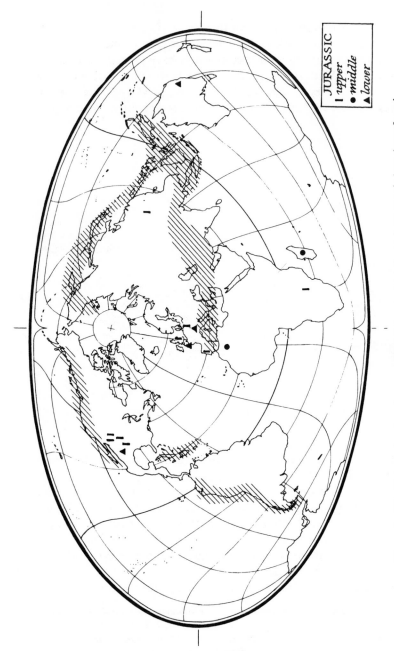

Figure 49. World map, showing the general localities at which Jurassic tetrapods have been found. The shaded areas represent regions of major submergence.

time has recently been attested by the discovery of a rich deposit of early gigantic sauropod dinosaurs in the Kota beds of central India. The bones, which occur in great profusion, are below sediments containing characteristic Liassic fishes. Here is a sample of life as it must have existed widely throughout the world of that distant day.

These have been vignettes, and rather poor ones, of reptiles in an early Jurassic world.

The middle Jurassic or Dogger seas, in which there grew coral reefs to enclose clear lagoons, washed the shores of many islands where the lands of Europe now stretch in unbroken vistas of fields and mountains. And these seas, as did the cooler, preceding Liassic oceans, covered great areas in other parts of the world which are now continental highlands. The world was still a world of great expanded oceans, where ichthyosaurs and plesiosaurs held sway, oceans enclosing restricted continents, islands and archipelagos, where dwelt the land-living reptiles.

Some of the middle Jurassic land-living animals that lived in what is now England are to be seen in the fossils of the Stonesfield slates. Here we get an impression of a variety of life. Here were turtles and small flying reptiles. Here were dinosaurs, as might be expected – among them *Megalosaurus*, a gigantic predator, twenty or thirty feet in length, with a huge skull having large, dagger-like teeth in the jaws, with strong hind limbs on which it walked, and with remarkably small front limbs, obviously used only for grasping. This reptile shows the trend toward giantism so characteristic of many dinosaurs, and so well exemplified in the dinosaurs of late Jurassic times. Its presence in the Stonesfield slates would lead one to believe that there were various other giant dinosaurs living in the particular habitat where these sediments accumulated, and one can only regret that the fossil record is so very incomplete. In the Stonesfield slates, too, are the remains of a small mammal-like ictidosaur, *Stereognathus*, the last of the rodent-like tritylodonts which had lived so successfully on several continents through late Triassic and early Jurassic times.

But the fossils of particular significance in the Stonesfield slates are the jaws and teeth of small, archaic mammals known as triconodonts and pantotheres, the descendants of some of the advanced mammal-like reptiles of late Triassic age. At last the threshold had been crossed, and unmistakable mammals had appeared on the land. This was a significant event in the history of life. Among the ferns and undergrowth of a middle Jurassic landscape in England there

lurked the forerunners of the animals which eventually were to inherit the earth. These little Jurassic mammals, no larger than shrews
or small mice, would have seemed inconsequential to the dinosaurs
of those days, but within the pattern of their heredity they carried
the traits that were to succeed when the dinosaurs no longer ruled
the world. That still would be a long time in the future.

Some idea of dinosaurian progress is to be had from the middle
Jurassic Oolites and the Forest Marble of England, in which are
found the fossil bones of a large carnivorous dinosaur, *Proceratosaurus*, of some gigantic swamp-dwelling sauropods, *Bothriospondylus* and *Cetiosaurus*, in which the body and limbs are heavy, the neck
and tail long, and the skull relatively small, and of a plated dinosaur,
Omosaurus. This record of dinosaurian development, even though
fragmentary, shows that various ruling reptiles of the Jurassic period
had attained the status of giants, a fact that was indicated, as we have
seen, by the presence of *Megalosaurus* in the correlative Stonesfield
slates and at an earlier date by the appearance of giant sauropods in
the Liassic Kota sediments of central India. The dominance of dinosaurs over the land had been established.

This dinosaurian dominance is further attested by recent discoveries of fossil bones in the middle Jurassic sediments of Morocco,
where are found the large predator, *Megalosaurus*, and the gigantic
swamp-dweller, *Cetiosaurus*, living with a long-snouted crocodile,
Steneosaurus. An impression of the same general assemblage of great
reptiles is to be had farther to the south from fossils of the crocodile,
Steneosaurus, and the giant sauropod, *Bothriospondylus*, discovered in
Madagascar. The world was full of dinosaurs – but in most parts of
the world they left no bones to show us what they were like, or where
they lived. We can only speculate about what the full range of dinosaurian life, of all reptilian life for that matter, was like during the
days of middle and even early Jurassic history.

In view of the circumstances, such speculation is quite justified.
There is a considerable fossil record to show us the course of evolution among the ichthyosaurs and plesiosaurs during early and middle
Jurassic times, when oceans were extensive and lands were restricted;
but what about the evolutionary development of various land animals, of which we have had only passing glimpses, or even inferred
glimpses, during this long interval of geologic time ? With the rather
abundant record of late Triassic amphibians and reptiles that was
outlined in a previous chapter at hand, and with a good record of late

Jurassic amphibians, reptiles, birds and mammals that will be reviewed in the next chapter, perhaps some extrapolations can be made to fill in the faunal gaps of early and middle Jurassic age.

This was the age during which frogs became firmly established throughout the world in essentially their modern form. An ancestor of the frogs, *Protobatrachus*, in the Triassic beds of Madagascar, bridges the gap rather nicely between small, labyrinthodont amphibians and full-fledged frogs. We are therefore certainly justified in thinking that during early Jurassic times the frogs became what they are today – small, tail-less, leaping amphibians, with large heads, because such frogs are found in upper Jurassic sediments. This would lead one to think that during much of Jurassic time, and on through the remainder of the age of dinosaurian dominance, the streams and marshes resounded to choruses of frogs. The other amphibians that are with us today, salamanders and tropical coecilians, may very well have been living as far back as early or middle Jurassic time, but this is only a guess.

There were certainly lizards in the undergrowth of early and middle Jurassic forests, and they were very probably widely spread throughout the world. Along with them, at least in some parts of the world, were small rhynchocephalians, well suited to continue their success from that day to this, in contradistinction to the rhynchosaurs, those large and peculiar rhynchocephalians which spread so widely through the world during late Triassic times, only to become extinct at the end of the Triassic period. And keeping company with the lizards and the rhynchocephalians on land were many turtles, the inhabitants of rivers, ponds and uplands, and crocodilians, likewise the denizens of rivers and lakes. Very probably, as has been mentioned, the crocodilians ventured into the salt waters along coast lines.

There were reptiles in the air, too, the early pterosaurs, the bones of which have fortunately been found in several localities, not only in those already mentioned, of early Jurassic age, but also at some places where middle Jurassic rocks are exposed. These first backboned animals to embark upon true flight were unchallenged in the air during all of early and middle Jurassic time; it was not until the late years of the Jurassic that the first birds appeared.

But, above all, the years of early and middle Jurassic times were the years when the dinosaurs waxed mightily, as is made clear not only by the diversity of these reptiles in subsequent Jurassic history, but also as is indicated by the presence of their bones in the Indian, European and North African lower and middle Jurassic beds. No longer were they limited to the few structural types that were so characteristic of late Triassic landscapes. Instead, they must have inhabited the world in considerable variety. There were carnivorous theropods of many kinds, some of them small and lightly constructed, predators on lizards and a variety of small animals, others of large and even gigantic size, the hunters of other dinosaurs. It was during this geologic interval that the sauropod dinosaurs, adumbrated by the prosauropods of late Triassic times, grew into giants. One of the first of such giants, *Rhoetosaurus*, is known from fossils found in the lower Jurassic sediments of Australia. The evolutionary growth of these reptiles into the largest of all land-living animals obviously took place with amazing speed, geologically speaking, during the early part of the Jurassic period. In short, the sauropods became the greatest of the giants with the beginning of the lower Jurassic and retained this status through the remainder of the Mesozoic.

The occurrence of *Scelidosaurus* in the Liassic sediments of England is a reminder that the ornithischian dinosaurs had enjoyed a wide range of evolutionary radiation by the opening of the Jurassic period. This dinosaur is a rather specialized type, one of the stegosaurians, and it gives us solid proof that the plated dinosaurs, so characteristic of late Jurassic history, had diverged widely from some primitive ornithischian type at an early stage in their evolutionary development.

The most primitive of the ornithischian dinosaurs are the camptosaurs and their relatives, first appearing in the upper Triassic beds of South Africa. It is thoroughly and justifiably logical to suppose that some small, primitive camptosaur must inevitably have been the ancestor of the Liassic scelidosaur, but as yet we have no record of such a central, ancestral type in the lower Jurassic. Here is one of those quirks in the geologic record, for which allowances must be made when the evolutionary progress of life is being interpreted.

We have seen that by middle Jurassic times there were small, archaic mammals living in Europe. Very probably they inhabited other continents as well. In view of the disappearance of all mammal-like reptiles except the ictidosaurs at the end of the Triassic period, and the decline of the ictidosaurs during the early phases of Jurassic history, it seems evident that the final transition from reptile to mammal took place in early Jurassic times. By the beginning of the middle Jurassic the mammal-like reptiles had come to the end of their interesting development, and their final exit from the great drama of animal evolution was owing in part to the fact that their immediate descendants, the first mammals, were able to take over to better advantage the niches that these progressive reptiles had occupied.

This has been a summary, based in part upon a limited amount of fossil evidence and in part on probabilities without any supporting fossil evidence, of the evolutionary development of amphibians, reptiles and mammals during the early and middle parts of Jurassic history[*]. From such a summary it can be seen that there must have been a new burst of evolution among reptiles which established a new hierarchy of rulers in the world, rather different from the dominant reptiles of Triassic times. With the advent of the Jurassic the two orders of dinosaurs came into their own, to begin their long and undisputed rule of the land. With them were the crocodiles, the lizards, the turtles, and in the air the flying reptiles. With them, too, were on the one hand amphibians of modern mien, and on the other, the first, very small, archaic mammals. Such was the association of tetrapod vertebrates immediately preceding the spectacular assemblages of reptiles and other animals that appeared in such full panoply as the Jurassic period drew to a close.

[*] See 'Page Corrections and Emendations' in Addendum.

Chapter 8

Dominance of the Dinosaurs

IF IN OUR MIND'S EYE we journey back through the ages to late Jurassic time, we enter a tropical world inhabited by many large and even gigantic reptiles. It is a world dominated by great dinosaurs. It is a world of giants, known to us from their many bones. Our knowledge of late Jurassic vertebrate life is broad and in many respects detailed – a decided contrast to the fleeting and fragmentary views of early and middle Jurassic backboned animals that have been vouchsafed to us from scattered exposures of sediments found in Europe and a few other places. From the fossils of reptiles and other vertebrates of late Jurassic age we are able to build up a rather full picture of tetrapod life on the continents, which shows us a variety of animals large and small, the hunters and the hunted, the dwellers on dry land, in marshes, in streams and ponds, in trees and in the air. And this record is supplemented by the fossil remains of marine reptiles. All in all, the evidence of ancient life as preserved in upper Jurassic rocks is abundant, and its interpretation has yielded rich rewards to the paleontologist.

This abundant and varied fossil record of life on the land comes in the main from three regions. One of these regions is in the Rocky Mountain states of North America, where the Morrison formation is widely exposed. A second region is in southern England and parts of western Europe, where the Oxford, Kimmeridge, Portland and Purbeck beds, and their equivalents, come to the surface in cliffs, banks and quarries. The third region is located in East Africa, in the general vicinity of Lake Tanganyika, where the famous Tendaguru beds have yielded spectacular fossils*.

Of these three regions the western North American area encompassing the Morrison exposures is the most extensive and the most prolific of fossil reptiles. Here is the locale of the elaborate and exciting expeditions that were carried on with such vigor and success by

*See 'Page Corrections and Emendations' in Addendum.

Othniel Charles Marsh and Edward Drinker Cope during the decades immediately following the American Civil War. Here are the beds that yielded the first abundant and complete skeletons of varied dinosaurs, large and small, skeletons that opened new vistas of past life to scholars and to the interested public all over the world. Here was the habitat of the reptiles that long ago filled and dominated an ancient North American continent. A survey of the Morrison fauna gives us as complete a picture of life on the land during late Jurassic times as can be had in the present state of our knowledge.

The Morrison formation, named for the little town of Morrison, Colorado, in the foothills of the Rocky Mountains immediately west of Denver, occurs as great linear bands of sediments associated with mountain uplifts in Wyoming, Idaho and Utah, Colorado, Arizona and New Mexico. In many areas it appears as continuous exposures for mile after mile, frequently forming colorful cliffs and badlands (the name used in North America for strangely and often weirdly eroded rocks, barren of vegetation), which appear very prominently in sweeping vistas across mountain and desert. The bones of dinosaurs and contemporary reptiles are not at all uncommon in these Morrison sediments, and were dinosaurs as easy and as inexpensive to collect, to prepare and to house as are fossil clam shells, there would be numberless bones and skeletons in almost every high school, local museum and university throughout western North America. But dinosaur skeletons, particularly the remains of giant dinosaurs, are extremely difficult and costly objects because they consume untold amounts of time in their collection and their preparation. Hence only a few of the larger or more favorably located institutions have attempted to collect Morrison dinosaurs and other reptiles. The localities where Morrison dinosaurs have been collected in greatest abundance are Como Bluff in Wyoming, Canyon City in Colorado, the area now known as Dinosaur National Monument along the border between Colorado and Utah, and the San Rafael Swell of Utah.

Dinosaur National Monument deserves passing mention. Here, where in past years the Carnegie Museum of Pittsburgh excavated great quantities of dinosaur bones, the National Park Service of the United States has now established a display *in situ*. A museum building has been constructed over an almost vertical cliff, where the bones of Morrison dinosaurs are being exposed, to be left on permanent view in the rock.

The Morrison formation, which may reach considerable thicknesses, is seen as shales and sandstones, the shales often rather colorful, in shades of purple, red, green, and gray. Most of the reptiles have been found in the uppermost shales of the formation, these being distinguished in Utah and the Colorado Plateau as a formational subdivision named the Brushy Basin member.

These shales give evidence of a tropical, humid climate, and of great rivers and many streams that came from higher lands to the south, to flow across a low, alluvial plain of vast extent. And on this great lowland lived a host of reptiles of all kinds. Vegetation must have been abundant, because the land was evidently inhabited by great herds of gigantic, plant-eating dinosaurs, the most spectacular being the huge sauropods, so very characteristic of late Jurassic continents throughout the world.

Indeed, if there is any one thing for which the Morrison beds are noteworthy, it is above all the abundance of gigantic sauropod bones and skeletons contained within these sediments. The discovery of such great bones at Como Bluff, Wyoming, first led Professor Marsh to explore and excavate at this locality, and from that day to this the search for giant dinosaurs has been a prime motive behind the numerous paleontological expeditions that have worked at various Morrison localities. It is interesting to recall that members of the first American Museum of Natural History expedition to the Morrison sediments at the Como Bluff locality found a cabin that had been constructed of large sauropod bones by a local sheepherder. At this place, appropriately designated as the Bone Cabin Quarry, these big bones, which were scattered all over the ground, were the most readily available building materials. This is but one indication of the abundance of Morrison sauropods.

Dinosaurs lived in enormous numbers and considerable variety when the Morrison sediments were being deposited. Consequently the Morrison landscape may have been in a very general way similar to the plains of modern Africa, where hordes of antelope belonging to many genera and species cover the veldt. But, of course, the Morrison scene was on a grand scale; instead of gazelles weighing fifty or sixty pounds, and large antelope and zebras weighing several hundred pounds, the flood plains of rivers and streams were populated by sixty and seventy foot sauropods, weighing fifteen to forty or fifty tons, and even more.

These figures are some indication of the variety of Morrison sauropods. There were at least a dozen genera, and, of course, many more species in the Morrison scene. All of them were built along a common structural plan: a heavy body supported by very massive legs and broad feet, a long neck and long tail, and a relatively small skull with comparatively weak jaws and a limited number of blade-like or pencil-shaped teeth. *Diplodocus* is a very long, slender sauropod, perhaps weighing no more than about fifteen tons in life. The other extreme is seen in *Brachiosaurus*, a huge sauropod with high shoulders and a very massive neck, that may have weighed as much as eighty tons and more.

It is to be assumed that the sauropods were water-living types, spending much of their time in swamps and in rivers and lakes, where their massive bodies were buoyed up by the water, and where they fed upon the vegetation of the bottom or of the shoreline. In all of them the nostrils are located high on the skull, a sure indication of aquatic habits, and an adaptation that very probably allowed these huge reptiles to wade or swim with the body largely submerged and the head thrust above the surface of the water, periscope-fashion, so that the animal might breathe and keep a sharp lookout for enemies.

The giant herbivorous dinosaurs certainly had enemies, in the form of the large carnivorous dinosaurs, the carnosaurs exemplified by such genera as *Allosaurus* (more properly *Antrodemus*) and *Cera-tosaurus*. These aggressive, bipedal dinosaurs, in which the skull is excessively enlarged, thus allowing for long jaws armed with scimitar-like teeth, were the arch predators of their time. They followed the sauropods (as is indicated by trackways found in Texas) and very likely attacked these giant dinosaurs when the big herbivores ventured too far away from the water for their own safety. The carnivores very likely fed on carcasses whenever they found one.

Certainly their diet was not limited to the sauropods, and they undoubtedly attacked other herbivorous dinosaurs, such as the small, inoffensive camptosaurs and the plated stegosaurs, that lived so abundantly in Morrison times.

Some of the Morrison dinosaurs are quite small, as for example *Ornitholestes*, a lightly built little carnivore no more than four or five feet in length. This agile little predator must have frequented undergrowth, to prey upon lizards and other small animals, which it caught with its quick jaws and claws. *Camptosaurus*, a rather primitive ornithischian, is another Morrison dinosaur, sometimes no larger than *Ornitholestes*. This herbivore shared the plants upon which it fed with *Stegosaurus*, one of the most bizarre of the ornithischians, a rather large, ungainly dinosaur, with two rows of upright plates along the back and spikes on the end of the tail. All of these various dinosaurs certainly gave an appearance of considerable variety to the Morrison scene.

The dinosaurs are, of course, the most spectacular of Morrison reptiles, but there were many others, as has been said. There were various crocodilians and turtles, lending a rather familiar aspect to the fauna. There were lizards and rhynchocephalians, too, although the evidence for these reptiles is very scanty. And there were amphibians, in the form of frogs.

But perhaps the most significant of Morrison animals were the mammals, known at the present time from a single small pocket – Quarry nine – at Como Bluff, Wyoming. Even though their occurrence is restricted to this one place, they show considerable diversity, being represented by a good array of genera distributed among several families and four orders. From this assemblage in one very small deposit we get the impression of a world in which the undergrowth was abundantly populated by quick, small mammals, incessantly on the move. They were not obvious in the large view, just as today small rodents and insectivores that live in such remarkable numbers in the ground and under the grass and leaves are seldom seen. But they were there.

These mammals were adapted for a rather secretive life, hidden in the thick foliage of the ground or in trees, where they were reasonably safe from the numerous reptiles that surrounded them. They were for the most part carnivorous, and perhaps fed to a large degree upon insects and worms, although some of them very probably ate fruits. All of them have differentiated teeth: nipping incisors, piercing canines and cusped cheek teeth, obviously derived from the differentiated teeth of their therapsid ancestors.

The various specializations of the teeth, especially the cheek teeth, suggest that these mammals represent several lines of evolution independently and simultaneously derived from reptilian ancestors. These were 'experiments' one might say, in mammalian evolution, most of them destined to failure. Thus the triconodonts have cheek teeth, in each of which are three sharp cusps: a large central one, with small ones in front of and behind it. In the symmetrodonts there are three cusps arranged in a triangular pattern, obviously a better adaptation for crushing food than the fore and aft pattern of the triconodonts. The pantotheres are mammals in which the cheek teeth also show a triangular pattern, but a pattern more complex and more completely interlocking than that of the symmetrodonts. Finally there are the multituberculates, so named because in these mammals there are elongated teeth in the back of the jaws, each tooth possessing several rows of fore and aft cusps. It is assumed that these mammals could crush and slice fruits, pods and nuts with their enlarged, multicuspid teeth, employing a backward and forward motion of the jaws as do many modern rodents.

The triconodonts and symmetrodonts were destined to become extinct at the end of Jurassic times. The multituberculates were more successful, and persisted through the remainder of the Mesozoic and on into the beginning of Cenozoic times, when they finally disappeared, seemingly displaced by the true rodents. Finally the pantotheres were the most important of the Morrison mammals, for it is obvious, by reason of the similarities of tooth and bone structure, that from them there arose the marsupials and placentals that were to inherit the earth after the extinction of the dinosaurs.

Such is the nature of the Morrison fauna, a collection of backboned animals dominated by huge dinosaurs, but including as well various other reptiles and a seeming host of archaic mammals. It is a fauna that lived successfully through a long time span and over a large part of what was then North America. It is a fauna that had its counterparts in closely related faunas living in Europe and Africa, as we shall see.

What is now Europe continued in late Jurassic times to be a region of tropical islands surrounded by coral seas, as it had been in the preceding part of this geologic period. Consequently the upper Jurassic beds of this region contain the fossil bones of reptiles which lived on lands sloping down to the sea, and also the contiguous remains of marine reptiles. Moreover there are occasionally found the skeletons of flying animals that had fallen into quiet lagoons, to be buried and fossilized. It is a mixed record.

Since the late Jurassic geography of the European region was so different from that of North America, the difference being between an islanded sea and a broad continent, there are bound to be differences, in part hinted at above, in the fossil records of the two regions. But there are other differences, too. The fossil beds to a degree are more limited in extent than is the Morrison formation, partly because in this area there were not the vast river flood plains for the interment of skeletons as was the case throughout western North America. Because of this factor, together with the forces of erosion, fossil remains of reptiles are generally not as abundant in the European region as in North America, so that the record is less complete than that of the Morrison beds, with which it may be compared. Conversely, because of the contiguity of land and shore, of beaches and coral lagoons, the European record preserves some facets of ancient vertebrate life that are missing in the Morrison sediments.

In southern England the upper Jurassic rocks form a sequence, in order of increasing age: Purbeck, Portland, Kimmeridge and Oxford. The Oxford beds are clays, formed near the shore, in which are contained the skeletons of plesiosaurs and ichthyosaurs, together with remains of crocodiles, dinosaurs and other reptiles. In the black Kimmeridge shales of subsequent age are found similar associations of reptiles. The Portland beds, overlying the Kimmeridge, are fine-grained limestones deposited in coral seas, and at the top of the sequence the Purbeck beds are of particular significance to the paleontologist because of their contained mammalian remains.

Related sediments are found on the European continent, especially in France, Germany, Spain and Portugal. Of especial interest are very fine-grained limestones, evidently deposited in the bottoms of quiet, shallow lagoons, at Solnhofen and Eichstätt in southern Germany, at Cirin in France and at Lerida, Spain, in which are contained the delicate skeletons of small animals.

The same complex of dinosaurs lived on the Jurassic islands of the European region as wandered across the Morrison landscapes of North America. Here were giant sauropods and the large carnivores that preyed upon them, small carnivores, herbivorous camptosaurs and plated stegosaurs. The picture, though similar in its general aspects, differs in details. For example, the genera are on the whole different. *Cetiosaurus* and *Bothriospondylus* in Europe are the counterparts of the giant sauropods of the Morrison. *Megalosaurus* played the role in that region that *Allosaurus* did in North America, and similarly *Compsognathus* in Europe was the hunter of small game as was *Ornitholestes* of the Morrison. *Cryptodraco* may be compared with the Morrison *Camptosaurus*, and *Dacentrurus* (or *Omosaurus*) with *Stegosaurus*.

There were many crocodiles of different kinds. Among the fossil bones that remain as evidence of these particular reptiles are those of marine crocodiles, known as geosaurs or metriorhynchids, showing transformations of the tail into a powerful, fish-like swimming fin and the limbs into paddles, these being adaptations for fast swimming. The geosaurs were obviously full-fledged marine reptiles that probably never came out on land, the only archosaurians to become completely adapted for marine life.

Of course, there were turtles on the Jurassic islands of Europe, and lizards and rhynchocephalians as well. And in the contiguous waters were the ever-present plesiosaurs and ichthyosaurs.

In the fine-grained lithographic limestone of Solnhofen are found exquisitely preserved skeletons of pterosaurs, or flying reptiles, some

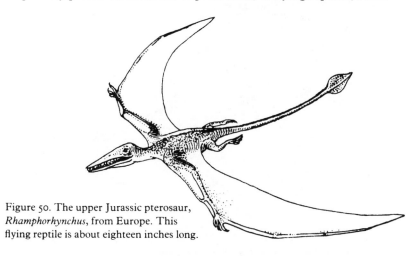

Figure 50. The upper Jurassic pterosaur, *Rhamphorhynchus*, from Europe. This flying reptile is about eighteen inches long.

of them, such as the beautiful skeleton of *Rhamphorhynchus*, showing quite plainly the wing membranes and the membrane of a little rudder at the end of the long tail. But of unusual importance was the discovery, years ago, in these limestones of the skeletons of *Archaeopteryx*, the oldest known bird. Three skeletons are known[*], as well as supplementary fossils. These skeletons would have been classified as reptilian when they were discovered, were it not for the excellent preservation of feather imprints with them, showing quite clearly the attachment of long wing feathers to the arms, and tail feathers to the axis of a long, bony tail. Here is a truly intermediate form between two great classes of vertebrates, a connecting link, bridging the gap between reptile and bird. *Archaeopteryx* gives a cogent basis to the oft-repeated statement that birds are essentially 'glorified reptiles'.

137

[*]See 'Page Corrections and Emendations' in Addendum.

Finally, there should be mentioned the fossil mammals of the Purbeck beds of the English Channel coast. These mammals are closely related to triconodonts, symmetrodonts, pantotheres and multituberculates of the Morrison beds; indeed in several cases the same genera are found in both regions. Thus the Purbeck mammals show the close relationships of geography and age that held between Europe and North America during late Jurassic times. And from them one may suppose that in the European islands, as in North

Figure 51. The first bird, *Archaeopteryx*, about two feet long, from the upper Jurassic Solnhofen limestone of southern Germany.

America, the microenvironments of undergrowth and treetops were numerously inhabited by these small, ever-active mammals. Their fossils add the final bit of evidence to show us how very similar was land life throughout the northern hemisphere.

But the similarities during late Jurassic time among land-living reptiles across thousands of miles of the earth's surface were not confined to the resemblances that we have just seen in the northern hemisphere. They may be traced southward into east Africa, an area separated from Europe by almost as much distance as is western North America. They give proof of the essential unity of environments and of life over a large part of the earth's surface at this stage of earth history.

The Tendaguru beds of Tanganyika, in East Africa, are composed of an interesting alternation of terrestrial sediments containing the bones of dinosaurs and other reptiles, and marine beds with sea shells. It is a continuous sequence that extends from the middle Jurassic into the lower Cretaceous, and the shells that are found in the marine phases of this series of deposits can be correlated closely with the standard European sequence of late Jurassic and early Cretaceous fossil-bearing formations. This is a fortunate circumstance, because it affords the opportunity of determining the relationships of the bone-bearing horizons to marine horizons of undoubted age. So it is

Figure 52. The Jurassic marine crocodile, *Geosaurus*. Skeletons of this reptile, found in Europe are about eight or ten feet in length.

that the sediments in which are enclosed the bones of large dinosaurs, obviously closely related to the Morrison dinosaurs, are sandwiched between marine beds carrying invertebrates of late Jurassic age. Such evidence reinforces that already reviewed which points to the essentially contemporaneous ages of the Morrison and the European Kimmeridge and Purbeck. It gives additional proof of a wide distribution of closely related reptilian faunas, dominated by gigantic dinosaurs.

It seems that the Tendaguru reptiles lived along a river course, or perhaps a complex of rivers, in the near vicinity of the debouchment of these waters into the ocean. It is very possible that the mouth of a large river emptied into a bay or inner seaway, protected by an outer bar. The skeletons of reptiles living in this environment were occasionally buried beneath the sands and muds of the sweeping rivers, to be fossilized. At intervals during a long span of time the sea would invade the region locally, and the shells of marine invertebrates would be deposited in the offshore deposits, on top of the river-lain sediments. The sea would then retreat, and there would be another cycle of river deposits with included bones. In such manner was this significant alternating series of sediments accumulated.

The Tendaguru reptiles have a familiar look. Massive semi-aquatic sauropods dominate the scene, just as they do in the Morrison fauna, although not in such variety. Among them the greatest of the giants, *Brachiosaurus*, is here as it is in North America, which leads one to think that these enormous dinosaurs migrated widely during the time of their dominance, pushing across intercontinental land bridges, possibly even moving along chains of connecting islands by swimming across sea channels between the lands*. Other Tendaguru sauropods are *Tornieria*, a relative of the Kimmeridgian *Cetiosaurus*, and *Dicraeosaurus*, similar to the Morrison *Diplodocus* in many respects, but smaller.

The carnivores are here, as might be expected. *Megalosaurus*, so characteristic of the upper Jurassic deposits of Europe, quite obviously was an inhabitant of the African scene, and the Morrison genera, *Allosaurus* and *Ceratosaurus*, may very possibly have been present. There were small carnivores as well, as indicated by the remains of a little dinosaur, *Elaphrosaurus*, similar to the Morrison *Ornitholestes*.

As for the ornithischian dinosaurs, there lived in Tendaguru times a stegosaur, *Kentrosaurus*, very like the Morrison *Stegosaurus*, but with smaller plates along the back and seemingly with spikes also on the back in addition to those on the tail. *Dysalatosaurus*, a camptosaur related to the Morrison *Camptosaurus*, completes the roster of Tendaguru dinosaurs.

The flying reptiles, *Rhamphorhynchus* and *Pterodactylus*, so typical of the upper Jurassic deposits of Europe, are found in Africa. This is not surprising, because these reptiles very probably were able to range over great distances, as do many modern birds. The fact that they have not been discovered in the Morrison sediments, for instance, is almost certainly owing to their lack of preservation and possibly the accidents of collecting in this region. The long-snouted crocodilian, *Steneosaurus*, so characteristic of the middle and upper

*See 'Page Corrections and Emendations' in Addendum.

Jurassic deposits in Europe, is also in the Tendaguru fauna, one more link in the chain of reptilian evidence connecting this area with Europe in these final days of Jurassic history.

As has been almost tediously evident in this review, western North America, England and Central Europe, and East Africa are closely linked by reason of the strong resemblances between their late Jurassic faunal assemblages. In all of them the giant dinosaurs are dominant, associated with other dinosaurs of lesser proportions. In all of them there are other reptiles, which, if only the fossil record were more complete, would show about as much community of occurrence as do the dinosaurs. There are similar turtles, crocodiles, lizards and rhynchocephalians in North America and Europe, and in both of these regions there are archaic mammals. There are similar crocodiles and flying reptiles in Europe and Africa. Extrapolating from such facts, one can think with good reason that all of these reptiles were as widely distributed, and as characteristic of the faunas on the various continental blocks, as were the dinosaurs. The world was a place of abundant life.

What evidences of this life do we find in regions other than those that have been reviewed? The best record beyond the limits of the North American, European and African areas is to be found in western China, in the province of Szechwan, and has been made known only within the past decade as a result of explorations and studies by Chinese scientists. Some of the fossil evidence from Szechwan is fragmentary, but some of it is based upon reasonably complete materials, so that the outlines of late Jurassic life in that part of the world are beginning to appear. The fossil collections from Szechwan should certainly be augmented in future years*, with the good possibility that this region may in time rank with those already described as the locale for the study and interpretation of upper Jurassic land-living animals.

Here, as in the other regions that we have surveyed, the fauna has a familiar upper Jurassic look. But in China it is, as presently known, composed almost entirely of dinosaurs. The most spectacular of the herbivores are, as might be expected, large sauropods – for example, *Omeisaurus* and *Mamenchisaurus*, this latter form showing certain characters that may relate it to the Morrison *Diplodocus*. And, of course, there are the giant carnivores that go along with these big plant-eaters in late Jurassic faunas all over the world: an allosaur called *Chienkosaurus* and a megalosaur called *Szechuanosaurus*.

141

*See 'Page Corrections and Emendations' in Addendum.

Sinocoelurus is one of the small carnivores, a counterpart of those little predators, the coelurosaurians, which we have seen in the other upper Jurassic faunas. Finally, in this Asiatic region the ornithischian dinosaurs are represented by a camptosaur, *Sanpasaurus*, and a stegosaur or plated dinosaur, *Chialangosaurus*. The one other upper Jurassic reptile found in Szechwan is a crocodilian, *Hsiosuchus*, a form rather remarkable for some of its primitive characters.

Any other evidence for land-living reptiles in late Jurassic times is indeed scattered. In Manchuria there has been found a rhynchocephalian, *Monjurosuchus*, associated with upper Jurassic plants and insects, and relatively near, in Mongolia, is an upper Jurassic lizard, *Yabeinosaurus*. This evidence, together with the discovery of an upper Jurassic turtle in China, about completes the known evidence for Asia.

Perhaps, having reviewed the late Jurassic land-living vertebrates of the world, it may be useful to step back as it were, and take a very general comparative view of them, as they are found in the principal regions of discovery, such as is given in Table 11.

Table 11. *Terrestrial vertebrates of the late Jurassic period and the principal regions of their discovery* *

	NORTH AMERICA Morrison	EUROPE Purbeck Portland Kimmeridge	EAST AFRICA Tendaguru	ASIA SZECHWAN Red Beds MANCHURIA MONGOLIA
Frogs	+	+		
Turtles	+	+		+
Rhynchocephalians	+	+		+
Lizards	+	+		+
Crocodilians	+	+	+	+
Coelurosaurs	+	+	+	+
Carnosaurs	+	+	+	+
Sauropods	+	+	+	+
Camptosaurs	+	+	+	+
Stegosaurs	+	+	+	+
Pterosaurs		+	+	
Birds		+		
Mammals	+	+		

Little has been said so far about the marine reptiles, which were numerous and varied at this stage of Mesozoic history, just as they had been in earlier Jurassic times. As might be expected, their re-

*See 'Tables and Diagrams' in Addendum.

mains are particularly evident in the European region, where lands even at this late date of Jurassic history were relatively restricted, and where tropical seas were extensive. Here are found icthyosaurs, little different from the icthyosaurs of earlier Jurassic times, and here are found plesiosaurs; long-necked types with small skulls, and short-necked forms, the pliosaurs, with rather large, long-jawed skulls. The marine waters of this part of the world were inhabited, too, by the marine crocodiles, or geosaurs, already alluded to.

The geosaurs may very well have been widely distributed through the oceans of the world in late Jurassic times, but the only other place outside Europe where to date bones have been found is in marine sediments of South America, where ichthyosaurs also occur. However deficient the evidence for the geosaurs may be at present, that for other marine reptiles gives us an idea that the ichthyosaurs and plesiosaurs swam as widely in the oceans as the dinosaurs roamed on the land. Brief late-Jurassic marine incursions in North America, specifically as preserved by the rocks of the upper Jurassic Sundance formation, show that ichthyosaurs and pliosaurs lived in oceans that once covered the mountain region of the western States. The short-necked plesiosaurs are also found in certain upper Jurassic rocks of Africa and of China – here again in Szechwan.

This discussion has left large parts of the world unaccounted for. What was life like in eastern North America during late Jurassic times ? What was the South American continent like, and what were the reptiles that lived on it ? For that matter, how much of a South American continent was there ? Were there dinosaurs in parts of Africa beyond the eastern segment of the continent ? How much land area made up the Asiatic block, and what animals lived on it ? There are many questions for which we do not have definite answers. There is much still to be learned.

Our lack of knowledge about the late Jurassic animals with backbones in many parts of the world may be due in part to the lack of sufficient exploration and study in these regions. For example, the recent work in Szechwan gives some indication of fossils still to be discovered and reptiles to be studied and described from that particular region in Asia. Other parts of the vast Asiatic continent and likewise of Africa, as well as of South America, should add materially to our knowledge of late Jurassic life during the years to come. But in those parts of the world where geological exploration and study have been concentrated during the past century, particularly western

Europe and North America, it seems likely that any new knowledge about late Jurassic tetrapods will come from the Jurassic beds that already have been mapped and thus are rather well known.

In large areas on the several continents there are no upper Jurassic continental rocks to be seen; either they were never deposited, or have been lost as a result of the powerful forces of erosion acting through long periods of time, or have been so deeply buried under a mantle of younger sediments that no longer are they available to the fossil hunter. Of course, this is true for sediments of any age, but it seems to be particularly true for continental Jurassic beds. The record is far too incomplete to satisfy the inquiring paleontologist; there is an ancient lost world about which we can only speculate.

But the record that we do have brings out one feature of late Jurassic life which already has been made apparent, but which may very well be commented on once more at this place. This is the strong trend toward giantism among many Jurassic reptiles, especially the dinosaurs. The land was inhabited by giants much larger than any animals of previous geologic ages, as is particularly seen in the faunas of late Jurassic age. Giants dominated the Morrison scene, as they did the Kimmeridge and the Tendaguru landscapes, and doubtless other regions of the world as well. This spread of giants through the world as Jurassic time ran its course carries with it some significant implications about what the world was like in those days.

In the first place, giants require living space. For instance, large land mammals today do not live on small islands; they are absent from such environments, even when such islands are accessible, because there is not sufficient living room for them. Or they may be represented by dwarf relatives. The island of Celebes does not support large wild buffaloes, but it is inhabited by a dwarf buffalo, *Anoa*. Restricted as some lands may have been during the late Jurassic time, there were nevertheless areas of sufficient extent to allow for the development of giants, not as limited populations, but in vast numbers and in considerable variety. So if one may make analogies, it seems reasonable to suppose that the giant dinosaurs of late Jurassic time found their living space in large expanses of jungle and plain, as was obviously the case for the Morrison reptiles, or that they must have lived on extensive island groups, where individual islands were of considerable size or where these reptiles could easily swim from one island to another. This was probably the case in the European region.

Concomitantly, giants require large amounts of food. Elephant herds in Africa today roam over large territories to feed, and it seems likely that the herbivorous dinosaurs also may have roamed widely, through marshes and along waterways, in search of food. Of course, these dinosaurs, since they were reptiles with relatively low metabolic rates, did not require as much food as might be supposed. Yet even so, when one considers their size and their apparent numbers, one can only conclude that food was very abundant during this stage of geologic history. Such would seem to have been the case. The late Jurassic dinosaurs lived in environments where there was thick tropical vegetation: cycads, conifers, ginkgos, horsetails, ferns and other plants. The great herbivorous dinosaurs fed upon this supply of green food, and in turn furnished a large source of energy for the giant meat-eating dinosaurs. Thus the sufficiency of food and of living space probably were the prime factors that favored the spectacular trend to giantism among the late Jurassic reptiles.

The wide dispersal of these giants throughout the world is definitive proof of the wide range of tropical climates at the time they lived, for the great dinosaurs could hardly have inhabited any but tropical and warm, subtropical environments. The world probably was in late Jurassic time uniformly tropical to an extent that had not been the case since the Carboniferous, and that was never to be the case again. Such a world was favorable to reptilian giants[*].

What about the lesser animals ? There were certainly great numbers of land-living vertebrates that were not giants, as is shown by the fossils of smaller reptiles and by those of the very tiny mammals from Quarry nine of the Morrison beds and from the Purbeck sediments. These animals also found the extensive tropical environments favorable to their ways of life. There were lizards living along with dinosaurs in the late Jurassic scene, just as today there are rodents living with elephants in Africa. But the proportion of total weight, or biomass, of the giants to the total weight of all land-living animals must have been spectacularly large during late Jurassic times as compared with what it is today.

With such rather random considerations in mind we come to the end of this survey of late Jurassic reptiles, birds and mammals, and of the world in which they lived. As we have seen, that world was a globe widely covered by tropical seas, above which there rose low continents and islands, clothed with tropical verdure. In the seas and on the lands various reptiles wandered far and wide. The seas

[*]See 'Page Corrections and Emendations' in Addendum.

belonged primarily to the ichthyosaurs and the plesiosaurs, the lands primarily to the dinosaurs, many of which were veritable giants. Although there were amphibians and undoubtedly great numbers of very small, archaic mammals on land, and the first, primitive birds in the air, the world nevertheless was ruled by the reptiles. Reptiles populated the earth in numbers and variety never before attained; reptiles dominated land and sea as they had never before dominated these habitats. The close of the Jurassic period was in truth a climax in the Age of Reptiles – a climax that set the scene for the further and even more successful evolution of these animals in the succeeding geologic period. One phase of reptilian evolution was coming to an end; another and even more spectacular phase of this evolutionary development was to begin. The story of tetrapod vertebrates in the Cretaceous period, the time when the reptiles reached the very zenith of their evolutionary dominance, will be the subject of the next chapters.

Chapter 9

A New World Foreshadowed

WITH THE OPENING OF the Cretaceous period shallow seas spread across the continents, so that once again, as at the beginning of Jurassic times, life on the land was restricted. The continents on which the giant dinosaurs and their lesser relatives had lived during the late Jurassic seemingly were not as extensive as those of today, even though, near the end of Jurassic history, there was some mountain folding, especially in western North America. During the transition from the Jurassic to the Cretaceous these land areas were reduced beyond their late Jurassic extent. Late Jurassic continents were generally low, so that throughout much of the world no great geologic revolutions were necessary to bring about the flooding of large segments of these land masses by the oceans. Evidently the various continental blocks sank slightly, as so frequently has happened during the history of the earth, and salt waters advanced across their depressed portions to form shallow seas.

Consequently, at the beginning of Cretaceous times the advancing seaways occupied the troughs and low areas on the continents which had formed the basins for late Jurassic seas, and then as the years wore on the seas advanced beyond these basins to flood ever-increasing expanses of what had been dry land. An early Cretaceous sun shone down upon glittering waves, undulating in regions which had long been far removed from the borders of the oceans. Much of the southern part of North America and the isthmian region were thus flooded. There were transgressions across what is now Arctic Canada as well. Broad tongues of salt water spread northward from the Tethyan sea, which as we have seen formed a long east to west trough cutting through south-eastern Asia, northern India and the present Mediterranean region during earlier Mesozoic time, to inundate large areas in northern Europe. Eastern Asia was also covered with oceanic waters, as were parts of the northern and eastern regions of Africa. A large part of central Australia also was beneath the sea. Perhaps there was some flooding of South America as well, but on this point the record is as yet indefinite. So the advance of Cretaceous seas began, an advance that was to continue intermittently through the extent of the period.

Of course, this expansion of oceans during lower Cretaceous times is variously reflected in the fossil record. The stony floors of ancient sea bottoms are widely spread, with their included remains of sea shells, and here and there the bones of marine fishes and reptiles. Deposits containing the bones of land-living animals are by contrast very scattered. All in all the fossil record of the lower Cretaceous is, in its occurrence, largely a repetition of the extensive marine deposits and limited continental beds so characteristic of early Jurassic history.

Perhaps these remarks will give the impression that our knowledge of lower Cretaceous backboned animals is not particularly extensive, and this is generally true, especially as it concerns the reptiles[*]. But it must not be thought that a rather incomplete record of land-living vertebrates necessarily implies the lack of significant knowledge of other forms of life. We do know the trends of evolution among various organisms of early Cretaceous age, and our knowledge reveals two very crucial evolutionary developments at this stage of earth history.

One of these was the beginning of the great radiation of teleost fishes – the bony fishes of the modern world. Until the close of Jurassic times the waters of the earth, both the inland rivers and lakes and the vast expanses of the oceans, were inhabited by comparatively primitive bony fishes, with heavy, shining scales. But with the transition from the Jurassic to the Cretaceous the first telosts appeared, fishes with very highly developed bony skeletons, but with rather thin, elastic scales, no longer composed of thick bone, yet none the less providing the fish with an efficient, light-weight, flexible outer covering. The first teleosts were similar to modern sardines, and from such beginnings these fishes inherited the waters of the earth. As the Cretaceous period ran its course the teleosts became ever more numerous and more varied, finally to dominate by numbers the rivers, the lakes and the oceans of the earth. This great revolution in the development of fishes brought a modern appearance to Cretaceous seas. Today teleost fishes are by far the most numerous and widely varied of the vertebrates. Many species of bony fishes live in the oceans in incredibly vast numbers.

[*] See 'Page Corrections and Emendations' in Addendum.

1 The Lower Permian Wichita beds of northern Texas. These are typical exposures in the famous Texas 'red beds', and the locality, Briar Creek, is one from which many fossil amphibians and reptiles have been recovered. The brick-red clays and sandstones are eroded into shallow gullies and banks above which are expanses of grassland and mesquite. Alfred S. Romer, a noted student of Permian vertebrates, on the right.

2 The Upper Permian *Cistecephalus* zone in the Lower Beaufort beds of the Karroo Series of South Africa. The several zones of the Beaufort, which reach considerable thicknesses, as may be seen, are made up of clays, shales and sandstones, in which fossils are found at many levels. We see here the evidence of long-continued deposition by rivers and ponds on great flood-plains. Note the dolerite dike cutting across the horizontal sediments.

3 Life of Early Permian time. Here are seen some of the amphibians
and reptiles that lived when the Wichita and Clear Fork sediments
were being deposited, in what is now northern Texas. On the left is
the large, fin-backed pelycosaur, *Edaphosaurus*, about ten feet in length,
and facing it another pelycosaur of similar size, the piscivorous

Ophiacodon. In the water are two small nectridian amphibians, *Diplocaulus*, and the small labryrinthodont, *Trimerorhachis*. This was a tropical, low-land environment, with coal forest vegetation growing in swamps, on pond and river margins and across the intervening land areas.

4

5

4 The Upper Triassic Red Beds and Cave Sandstone of the Stormberg Series of South Africa. The Cave Sandstone forms steep cliffs and smoothly rounded surfaces, while generally below it the Red Beds make the long slopes. However these two units may interdigitate. Above the Cave Sand stone in Basutoland and adjacent areas are the great thicknesses of the Drakensberg volcanics.

5 A gully or *sanga*, as it is called in Brazil, exposing the bright red sediments of the Upper Triassic Santa Maria formation, near the settlement of Pinheiros, in the state of Rio Grande do Sul. In the distance is seen the escarpment formed by the Serra Geral lavas, which cover the northern part of the state and much of the adjoining states of Santa Catarina and Parana. The superposition of great lavas over Upper Triassic reptile-bearing sediments in both Brazil and South Africa may indicate parallel, if not closely related, geologic and faunal developments in these two regions during the final stages of Triassic history.

6 The Upper Triassic Chinle formation, as exposed in Arizona. These colorful sediments make up the badlands of the Painted Desert, noted for its variegated hues. Red is the predominant color, but there are bands of yellow, white, brown, chocolate-colored, and purple clays and sandstones. This picture taken in the general vicinity of the Petrified Forest, shows the alternation of large sandstone lenses, which break down along joint cracks into huge blocks, with soft clays. Notice the parked vehicle with a tarpaulin stretched from it to form a sunshade, at a site where a phytosaur is being collected.

6

7

7 The Mesozoic sequence at Ghost Ranch, northwest of Abiquiu, New Mexico. The badlands in the foreground are composed of the fossiliferous, brilliantly colored soft clays of the Chinle formation, in which, at this locality, have been found numerous skeletons of the early dinosaur, *Coelophysis*, as well as many specimens of phytosaurs and other Triassic reptiles. Above the Chinle are steep yellowish cliffs of the Jurassic Entrada sandstone, these capped by a layer of white, Todilto gypsum. Beyond the cliffs are gentle slopes of the chocolate colored and purplish Upper Jurassic Morrison formation, which in many localities has yielded the bones of gigantic dinosaurs. At the top is an escarpment formed by the brownish sandstones of the Cretaceous Dakota formation.

8 Life of Late Triassic time, showing restorations of the animals and plants
that are now found as fossils in the Chinle beds of New Mexico and Arizona.
In the water is the gigantic labyrinthodont amphibian, *Eupelor,*
an animal some six feet or more in length. Lying on the bank is the crocodile-
like thecodont reptile, *Phytosaurus,* large individuals of which may be twenty
or thirty feet long. Behind the phytosaur, in the distance, is the armored
thecodont, *Desmatosuchus,* ten feet long, and in the foreground is the small,

bipedal thecodont, *Hesperosuchus*. In the left background are two individuals
of the early saurischian dinosaur, *Coelophysis*, reptiles about ten feet
in length. These animals lived in a tropical environment of moderate topography,
crossed by many sluggish rivers and dotted with lakes. Numerous volcanoes
rose above the general level of the land. Large, aruacariān trees
were abundant, stout scouring rushes or horsetails ten or fifteen feet high
were everywhere, and the ground was covered with abundant ferns.

9

9 The lower Jurassic or Liassic cliffs of the Channel Coast, near Charmouth, Dorset, England. In these alternating shales and limestones, of marine origin, are found the skeletons of aquatic ichthyosaurs and plesiosaurs, as well as some other reptiles. The early armored dinosaur, *Scelidosaurus,* was excavated near this locality, the fossil remains of a land-living animal whose carcass was swept offshore before burial.

10

10 The Upper Jurassic Oxford clays, as exposed in a quarry in Dorset. These sediments have yielded many fossils of crocodiles, turtles, plesiosaurs, ichthyosaurs, dinosaurs and other reptiles, to give us a glimpse of ancient life along the edge of a tropical sea.

12

11 The Upper Jurassic Morrison formation, at Dinosaur National Monument, Utah. Relatively soft clays and shales of light to brownish and purplish colors predominate in the Morrison, but there are layers of heavy sandstones as well. In the highly tilted sediments at this locality have been found many of the great Jurassic dinosaur skeletons to be seen in museums throughout the world.

12 Excavating Jurassic dinosaurs at the turn of the century in the Bone Cabin Quarry at Como Bluff, Wyoming. The men, famous in the annals of dinosaur hunting are from left to right, Peter Kaisen, Walter Granger and Richard Swann Lull. Beyond them are the fruits of their labors, many dinosaur bones encased in white plaster jackets, ready to be shipped to the museum.

13 Life of Late Jurassic time in western North America. The scene here
reconstructed is based upon our knowledge of the famous Morrison fauna
and contemporaneous plants. In the left foreground is the large carnivorous
saurischian dinosaur, *Antrodemus* or *Allosaurus*, a thirty foot long predator
upon other large dinosaurs. In the right foreground is the persistently
primitive small saurischian, *Ornitholestes*, about five feet long, and near it

a Jurassic turtle. Beyond is the plated ornithischian dinosaur, *Stegosaurus*, twenty feet long, and in the background and the distance are several individuals of the gigantic sauropod, *Apatosaurus*, some seventy feet in length. These dinosaurs lived in a tropical environment that extended widely throughout the world. Swamps and lowlands were typical, and there were conifers, cycads, and other gymnosperms, and ferns.

14

15

14 The Flaming Cliffs of Shabarakh Usu, Mongolia, formed by the wind-scoured Cretaceous Djadochta formation. This is the site at which many skeletons and eggs of the primitive horned dinosaur, *Protoceratops*, have been found.

15 The white Upper Cretaceous chalk cliffs of southern England. It is from these sediments that the name of the Cretaceous period is derived. In chalks of the same age in North America, notably the Selma and Niobrara formations, there have been found many skeletons of plesiosaurs, mosasaurs, giant flying reptiles, early birds, and some dinosaurs.

16

17

16 Hauling dinosaur bones out of the valley of the Red Deer River, Alberta, where the Oldman formation of the Upper Cretaceous Belly River series forms extensive badlands below the level of the prairie. The Belly River beds here consist of light colored clays and sandstones. This picture, taken some fifty years ago during the heyday of dinosaur collecting along the Red Deer River, shows an area that is now included within Dinosaur Park, maintained by the Province of Alberta. An automobile road now descends into the valley along the path of the old wagon trail.

17 The life of a fossil hunter fifty years ago in the Upper Cretaceous Edmonton formation, Red Deer River, Alberta. Barnum Brown, one of the great dinosaur collectors, is seen on the flatboat at the right. In the thick exposures across the river are seen the clays and sandstones composing the sediments of the Edmonton formation, from which many dinosaurs have been excavated.

18 Life of Late Cretaceous Belly River time in western Canada. In the
left lower foreground is the giant predator, *Gorgosaurus*, a saurischian
dinosaur, and confronting it, in the water, is the ornithischian dinosaur,
Corythosaurus. Both of these dinosaurs are about thirty feet long.
In the background are seen other corythosaurs as well as the armored
dinosaur, *Ankylosaurus*, a reptile about fifteen feet in length.

On the hill are two individuals of *Styracosaurus*, a horned dinosaur
some twenty feet long. These, among the last of the dinosaurs,
lived in a subtropical environment, characterized by many deciduous
trees, such as oaks, willows and sassafras. There were conifers,
as well, and a ground cover of ferns and other low plants.

19

20

19 Barnum Brown excavating the skeleton of a duck-billed dinosaur in the Upper Cretaceous Lance formation, south of Glasgow, Montana. Here we see various aspects in the excavation of a dinosaur skeleton. The skeleton has been outlined and the bones partially exposed. Some of the bones have been jacketed with burlap and plaster, as all will be before the skeleton is ready for shipment to the laboratory.

20 The Upper Cretaceous Hell Creek beds of Montana. In these light-colored sandstones are found the bones of the last of the dinosaurs.

On land there was at the same time another evolutionary development of the utmost significance to future life. This was the explosion, and one can call it hardly less than this, of the flowering plants. Until the end of Jurassic times the continents of the earth were clothed with monotonous green verdure, largely composed of primitive tree ferns, cycads, conifers and the like. Then with the passing of the years that we now call the early Cretaceous, the angiosperms or flowering plants appeared and evolved with great rapidity and along

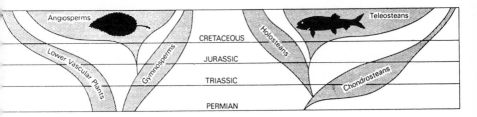

Figure 53. The great expansion of teleost fishes and of flowering plants in early Cretaceous time.

many lines of adaptation. The lands were brightened by the variegated colors of flowers on all sorts of broad-leaved plants. Trees of modern aspect grew in forests and glades; trees such as poplars, willows, oaks and sassafras. The dinosaurs, which in Jurassic time had wandered through primitive tropical jungles, walked during Cretaceous time in forests that would seem quite familiar to us.

It should be added that along with the rise of the flowering plants there must have been a burgeoning of modern insects, because flowers and insects to pollinate them go together. Insects of great variety and in incredible numbers probably populated the land, just as the teleosts populated the seas.

In truth, the world of modern living things was beginning to take form.

Early Cretaceous time, when these highly significant evolutionary events took place (as recorded by the fossils found in lower Cretaceous rocks), is one of the two recognized divisions of the Cretaceous. In contrast with the other Mesozoic periods, each of which has been accorded a threefold division, the Cretaceous is universally recognized as having just two parts: early and late, or lower and upper.

The original or type Cretaceous rocks are the gleaming white chalk cliffs of the southern coast of England, and these are of late Cretaceous age. But by extension and usage the name is now applied to all Mesozoic rocks of post-Jurassic age, whether they be of an age more or less comparable with that of the chalk cliffs, or whether they be earlier. Let us now return to the subject with which we are presently concerned, the lower Cretaceous rocks and the fossil bones contained within them.

By far the best fossil record of lower Cretaceous reptiles is contained within the Wealden beds of southern England and northern continental Europe. Here, in much of the same area where the reptile-bearing Jurassic deposits are found, one may trace sediments that tell the story of land and sea during the initial years of Cretaceous history. In southern England and across into northern France are sands and shales containing the fossil bones of many reptiles that inhabited a low continent never very far away from the seashore. As one proceeds southwardly the sediments grade into shallow water, marine beds, and farther on into deeper water marine sediments as one draws near the ancient Tethyan sea.

Immediately above the Wealden beds of England are the Greensands, which have yielded some reptilian remains, thereby extending our knowledge into the later phases of early Cretaceous history; yet as compared with the Wealden deposits the Greensands contain a rather sparse assemblage of reptilian genera. Bones from this upper part of the lower Cretaceous are also found in a few localities in north-western continental Europe.

The coastal plain of the eastern United States is also the site of extensive lower Cretaceous deposits, most of them of marine origin. But in the Arundel formation of Maryland are found scattered and fragmentary bones that give us a glimpse of the reptiles that once roamed the land in this part of the world. Only a few other such glimpses of the early Cretaceous reptiles of the western hemisphere are available, essentially as bones and skeletons in the Cloverly formation of Wyoming and Montana, and as impressive sauropod and carnosaur footprints in the Trinity beds of Texas. Our knowledge of lower Cretaceous reptiles in South America is at the present time rather limited.

A few scattered beds of supposed early Cretaceous age are found in Asia – in Mongolia, in Sinkiang and in Shantung. Dinosaurs have been excavated from these sediments, but in some cases the age of

Table 12. Correlation of Lower Cretaceous vertebrate horizons *

Lower Cretaceous

SOUTH AMERICA	NORTH AMERICA	ASIA	EUROPE	AFRICA	AUSTRALIA
Nequen	Arundel	On Gong (Mongolia)	Wealden	Northern Africa	Tambo
	Trinity	Ondai Sair		Uitenhage (S. Africa)	Rolling Downs
	Fredericksburg	Oshih	Lower Greensand		
	Washita	Iren Dabasu	Upper Greensand		
	Dakota	Sinkiang (China)	Gault		
	Cloverly	Shantung			

*See 'Tables and Diagrams' in Addendum.

the fossil reptiles is the subject of differences of opinion. For example, the deposits in Mongolia, at On Gong and at Oshih, are contained within isolated desert basins that cannot be correlated in any physical way with each other or with other areas beyond them. The fossils are rather suggestive of lower Cretaceous relationships, but they may very well be upper Cretaceous forms.

Fossil reptiles of probable lower Cretaceous affinities are found near Uitenhage, in South Africa, and in Malawi. Likewise, reptiles of this age are found in Australia, some of them land-living forms, others ichthyosaurs and plesiosaurs.

The correlation chart of Table 12 shows the approximate age relationships of these lower Cretaceous reptile-bearing sediments in different parts of the world.

Having made a brief excursion around the world for a look at the places where lower Cretaceous reptiles may be found, let us now come back to the English Channel coast and to the land just across the Channel, to consider in more detail the Wealden reptiles. For there can be no doubt that our best impression of lower Cretaceous reptilian life is to be had from a study of the Wealden fauna.

To the student of fossil reptiles mention of the Wealden immediately brings to mind visions of *Iguanodon*, the first dinosaur to be adequately described. The original specimens of *Iguanodon* were collected in southern England, and were studied by Dr Gideon Mantell, an eccentric physician who became interested in fossil reptiles to the eventual detriment of his medical practice. This was the dinosaur that was restored a century ago under the direction of Sir Richard Owen as a sort of rhinoceros-looking reptile with a horn on its nose. We now know *Iguanodon* to have been a bipedal ornithischian, a plant-eating dinosaur with powerful hind limbs and tail, with rather short fore limbs, the hands of which are distinguished by a large, pointed spike on the end of the thumb, the bone originally thought to be a nasal horn by mid-Victorian paleontologists. The discovery of a score or more of complete *Iguanodon* skeletons in a coal mine at Bernissart, Belgium, about eighty years ago, affords extraordinarily complete anatomical knowledge of this interesting dinosaur, and gives some slight inkling of the abundance of these reptiles during early Cretaceous times.

Iguanodon and its close relatives were not only present in Europe during early Cretaceous time, but also inhabited regions far removed from the European scene. A recent discovery of iguanodont footprints in rocks of Wealden age on the island of Spitzbergen shows that tropical climates and dinosaurs extended into what are now polar regions. Discoveries of iguanodonts in Australia give further proof that these lower Cretaceous dinosaurs ranged over a remarkably wide spread of latitudes.

Figure 54. The herbivorous ornithischian dinosaur, *Iguanodon*, from the lower Cretaceous of Europe. This, one of the first dinosaurs to be discovered and described, gave the early Victorian paleontologists some of the first clues as to the existence of gigantic land reptiles during the Mesozoic era. Skeletons of *Iguanodon* are thirty feet and more in length.

Iguanodon is but one of a number of Wealden dinosaurs, the remains of which have been found on either side of the English channel. Living with it were armored dinosaurs, one of the best known of which is *Polacanthus*, a bizarre reptile with very large spikes on the back. Also in these deposits is *Hypsilophodon*, discovered on the Isle of Wight, one of the more primitive of known ornithischian dinosaurs. This little reptile, some three or four feet in length, is a long-tailed, bipedal type, the supple hind foot of which suggests possible tree-climbing habits. *Hypsilophodon* is of particular interest to the evolutionist, because it demonstrates the survival of a primitive type into an age when it was living along with highly specialized animals for which it might very well have served as a structural ancestor.

Figure 55. *Hypsilophodon*, a small, lower Cretaceous ornithischian of primitive type. This little dinosaur, about five feet in length and found in southern England, may have been able to climb into trees.

There are gigantic sauropod dinosaurs in the Wealden fauna, the descendants of late Jurassic progenitors. The huge sauropods continued in Cretaceous times to be the largest of the herbivores, as they had been during Jurassic times, carrying on the mode of life of their Jurassic ancestors with little change, dwelling in swamps and feeding upon succulent aquatic vegetation.

As might be expected, there are large carnivorous dinosaurs in the Wealden fauna, among which *Megalosaurus* is prominent, these being the predators on other large dinosaurs. Small predators are present, too, the coelurosaurian dinosaurs that lived in the undergrowth and preyed upon a variety of small game.

The reptiles living with the Wealden dinosaurs were of various kinds. Turtles, crocodilians and flying reptiles, or pterosaurs, are known. There is every reason to think that many other reptiles also inhabited the Wealden land; lizards, for example, snakes, and possibly rhynchocephalians. There must have been numerous primitive mammals, descended from the mammals of the Jurassic Purbeck sediments, even though as yet there is no fossil evidence on this score. Likewise, there must have been primitive toothed birds in the air, along with the pterosaurs.

In the realm of definite knowledge, rather than of speculation, we know that there were plesiosaurs in the seas bordering the Wealden land of northern Europe.

The life of Wealden times probably continued into the later phases of early Cretaceous history, very likely without much change in its

Figure 56. *Polacanthus*, a plated dinosaur about fifteen feet long, from the lower Cretaceous of England.

essential components. Certainly *Iguanodon* lived on into lower Greensand times. And with this dinosaur there was an armored dinosaur, *Acanthopholis*. We know, too, that pterosaurs still flew among the trees and along the cliffs during the later days of the early Cretaceous. But we can only guess what other reptiles or birds or mammals then lived in northern Europe. The fossil record gives us no information about them at the present time[*].

In central Europe there have been found the remains of lower Cretaceous geosaurs or marine crocodiles, showing that these archosaurians still continued their mode of life successfully in waters inhabited by active and abundant plesiosaurs and ichthyosaurs. There were many fishes in the sea, and reptiles to prey upon them.

A discovery of particular interest is that of *Pachyophis*, a lower Cretaceous snake, found in the Balkans. This is the first record of a

[*]See 'Page Corrections and Emendations' in Addendum.

snake in the geologic column*. Snakes are essentially highly modified lizards, but exactly when their divergence from lizard ancestors took place, we do not know. It very probably was during the Jurassic period – at some time after the first appearance of the lizards in late Triassic times. Thus began a specialized and very successful line of reptilian evolution.

Such is our view of Europe during the early Cretaceous, in which we see a scene that was perhaps not unlike the late Jurassic scene preceding it. One gets the impression of many reptiles living on low lands that bordered the sea, with numerous huge dinosaurs dominating the landscape. And we may assume that this view was true for other parts of the world as well. Unfortunately, when we go to other parts of the world the view is very incomplete, to say the least.

The Arundel formation of eastern North America has, as mentioned, yielded a few bones of dinosaurs. These, fragmentary as they may be, are none the less sufficiently well preserved to show that at one time small carnivorous dinosaurs, aggressive carnosaurian predators, giant, swamp-dwelling sauropods, inoffensive camptosaurs and armored dinosaurs inhabited the land. There were probably many other dinosaurs, other reptiles, perhaps birds, and almost certainly ancient mammals as well. In recent years lower Cretaceous dinosaurs have been found in the Cloverly formation of western North America, which when described will expand the knowledge now available from the Arundel fossils, and will help to correlate the lower Cretaceous reptiles of this continental region with those of Europe. Mention should be made of an armored dinosaur, *Hoplitosaurus*, also known from the lower Cretaceous of the western states. Finally, this glimpse of early Cretaceous life in North America is augmented by the trackways of giant dinosaurs in the Trinity beds, previously mentioned, and by numerous teeth and jaws of archaic mammals, preserved in bone beds within these same sediments.

Crossing to eastern Asia†, which in Mesozoic times was probably connected with North America, we find only isolated bits of evidence here and there. In the Oshih formation of Mongolia is a beaked dinosaur, *Psittacosaurus*, which makes a rather good structural ancestor for the horned dinosaurs or ceratopsians of late Cretaceous age. *Psittacosaurus* has been regarded as possibly belonging to the early Cretaceous because of its primitive stage of development in comparison with even the most primitive of the horned dinosaurs, yet there is no reason why it should not belong to the end of the age.

*See 'Page Corrections and Emendations' in Addendum.
†See 'Page Corrections and Emendations' in Addendum.

Several large sauropod dinosaurs are known from this part of the world, and have been assigned to the early Cretaceous. These are *Mongolosaurus* from the On Gong formation of Mongolia, *Helopus* from Shantung and *Tienshansaurus* from Sinkiang. These discoveries, together with those of sauropods made in lower Cretaceous sediments in Europe, North America, Africa and Australia, demonstrate quite clearly that the sauropod dinosaurs continued their highly successful world-wide habitation of the continents, in spite of the influx of new

Figure 57. A possible ancestor of the horned dinosaurs, *Psittacosaurus*, from the Cretaceous beds of Mongolia. The skeleton is about six feet in length.

dinosaurian types that was taking place during early Cretaceous history.

We know that giant dinosaurs roamed across Australia in early Cretaceous time because of discoveries made in Queensland and in West Australia. The presence of iguanodonts, noted above, as well as of giant sauropods, is indicated by bones found in Queensland. Footprints from Queensland and especially from West Australia show that large megalosaurs were inhabitants of this land during the early phases of Cretaceous history.

The continent of Australia is also particularly noteworthy by reason of some of the lower Cretaceous marine reptiles that have been found there. Among the ichthyosaurs and plesiosaurs known from lower Cretaceous sediments in Australia, the most imposing form is the great pliosaur, *Kronosaurus*, fifty feet or so in length, with a huge skull and with jaws twelve feet or more long. The teeth are proportionately large. Here we see in the early Cretaceous a marine reptile playing a role in the oceans of that time that is assumed today by the great toothed whales. One may imagine *Kronosaurus* swimming through the water in pursuit of fishes, or perhaps of squids and

Figure 58. The gigantic Cretaceous plesiosaur, *Kronosaurus*, from Australia. This reptile, fifty feet or more in length, probably lived a life in Cretaceous seas similar to that of the great whales in modern oceans.

octopuses, as does the modern sperm whale; the convergence in structure and function between the giant plesiosaur of the past and the giant whale of today is truly striking.

These are some of the fossil reptiles known from lower Cretaceous rocks around the world. They lived at a time that would seem to have been an age of transition in their faunal relationships and their environment, a time between faunas dominated by gigantic sauropod dinosaurs living in jungles of primitive trees, and faunas dominated by new dinosaurs living in modern forests of broad-leafed trees, where brightly colored flowers bloomed profusely. It was a time when a new age was foreshadowed, and yet when survivors from an earlier age were still numerous on the earth. It was a time when the world was changing; when the old, archaic plant world in which the reptiles had so long held sway was giving way to a new and different world of plant life in which reptiles would reign for still many millions of years.

Some of the details of this world of transition, known from evidence that is all too insufficient, have been set forth in a general way. But what are some of the implications to be drawn from this outline of reptilian life of the early Cretaceous period?

In this time of advancing oceans there were the new bony fishes, the teleosts, which during Cretaceous history were destined to evolve along numerous radiating lines, to replace the more primitive, heavily scaled fishes that up until now had lived so successfully in river, lake and sea. The teleosts colonized the oceans where the marine reptiles lived, and so it was that during early Cretaceous times these reptiles had available to them a new and abundant food supply, rather different from that on which their Jurassic ancestors had fed. Yet the marine reptiles seemingly adapted themselves to the influx of teleost fishes in the seas without any significant changes in form and structure. Cretaceous ichthyosaurs and plesiosaurs and other marine reptiles pursued and fed upon teleosts, as their Jurassic forebears pursued and fed upon the heavy-scaled fishes of that earlier geologic period. These reptiles had attained on the whole such perfection of structure for the environment in which they lived, such complete adaptations for swimming in the oceans and feeding upon fishes, that they were able during the transition from Jurassic to Cretaceous times to switch from pursuit of the more primitive to the more advanced fishes with complete success. As we shall see, this new and abundant food supply of Cretaceous teleosts eventually attracted other reptiles into the ocean.

Moreover, as we shall also see, the modernization of plant life that took place during early Cretaceous times, the geologic expansion of the flowering angiosperms, made available to the land-living reptiles new sources of food, just as the expansion of the higher bony fishes provided new food supplies in the sea. Certainly there must have been a relation of cause and effect between the great evolutionary radiation of flowering plants that took place during the early Cretaceous and the amazing increase in variety and numbers of the plant-eating ornithischian dinosaurs that occurred during the late Cretaceous. The revolution in the plant world afforded new evolutionary opportunities for the dinosaurs, and for other reptiles. It led eventually to the final climax of reptilian life, but in early Cretaceous times this climax had not been attained; it was only foreshadowed. This climax of the Age of Reptiles, which was still to come during late Cretaceous time, is the subject to which we will now turn our attention.

Chapter 10

Zenith of the Dinosaurs

THE CLIMAX OF reptilian evolution, foreshadowed by the obviously incomplete fossil record preserved in lower Cretaceous rocks, was certainly attained during the forty million years or so of late Cretaceous history. This history as recorded in upper Cretaceous sediments is amply documented by numerous fossils the world around, a decided contrast to the lower Cretaceous record, which, as we have seen, though not so sparse as that of the lower Jurassic, none the less leaves much to be desired. Whereas the Wealden fauna is one of the few adequately known assemblages of lower Cretaceous land reptiles*, there are many varied upper Cretaceous continental faunas, found in considerable abundance at numerous localities throughout the world. Moreover, these are supplemented by abundant discoveries of marine reptiles, also found scattered over the surface of the globe.

Consequently our knowledge of upper Cretaceous reptiles is based upon large collections of fossils, thereby paralleling our knowledge of the upper Jurassic reptilian faunas in which dinosaurs of spectacular form and size are so dominant, and plesiosaurs and ichthyosaurs so prominent. Yet even though the delineation of late Jurassic life presents a picture of many startling and impressive reptiles living in an ancient, tropical world, the parallel picture of late Cretaceous life is far more complete and far more varied than that of earlier times. It shows us a great array of reptiles, living in a rather modern world of tropical, subtropical and warm temperate environments.

Why should this picture of upper Cretaceous reptiles be so much more complete than that of the preceding Jurassic and lower Cretaceous ones? Perhaps a number of factors were involved, as is very commonly the case when the geologic history of life is being deciphered, and of these the actions of earth processes, particularly of earth movements and of erosion and deposition, must have been

*See 'Page Corrections and Emendations' in Addendum.

particularly important. Lands sank beneath the seas and rose again. Seas advanced and retreated. Sediments were destroyed and with them the fossils they contained, and new sediments and new fossils were deposited. The accidents of burial and fossilization, and of the preservation of fossils through the ages, had much to do with the record of Cretaceous life, as it had with previous fossil records, but here the accidents were for us fortunate ones.

The transgressions of the oceans across the continents that had opened Cretaceous history continued through much of the extent of this geologic period, so that by the middle part of late Cretaceous time shallow seas had advanced over the land masses to an extent rarely exceeded in the long history of the earth. These inland seas spread far beyond the troughs in which they had been contained during late Jurassic history, and even beyond their lower Cretaceous limits, to flood many parts of the continents that had never before been invaded, or had been inundated only at occasional intervals far back in the Paleozoic.

Yet extensive as were these late Cretaceous shallow oceans, on the floors of which the skeletons of many marine reptiles and fishes were buried and protected through the millennia still to come, we nevertheless have a rich record of contemporary land life. This is the testimony of animals fortunately buried and fortunately preserved from that time until today. All of which illustrates very nicely the role that chance has played during past ages in the accumulation of the fossils on which we base our reconstructions of ancient life. The record of lower Cretaceous land reptiles is sparse; that of upper Cretaceous ones is full, and we have to make the best of it.

Toward the end of Cretaceous times, however, more than chance was involved in the preservation of land-living reptiles as fossils. At that stage of earth history, measured perhaps by the final ten or fifteen million years of the Cretaceous record, there was initiated a world-wide uplifting of the continents – a series of earth movements on a grand scale which reversed the trend of previous Cretaceous events. It was the beginning of what is known in geological parlance as the Laramide Revolution, the series of tremendous continental uplifts that in time drained away the shallow Cretaceous seas and gave to the continental blocks their modern outlines. It was the beginning of the great mountain chains of our modern world: the Himalayas and Alps, the Rockies and the Andes. These widespread uplifts of continents taking place as the Cretaceous period drew to its close caused the emergence of ever-expanding areas of land surfaces throughout the world, and as land areas became increasingly extensive the areas for the burial and preservation of land-living animals also became increasingly extensive. It is not completely accidental that the fossils of dinosaurs and other land-living reptiles which inhabited the earth during the closing stages of Cretaceous history are particularly abundant.

But the variety and abundance of reptilian life as revealed in the upper Cretaceous rocks must not be thought of as being due entirely to earth forces. As will be remembered from the last chapter, there were two evolutionary 'explosions' during early Cretaceous times that had a direct bearing upon the development of late Cretaceous reptiles: the great development of teleost fishes in the seas, which provided a food supply for marine reptiles beyond anything that had existed in previous ages, and the remarkable radiation of the angiosperms, or flowering plants, affording entirely new sources of energy for herbivorous animals.

So it was that the marine reptiles that had been so prominent in the Jurassic scene continued and multiplied during late Cretaceous times. This was especially true for the plesiosaurs, while reptiles whose immediate ancestors had lived on the land entered the sea, to partake of the abundant living to be found there. These latter were notably the mosasaurs, which are nothing more or less than gigantic lizards completely adapted to life in the ocean, and certain turtles.

The increase of reptiles in late Cretaceous time[*] is especially apparent, however, in the development of the dinosaurs. There are considerably more than twice as many genera and species of dinosaurs in the fossil record of late Cretaceous times than of any other stage in the evolutionary history of these reptiles, and this great increase among the rulers of Mesozoic lands may be attributed for the most part to the remarkable evolutionary radiation of the herbivorous dinosaurs in a world filled with flowering plants. The ornithopod dinosaurs, which had enjoyed a moderate degree of evolutionary variety in late Jurassic and early Cretaceous times as camptosaurs and iguanodonts, increased fivefold in late Cretaceous times, largely as a result of the diverse radiation of the duck-billed dinosaurs. Moreover, two new large groups, or suborders, of plant-eating dinosaurs arose during the Cretaceous period, the armored dinosaurs or ankylosaurs, and the horned dinosaurs or ceratopsians. Both of these dinosaurian groups became varied and numerous during the final

[*]See 'Page Corrections and Emendations' in Addendum.

stages of Cretaceous history, thus adding to the array of plant-eating dinosaurs throughout the world. And as might be expected, with so many different herbivores inhabiting the lands, there was an increase among the carnivores, the meat-eaters that preyed upon the inoffensive plant-consumers.

Of course, the increase of late Cretaceous dinosaurs is very spectacular and significant, and is one of the great facts of evolution during this phase of earth history, but the augmentation of reptilian life on the land during the final years of the Mesozoic was not confined to the dinosaurs alone. It would appear that there were increases among other reptiles as well – the crocodilians, the lizards and snakes, the turtles, and some of the lesser groups. It was a time of reptilian diversity that had not hitherto been attained, and was never again to be even remotely approached. It was truly the great climax of the Age of Reptiles.

Furthermore, it was a time when the birds and the mammals, previously of very primitive types, developed along the initial lines of their subsequent evolution. In short, the birds of late Cretaceous times became in all essential features modern birds, and among the mammals the marsupials and placentals made their appearance.

The localities at which upper Cretaceous reptiles have been found are too numerous to be satisfactorily discussed in anything short of a large and wearying monograph, but certainly the more important and productive ones can be taken up here. Even a survey of these more important localities and horizons can be confusing if they are considered on a world-wide basis in some detail, and with equal emphasis. Consequently the evolution of the reptiles during late Cretaceous times can perhaps best be comprehended by first limiting oneself to a single continental area, where the sediments are well exposed in sequence, and are richly fossiliferous. For such a simple survey, North America is the most revealing region to be considered.

In the western States and Provinces of North America are continental beds one above the other, or showing sequential relationships in age, the fossils from which tell a reasonably continuous story of evolution during the final years of Cretaceous history. Certainly the most famous of these sediments are the Belly River and Edmonton beds in Alberta and the Lance and Hell Creek beds in Montana and Wyoming, rocks which may be considered as forming an age series, with the Belly River at the bottom, the Edmonton in the middle, and the Lance and Hell Creek at the top. As one studies the reptiles from these formations, it is frequently possible to trace in some detail the minutiae of evolutionary progress among various dinosaurs and contemporary forms, from the bottom to the top, from the older to the younger. To reinforce the evidence of this fossil series, a similar time sequence may be seen to the south in the Mesa Verde formation of Colorado, the Aguja of Texas and the Difunta of northern Mexico, all of these being approximate equivalents of the Belly River; in the Kirtland and Fruitland of New Mexico, which may be equated with the Edmonton; and perhaps in the Animas of New Mexico, correlative with the Lance to the north. Finally, to complement the story of late Cretaceous reptilian evolution on the land, there are the Niobrara and Pierre formations of the western States, containing the bones of marine reptiles as well as those of the fishes upon which they fed. So here, in the high plains and mountains of western North America, is found contained within the rocks a record of the culminating phase of the Age of Reptiles, with all of its fascinating complexities of evolutionary development, of relationships between organisms and their environments, and of the distributions through forest and plain and across the seas, of reptiles, great and small, that lived before the Rocky Mountains had been lifted into the skies. Some fragments of this record are to be found along the Atlantic and Gulf coastal plains of North America, where the bones of dinosaurs, mosasaurs and other inhabitants of the late Cretaceous scene are constantly coming to light. Indeed, the first skeleton of a dinosaur to be discovered and described in North America was unearthed in Cretaceous sediments at a locality in New Jersey, just across the Delaware River from the city of Philadelphia.

It appears that north-eastern Asia was very closely connected with western North America during late Cretaceous times, so that dinosaurs and other reptiles were able to cross from the one region to the other. In outer Mongolia dinosaurs very similar to some of those found in the Belly River and later deposits of North America have been uncovered as undoubted testimony to this close geographical unity of the two Cretaceous continents. Upper Cretaceous reptiles are found in other parts of north-eastern Asia as well, especially in Kansu and Shantung. And the record is extended to the south-west into India, where the Lameta beds of the peninsular region have yielded the bones of dinosaurs and of other animals that lived with them.

Continental deposits of late Cretaceous age are rare in Europe,

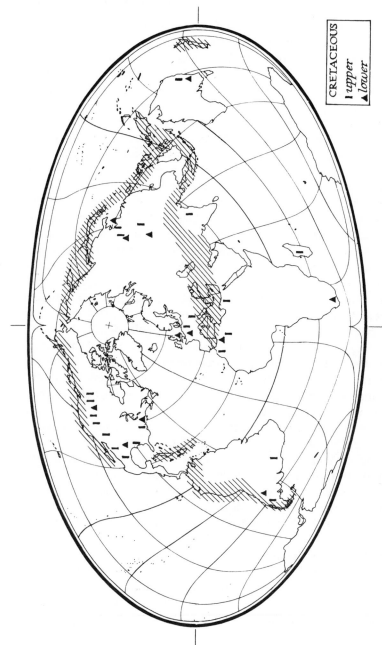

CRETACEOUS
1 *upper*
▲ *lower*

Figure 59. World map showing the general localities at which Cretaceous tetrapods have been found. The shaded areas indicate regions of major submergence.

and most of what is known is based upon discoveries made in Transylvania. But the marine beds of this region are justly famous; indeed, the name of the period is based, as has been mentioned, upon the chalk so beautifully seen in the white cliffs of the Channel coast. In the Maestrichtian of northern Europe, which includes the uppermost part of the chalk, are found marine reptiles, especially mosasaurs. The original skull of *Mosasaurus* was discovered in beds of this age in Belgium during the early days of paleontological exploration and research, and became an object of some importance, to be contended over by the opposing forces during the Napoleonic wars.

The African continent, in contrast with Europe, has yielded a considerable series of upper Cretaceous land-living reptiles, these being found across the northern border of the continent. They characterize the Baharija beds of Egypt, known for many years, and several localities in Morocco and in the Sahara desert, discovered and exploited during the past decade. Land-living reptiles of this age are also found on the island of Madagascar.

They are found, too, on the island continent, in the Opal beds of eastern Australia.

Finally, South America has proved to be a rich burial ground for upper Cretaceous reptiles, and it is probably safe to say that the investigation of these fossils on that continent is still in its preliminary stages. In recent years the bones of dinosaurs, crocodiles and turtles have been uncovered in the vicinity of Bauru, in the State of São Paulo, Brazil, and descriptions of these fossils, as yet largely unpublished, bid fair to make some important and exciting additions to our knowledge of late Cretaceous reptilian life. The Bauru locality is probably at the base of the upper Cretaceous, but most of the late Cretaceous fossil reptiles from South America are from high in the sequence, and have been found in Patagonia, a region that has yielded many bones of dinosaurs, crocodiles, turtles and other reptiles characteristic of this stage of earth history.

Such is a brief resumé of the more important upper Cretaceous localities and horizons from which the bones of fossil reptiles have been excavated. The relationships of these sediments, and of others that have not been specifically mentioned above, are shown by the correlation chart of Table 13.

The Red Deer River flows eastward from the Rocky Mountains across the southern part of Alberta, where in the south-eastern part of this Canadian Province it winds through the picturesque and

Table 13. *Correlation of Upper Cretaceous vertebrate horizons* *

Upper Cretaceous

SOUTH AMERICA	Patagonia; Bauru (Brazil)
WESTERN NORTH AMERICA (Northern)	Lance Hell-Creek; Edmonton; Belly River — Oldman, Foremost, Milk River, Judith River, Two Medicine; Pierre; Niobrara; Benton
WESTERN NORTH AMERICA (Southern)	Animas; Kirtland; Fruitland; Mesa Verde; Aguja; Difunta
EASTERN NORTH AMERICA	Monmouth; Matawan; Magothy; Raritan
ASIA	Bain Shire (Mongolia); Nemegetu (Mongolia); Lameta (India); Kansu; Shantung Sinkiang (China); Amur; Djadochta (Mongolia)
EUROPE	Chalk; Transylvania beds
AFRICA	Continental intercalaire Saharien; Baharija (Egypt); Morocco; Bushmanland (S. Africa); Madagascar
AUSTRALIA	Opal Beds

168

*See 'Tables and Diagrams' in Addendum.

barren badlands that make up the Belly River beds. And here, at a northern latitude of fifty-one degrees, in a land of short hot summers and long, cold winters, is one of the most richly fossiliferous regions in the world for the dinosaur hunter. Innumerable bones and many fine skeletons of dinosaurs and of other associated reptiles have been quarried from these badlands, particularly in the fifteen-mile stretch of the river to the east of Steveville, a stretch that is a veritable dinosaurian graveyard. The fossils are to be found on both sides of the river, where they occur in the upper part of the Belly River series, the portion named the Oldman formation, the lower part of the Belly River being the Foremost formation. In this superposition of Oldman sediments on Foremost beds there is recorded the withdrawal from west to east of a shallow Cretaceous sea, a retreat that began at the beginning of Belly River times and reached its maximum extent by the late Belly River, when this part of Canada was a low, forested land, inhabited by many different kinds of dinosaurs.

It must have been a land of abundant vegetation and of tropical or subtropical climates, a land of mild temperatures quite in contrast to the extremes which today typify this part of the world. The gigantic reptiles whose bones have been dug out of the Belly River sediments could hardly have lived in other than warm and rather uniform climates; the numerous herbivores among them obviously required a constantly abundant supply of plants for their survival. Thus we get an impression from the fossils of a great, low verdant plain, where herds of plant-eating dinosaurs roamed to feed upon the tropical vegetation, with the ever-constant danger of attack from their gigantic carnivorous enemies.

The overwhelming prevalence of herbivorous dinosaurs, so characteristic of late Cretaceous land faunas, is readily apparent when one surveys a list of Belly River reptiles. Such a list reveals about four times as many genera of plant-eating dinosaurs as there are of carnivores, the herbivores showing a range of diversity that embraces dome-headed troödonts*, various crested hadrosaurs or duck-billed dinosaurs, horned dinosaurs and several kinds of armored dinosaurs. Almost all of these plant-eaters are giants, and most of them were evidently very abundant. The fossil evidence reveals just one gigantic carnivore in the Belly River assemblage associated with the varied herbivores, the other carnivores that have been found in these beds being relatively small and lightly built dinosaurs, evidently predators upon small game.

*See 'Page Corrections and Emendations' in Addendum.

If one were able to look out upon the Belly River landscape during the days of the dinosaurs instead of analyzing lists of fossils, the numbers and variety of these plant-eating dinosaurs would surely have been most impressive. Their numbers probably would have been comparable with the great herds of gazelles and wildebeest,

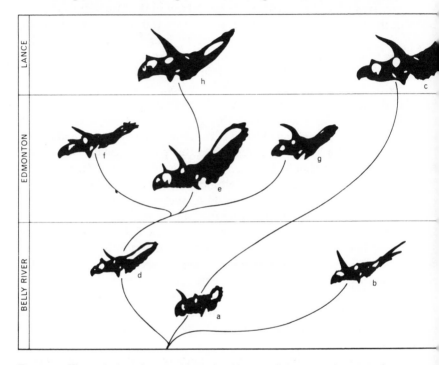

Figure 60. The evolution of the duck-billed and horned dinosaurs, as interpreted from fossils found in the upper Cretaceous sediments of western North America. Here we see a sequence of forms from three successive series of sediments. The phylogeny of the horned dinosaurs shows the short-crested forms on the right (a–c) and the long-crested forms on the left (d–h), as simultaneous radiations from a common ancestor. The genera are as follows: a. *Monoclonius*, b. *Styracosaurus*, c. *Triceratops*, d. *Chasmosaurus*, e. *Pentaceratops*, f. *Anchiceratops*, g. *Arrhinoceratops* and h. *Torosaurus*. The phylogeny of the duck-billed dinosaurs shows the conservative

antelopes, buffaloes and zebras that may still be seen in some of the protected areas of Africa – only on an enlarged scale. It would have been a gathering of the giants[*].

Along the water courses would have been the crested duck-bills, dinosaurs which habitually lived in rivers and lakes, but which came

[*]See 'Page Corrections and Emendations' in Addendum.

out on the shore frequently, as do modern hippopotamuses. Almost all of them were large, and all of them had the front of the skull and jaws elongated and broadened, like the beak of a gigantic duck, for shoveling in the mud beneath the water. These dinosaurs, cousins of the more primitive camptosaurs and iguanodonts, which inhabited

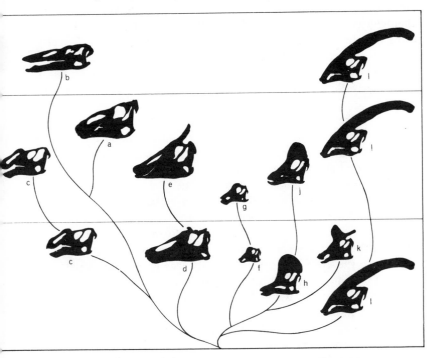

flat-headed forms on the left (a–d), the spike-skulled forms in the middle (d–e) and the varied crested forms on the right (f–l), all descended from a common ancestor. The genera are as follows: a. *Edmontosaurus*, b. *Anatosaurus*, c. *Kritosaurus*, d. *Prosaurolophus*, e. *Saurolophus*, f. *Procheneosaurus*, g. *Cheneosaurus*, h. *Corythosaurus*, j. *Hypacrosaurus*, k. *Lambeosaurus*, and l. *Parasaurolophus*. Note in both of these phylogenies the relative variety of forms in the Belly River and Edmonton stages as compared with those of the Lance-Hell Creek stage.

the world during late Jurassic and early Cretaceous times, evolved rapidly and along varied specialized lines during the final years of the Mesozoic. In the Belly River scene there was *Kritosaurus*, with the nasal bones somewhat swollen, to form a low crest or ridge in front of the eyes. There was *Prosaurolophus*, in which these bones have been carried back over the top of the skull to form, with the frontal bones, a sort of bony spike rising above the top of the head. Then there were the various hollow crested types, in which the nasal bones and frequently other contiguous skull bones are greatly enlarged, to form hollow structures on the top of the skull, these containing in life loops of the nasal passage. In *Corythosaurus*, perhaps the most characteristic of Belly River duck-bills, the crest is shaped something like the crest of an ancient Greek warrior's helmet. In *Lambeosaurus* it is rather hatchet-like in form. In *Procheneosaurus* it is a broad swelling over the skull, and in *Parasaurolophus* it forms an enormously elongated, curved crest extending back over the shoulders.

All of these crests had something to do with the nasal apparatus; perhaps they increased the sensitivity of smell in the duck-billed dinosaurs. But why should they have been of such diverse form? It is a question not easy to answer, separated as we are from the duck-billed dinosaurs by millions of years of time.

A parallel diversity in skull structure is to be seen in the horned dinosaurs of the Belly River formation. In these dinosaurs there is a great expansion of the back of the skull to form a broad frill extending over the shoulders, and various expressions of horns on the nose and above the eyes. The frill seemingly was largely for the attachment of jaw muscles; the horns need no general explanation.

Monoclonius of the Belly River has a long horn on the nose and very small nubbins of horns above the eyes. The same is true for *Styracosaurus*, with an additional array of long horns or spikes extending out from the margins of the frill. In *Chasmosaurus*, a ceratopsian of modest size, there are well developed, but not large, horns on the nose and above the eyes. In all of these dinosaurs the horns evidently evolved for protection against attack by giant predatory dinosaurs, possibly for sexual combat. Again, why should there have been the diversity that is seen among the horned dinosaurs?

A development somewhat analogous to that of the horns in the ceratopsians is seen in the astonishing variety of horns characteristic of the modern African antelopes. It might seem that among modern antelopes a pair of rather simple, straight or slightly curved horns would be completely sufficient and thoroughly efficient for life in the bush or on the veldt. Yet the antelopes of Africa show great diversity in the form of the horns, some of them having straight horns, some curved horns, some spirally twisted horns, and so on. It has often been maintained that the various horn shapes in the antelopes are non-adaptive – that such horn shapes evolved in the different antelope species by mutations neither particularly advantageous nor deleterious. The several horn types were sufficiently good for their purposes, and so they continued.

Recent studies indicate, however, that this explanation is quite wrong. It may be doubted whether animal features can evolve in a non-adaptive way, and this is certainly true for structures as large and important as horns. Actually the variety of horn types in the African antelopes would seem to be correlated with patterns of sexual combat, the horns being of such form as to allow the battling males to fight it out without killing each other.

This example is cited to show how complex may be an answer to a question of form and function. Without close observation of antelopes in their native habitat, their array of horns might remain a baffling problem.

So the question of why there should have been such diversity of horns and frills in the ceratopsian dinosaurs is a question to which there must be a logical answer, but an answer that may elude us for a long time. Since we can not observe the behavior of these long-extinct reptiles we can only speculate as to the various purposes for which they used their great horns, or the details of how they used them.

The armored dinosaurs of the Belly River scene were of several kinds, but all of them were heavily protected by great coverings of bony plates over the back and sides, on the legs, on the neck and over the skull. The adaptation for protection against attack, is as in the horned dinosaurs, quite obvious. The difference between them is in details, especially in the development of clubs and spikes on the end of the tail, with which they might flail their enemies. In *Palaeoscincus* the tail terminates in a rather normal fashion, but in *Ankylosaurus* there is a massive excrescence of bone at the end of the tail, to form a huge club that in life must have made a very efficient weapon of defense.

One other plant-eating dinosaur of the Belly River fauna that should be mentioned is *Troödon*, more properly *Stegoceras*, a rather small form in which the top of the skull is greatly thickened into a sort of knob or dome. The interpretation of this adaptation is a puzzle that has never been satisfactorily solved[*].

Even though there were several adaptations for protection among

173

the herbivores it is a fact that the giant predators of the Belly River were lacking in variety; there seemed to be no opportunities for a diverse array of large carnivores. *Gorgosaurus**, the one known genus, had all of the requisites necessary for a predator on giant dinosaurs – it fulfilled its role quite well. It may be compared with the lion today, which over large tracts of the African veldt is the principal predator upon various species of antelopes, and zebras.

Thus there was a balanced relationship between the hunter and the hunted in Belly River times, as always has been the case during the long years of earth history. The giant predators were amply supplied by the great herds of plant-eating dinosaurs, yet these latter were sufficiently able to escape from their enemies, to withstand predatory onslaughts, or to fight back, so that their numbers were as great as could be supported by the supply of plant food.

This delineation of the Belly River fauna has so far been concerned with the large dinosaurs, because these are the most numerous and in many respects the most interesting of the Belly River animals. But it must not be forgotten that there were other reptiles living on the Belly River plain, reptiles that carried the pattern of hunter and hunted down to less than giant dimensions, reptiles that would in many cases seem hardly out of place in the modern world.

Such were the smaller dinosaurs, notably *Ornithomimus*, a lightly built, fast-running biped with a small, toothless skull. This dinosaur, comparable in size to a modern ostrich, probably lived an ostrich-like life, running across the open ground and feeding on a varied diet. Such also were the turtles and the crocodilians, very much like the turtles and the crocodilians of the modern world. There were undoubtedly lizards and snakes in the Belly River fauna, too.

One other reptile known from the Belly River fauna in addition to those that have been discussed is *Champsosaurus*, an eosuchian. This is a sprawling reptile of moderate proportions, perhaps four or five feet in length, with elongated jaws, set with sharp teeth. *Champsosaurus* was a land-living reptile; perhaps it filled a niche similar to that occupied today by some of the very large, tropical lizards.

There must have been innumerable small mammals living under the feet of the Belly River dinosaurs, the animals which usually are not seen, but which in truth far outnumber their large and spectacular neighbors, but of these we have little evidence†. Conditions

* See 'Page Corrections and Emendations' in Addendum.

† Numerous mammal bones have recently been found in the contemporaneous Mesa Verde formation.

that accounted for the burial and preservation of the bones of countless gigantic dinosaurs may not have been generally conducive to the fossilization of small, delicate animals. There are some scattered fossils of a Belly River opossum, *Eodelphis*, which is not very different from the modern North American opossum. Here, among the marsupials, is an animal that like the turtles has retained its basic adaptations through great spans of geologic time, an animal that has seen other dynasties, reptilian and mammalian, come and go. And it is still with us. A few other mammal bones are known.

A single bird, *Caenagnathus*, has been found in the Belly River sediments. There is every reason to think that by Belly River times birds generally similar to modern birds were abundant in the air.

This glimpse of the Belly River fauna shows us what reptilian life on the land was like in late Cretaceous times, perhaps ten or fifteen million years before the close of Mesozoic history. It is a sample from which a view with wider horizons may be projected, a view that encompasses not merely a few hundred or thousand square miles in what is now Alberta, but rather a major part of the continent. For it must not be thought that giant dinosaurs so numerous and so varied as those which are contained within the Belly River fauna, together with great numbers of lesser reptiles, birds and mammals, were by any means confined to the region in which their bones have been found. Indeed, fossils occur in regions adjacent to the Belly River region, which represent extensions of this fauna beyond its type area. Such, for example are the Judith River fossils, from northern Montana, and the fossils of the Two Medicine formation, exposed along the Milk River, east of Glacier Park, in Montana. But what interests us are not the nearby faunas but rather the possible evidence that Belly River dinosaurs and crocodiles and turtles and other animals lived far beyond the vicinity of the present western Canadian–American boundary. Large animals in great numbers occupy large areas of land; this must have been true for the Belly River reptiles.

That such was the case has been underlined within recent years by the discovery of a reptilian fauna in the Aguja beds along the Texas border, where the Rio Grande River makes its great bend to the south and then to the north again, as it flows eastwardly to the sea. Here, in the Big Bend region are found dinosaurs closely comparable to the Belly River dinosaurs. And with them are other reptiles, notably a gigantic crocodile, *Phobosuchus*, to be compared with remains of this same reptile that have been found in the Judith River beds of Montana. *Phobosuchus*, known from a huge skull and parts of the skeleton discovered in the Aguja sediments, is a crocodile grown to giant proportions, a crocodile that in life must have been fifty feet in length, living quite probably as a predator on young dinosaurs.

A reptile in the Aguja sediments that is not known in the Belly River beds, or in any of the other more northerly horizons of this age, is a gigantic swamp-dwelling, sauropod dinosaur, a lineal descendant of the great sauropods that so dominated the late Jurassic scene. Could it be possible that the range of the huge sauropods did not extend into the northern part of the continent during late Cretaceous times ? Could it be that they were dinosaurs with a southern distribution, at least in the western hemisphere, limited by reason of their immense size to regions which were truly tropical, perhaps unable to live in more northerly latitudes, even though in those days the temperatures at fifty degrees latitude would fall quite easily within the range that we regard as subtropical or warm temperate ? This argument is largely an exercise in speculation, and perhaps some future discoveries in Montana or Alberta will disclose the bones of late Cretaceous sauropods. But it does seem probable that bones as large as those of sauropods would hardly escape being preserved in a fossil assemblage as rich as the Belly River, or would remain completely undiscovered, even though rare. So the explanation of a geographical limitation to southerly latitudes is offered for what it is worth.

To the south-east of the Big Bend region, particularly in the Difunta formation near the city of Saltillo, Coahuila, Mexico, there have been found dinosaur bones that would seem to extend the Belly River fauna to the south. And finally, in the coastal plain sediments of New Jersey, are fragmentary bones indicating, so far as can be determined, reptiles of Belly River affinities along the eastern edge of the continent. Thus our vision of the Belly River fauna as an assemblage of varied and quite abundant dinosaurs, with accompanying crocodiles, lizards, snakes, turtles, small mammals and birds spread across large areas on the North American continent, is not entirely a projection of the imagination. There is adequate evidence to show that reptiles and other land-living vertebrates were widely dispersed across the land in those far distant days.

The Red Deer River, which flows eastwardly in that area where it has exposed the Belly River beds, is, in its upper reaches, a predominantly north and south water course. And here, to the north of the Belly River exposures and south of the city of Edmonton, its banks are formed by the badlands of the Edmonton beds. These sediments, clearly higher in position than the Belly River beds, and therefore later in age, contain the bones of numerous dinosaurs and other reptiles. The fauna is not as rich as the earlier Belly River fauna, but it is none the less sufficiently well preserved to afford the opportunity for making close comparisons. Fortunately for the paleontologist there are in these two regions two reptilian faunas, separated from each other by a distance of perhaps a hundred miles, and by a time interval of several million years. Many of the reptiles in the Belly River fauna are obviously the ancestors of reptiles in the Edmonton fauna. One can see here the course of evolution through the years, one can see the changes that occurred among various dinosaurs over a considerable span of geologic history. One can get a feeling of the fourth dimension, time, so invaluable to the student of evolution.

Generally speaking, the Edmonton scene, like the earlier one, was dominated by varied plant-eating dinosaurs, accompanied by their predators. And there were undoubtedly other reptiles present besides the dinosaurs, but except for evidence of some turtles, and one plesiosaur discovered in brackish water deposits within the Edmonton formation, the fossil record is blank.

The dinosaurs are sufficiently numerous to show the way in which the evolutionary succession from Belly River to Edmonton time took place. Some genera continued right through from the earlier to the later age. Some genera that were typical of the Belly River failed to survive into Edmonton time; they were for the most part replaced by their descendants or by related genera. And some genera were completely new elements in the Edmonton fauna, with no close forebears in the Belly River assemblage, genera that perhaps entered this part of the world from a distant region.

Replacement, so often seen in the evolutionary history of animals and plants, is nicely demonstrated by the duck-billed, armored and horned dinosaurs during the progression from Belly River to Edmonton time. Thus the crested duck-bills, *Procheneosaurus*, *Lambeosaurus* and *Corythosaurus*, characteristic of the Belly River, did not survive into later times, but rather were replaced by other crested duck-bills such as *Hypacrosaurus* with a hollow crest, and *Saurolophus* with a spike-like solid crest, this last-named dinosaur also appearing in Asia at about this same stage of earth history. In a similar fashion new horned dinosaurs, *Arrhinoceratops* and *Anchiceratops*, appeared on the Edmonton scene as replacements for some of the Belly River ceratopsians, and the armored dinosaur, *Edmontonia*, possibly for some of the earlier armored types. It is not easy for us to see why the older dinosaurs did not continue into Edmonton time, because on the face of it they would appear to our eyes to have been as thoroughly adapted for living in the Edmonton environment as they were for that of the Belly River, and certainly as nicely adjusted for the kinds of lives they led as those later dinosaurs which replaced them. Why did they not continue as did the duck-bill *Parasaurolophus*, for example, or the meat-eaters, *Ornithomimus* and *Gorgosaurus*? They seemingly did not, and there we must leave the question.

Some of the gaps in the Edmonton fauna may be the result of the accidents of preservation or of discovery rather than of any real absence. This is almost certainly true for the armored dinosaurs, *Palaeoscincus* and *Ankylosaurus*, present in the earlier Belly River and the later Lance faunas. But if the record has lost some of its details, it has gained others, for in Edmonton time there appeared some new dinosaurs to lend added variety to the scene. Such is *Thescelosaurus*, a rather primitive ornithopod dinosaur related to *Hypsilophodon* of the Wealden of England, and *Leptoceratops*, a very primitive horned dinosaur. Here once again we see the persistence of primitive structural types – the continuation of animals which in their general anatomy might very well serve as ancestors to their large, specialized contemporaneous relatives.

It is particularly interesting to see some large, flat-headed duck-bills appearing in the Edmonton fauna along with their crested relatives. The crested duck-bills were destined to become extinct before the end of Cretaceous times, leaving the flat-headed hadrosaurs to carry on this large line of dinosaurian evolution to the very end of the period, and the beginning of this shift in duck-bill types, resulting in a mixture of the old with the new, is to be seen in Edmonton fossils.

The end of this progression of North American reptiles through time comes with the Lance fauna, the uppermost and youngest record of the Cretaceous on the continent. The Lance fauna, like that of the Belly River, is an abundant one, known from many fossils collected in Wyoming and adjacent states, and the evidence of its fossils is supplemented by those of the Hell Creek beds, which occur in Dakota and Montana.

The dinosaurs of the Lance are in many cases dinosaurs grown large from their Belly River forebears. So we see *Gorgosaurus*, a giant carnivore of the Belly River and Edmonton, replaced by *Tyrannosaurus*, justly famous as the greatest among the meat-eating dinosaurs. The characters that distinguish *Gorgosaurus*, that determined its success as a predator, are accentuated in *Tyrannosaurus*. This dinosaur is not only generally larger than its earlier relative, its skull and teeth are larger, actually and proportionately, its hind limbs stronger, its fore-limbs even more ridiculously small. In short, *Tyrannosaurus* is the logical end result in the evolution of the giant predatory dinosaurs.

This increase in size among Lance and Hell Creek dinosaurs over those of the Belly River is seen in other lines of evolution as well. The Lance duck-bill, *Anatosaurus*, is certainly one of the largest of these dinosaurs, while the related and contemporaneous dome-headed dinosaur, *Pachycephalosaurus*, is a true giant in its own evolutionary line. Likewise, the horned dinosaurs of the Lance, *Triceratops* and *Torosaurus*, are considerably larger than those of earlier times. And in this connection should be mentioned the presence of a giant sauropod, *Alamosaurus*, in the correlative Cretaceous beds of New Mexico. This sauropod is perhaps no larger than the sauropods of the earlier Aguja beds of this southern region. But it does continue giantism in the sauropod line to the very end of Cretaceous history in North America.

It must not be thought that all of the dinosaurs grew ever larger during late Cretaceous history. Relatively small, lightly built theropods continued through the long time span encompassed by the Belly River, Edmonton and Lance, with no appreciable change in size or in structure. *Ornithomimus* – the ostrich dinosaur – for example, was beautifully adapted for the type of life it led in Belly River times, and it lived this same life through Lance time. The pattern was perfected; there were no advantages for survival by becoming larger. The armored dinosaurs of the Lance are also essentially similar to those of the Belly River.

The plains and savannahs of western North America in Lance times supported an abundant array of animals in addition to the dominant and spectacular dinosaurs. There were many turtles and there were crocodilians. Lizards, snakes and frogs lived in the undergrowth, along the streams and in the ponds and lakes. And although the fossil record gives us no evidence, we can be sure that there must have been many birds in the air.

Of particular importance, however, were the mammals, which thrived in great numbers during Lance time. The ubiquity of these animals during the closing years of Cretaceous history is becoming increasingly apparent as a result of new collecting techniques that have been developed during the past decade or so. By washing and screening large masses of Lance sediments it has been possible to recover thousands of specimens of Cretaceous mammals, tiny jaws and parts of skeletons, and teeth in prodigious numbers. These fossils give us a glimpse of the hordes of small mammals that inhabited the land during the last days of the dinosaurs, mammals no larger than modern mice and shrews, lurking in burrows, busily pushing their way through thick vegetation, or climbing in the trees.

Many of these Lance mammals were multituberculates, perhaps similar in mode of life to modern rodents, with multicuspid teeth in the cheek for the purpose of grinding fruits and husks. The majority of them were, however, marsupials, close cousins of modern opossums. Some of them were placental insectivores, related to modern shrews and hedgehogs. All of these Lance mammals outlived the dinosaurs, but the multituberculates were destined to become extinct early during the Age of Mammals, whereas the marsupials and the insectivores continued into modern times. The marsupials have enjoyed a modest degree of evolutionary success. The placental mammals, descendants from the Cretaceous insectivores, have now inherited the earth, and are today supreme. One of them, man, dominates the earth as it has never before been dominated, even in the days of the dinosaurs.

While dinosaurs and contemporaneous animals were thus populating the landscapes of North America in great numbers and with wide variety during the latter part of Cretaceous history, other reptiles were filling the seas. Great numbers of ichthyosaurs, plesiosaurs and mosasaurs were established far and wide through the oceans of the world, where they made an abundant living on the vast schools of bony fishes, which had by this time become pre-eminent in the waters of the earth. By the late Cretaceous reptiles were universal around the globe – on land, in the air and in the water.

In North America the record of marine reptiles is particularly well shown in three formations that are widely exposed through the western states – the white Benton limestone overlain by the Niobrara limestone and chalk, and above this the black Pierre shale. These formations, which frequently are found together, come within the confines of late Cretaceous time, the Benton and Niobrara being perhaps somewhat older than and the Pierre more or less equivalent to the Belly River in age.

These marine sediments are, of course, the remaining visible evidence of some of the inland seas that were so extensive during Cretaceous times. Even though lands stretched far and wide as the Cretaceous period drew towards its close, offering broad stages upon

Figure 61. The upper Cretaceous long-necked plesiosaur, *Elasmosaurus*, from North America, about forty feet long, which lived in shallow inland seas and preyed upon fishes.

which the dinosaurs played their final roles, these seas persisted through the middle of the continent and around its borders.

Two groups of marine reptiles inhabited the Benton seas, the fish-like ichthyosaurs, and various plesiosaurs, some of these latter being pliosaurs and some elasmosaurs. The pliosaurs, as has been said, are short-necked plesiosaurs with long skulls and jaws; the elasmosaurs are long-necked plesiosaurs with relatively small skulls. It would seem that the plesiosaurs of these two groups lived rather different lives, the pliosaurs perhaps pursuing fishes through the waves as did the ichthyosaurs, the elasmosaurs probably swimming slowly along the surface and catching fishes by darting the long, snake-like neck this way and that to either side. Both adaptations were successful; both groups of plesiosaurs lived abundantly.

The ichthyosaurs seemingly were on the way to extinction. Only a single genus is known from the Benton formation, and this is the

last of North American ichthyosaurs. These reptiles, so very successful during a great part of Mesozoic time, seem to have died out well
before the end of Cretaceous history – for what reason it is difficult
to say. Certainly they were wonderfully adapted for a life of fast
swimming in ocean waters, and one would think that with the ever-
increasing numbers and variety of teleost fishes in late Cretaceous
seas the ichthyosaurs would have prospered. They did not; they
disappeared. Perhaps the pliosaurs were able to compete with them,
and shoulder them out of the marine niche they had occupied for
such a great span of time, but this is only a supposition. Like so many
extinctions, that of the ichthyosaurs, at a time when environments

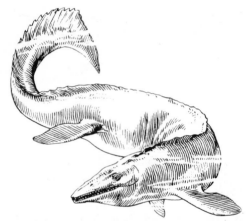

Figure 62. The gigantic upper Cretaceous marine lizard, *Tylosaurus*, from North
America. This great predator is some thirty feet in length.

and food supplies seemed favorable to their continuation, probably
will remain a mystery to us.

But if the mid-continental seas of late Cretaceous times were impoverished by the disappearance of the ichthyosaurs at the end of
Benton time, they were enriched by the increase of other marine
reptiles in the Niobrara seas. Here again were numerous long-necked
elasmosaurs and short-necked pliosaurs, apparently living in greater
numbers and greater variety than ever before. And in addition there
were large numbers of mosasaurs, newcomers to the oceans of the
world.

The mosasaurs were gigantic marine lizards, closely related to the
monitor lizards that live today throughout the Old World, and their

rapid adaptation for a life spent entirely in the ocean was certainly a response to the increase of bony fishes, on which they fed. Some of the mosasaurs attained lengths of thirty feet and more, with the tail narrow and deep – a sculling oar for propelling them through the water, with the limbs modified into paddles. But otherwise these were essentially monitors, and the resemblances of the skull of a large mosasaur to the skull of a modern Komodo lizard are indeed striking.

Within the limestones and chalk beds that today constitute the Niobrara formation are found, in addition to the many plesiosaurs and mosasaurs, the fossil bones of flying reptiles and of birds, these

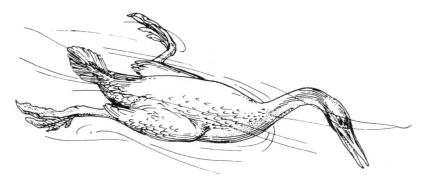

Figure 63. An upper Cretaceous diving bird, *Hesperornis*, from North America. *Hesperornis*, about the size of a loon, was probably very loon-like in its habits. It was flightless, and therefore confined to the water and to nearby shores.

latter very much like modern birds except that some of them may retain some teeth in their jaws, a reminder of their reptilian ancestry. One of them, *Hesperornis*, was a diver like a modern loon, and even at this early time in avian history was so specialized as to have lost its wings! The flying reptiles were pteranodonts, of which the genus *Pteranodon* is particularly characteristic. *Pteranodon*, one of the last of the flying reptiles and certainly the largest*, had a wingspread of twenty feet and more, a long, beaked skull (the beak completely toothless, like the beak of a modern bird) and a comparatively small body, no larger in bulk than the body of a turkey. In short, *Pteranodon* must have been primarily a glider, soaring through the air on enormous wings, dipping down to the surface of the sea to scoop up fishes.

*See 'Page Corrections and Emendations' in Addendum.

Time advanced, and the Pierre seas developed, seas that occupied the center of the continent at a time when the dinosaurs were reaching their great climax on the Belly River plains. And in the Pierre seas the marine reptiles continued their dominant roles. Here once more were long-necked elasmosaurs as in the Niobrara sea, but elasmosaurs of gigantic size, some of them forty feet and more in length, half of this length being taken up by the long neck. And with these long-necked elasmosaurs there were many mosasaurs. Furthermore, certain turtles had by now entered the ocean, to become fully adapted marine reptiles. In the Pierre seas lived *Archelon*, a huge marine turtle with a shell ten feet or so in length, with large paddle-like limbs by which it propelled itself. This great sea turtle and others

Figure 64. The largest and one of the last of the pterosaurs or flying reptiles. *Pteranodon*, from the upper Cretaceous of North America, has a wing span of more than twenty feet.

related to it were parallel forerunners but not ancestors of modern sea turtles.

This picture of marine reptiles in successive mid-continental seas during millions of years of late Cretaceous history applies to other regions as well. Plesiosaurs and mosasaurs are found in Cretaceous beds around the margins of the North American continent, in northern Europe, and in many other parts of the world. It is not surprising that these marine reptiles are widely distributed, because they obviously were able to swim freely through the tropical seas that covered much of the earth's surface.

This somewhat extended discussion of reptilian life during late Cretaceous times, as it is revealed by fossils found within the interior of North America, may be taken as fairly typical of life on other continents as well. The North American record is at the present time the most complete one known, and by looking at it in detail we may obtain a good and valid idea of reptilian life everywhere. Fossils from other parts of the world serve mainly to supplement and to reinforce the evidence of those found in North America.

Within the past few decades a great deal of exploration has been carried on in Central Asia, first by American paleontologists, subsequently by the Russians and Chinese, and when all of the fossils that have been and will be gathered from these and from future expeditions are known, it seems probable we shall have an array of dinosaurs and other reptiles from that continent quite comparable in numbers and variety to the fossil record of North America. Already much has been learned, and what we know at this time from the Asiatic fossil fields indicates that there was a close relationship between this continental area and north-western North America during the late years of Cretaceous history.

To take the dinosaurs as an exemplification of this, it is quite apparent that the tropical lowlands forming the landscapes of what are now Mongolia and northern China, were inhabited by dinosaurs very much like those living in the Belly River, Edmonton and Lance environments. There were varied plant-eaters, most of them giants of their kind, with the accompanying predators which fed upon them, the result being that eastern Asia was populated by crested hadrosaurs, by armored dinosaurs, by horned dinosaurs and by great carnosaurs. And in addition there were the smaller dinosaurs as well in the Asiatic scene. Many of these Asiatic dinosaurs, even though closely related to their North American counterparts, are distinctive enough to warrant inclusion in distinct genera, yet in addition to these close cousins of the New World dinosaurs, there are some Asiatic genera identical with those of North America, showing that there was reasonably free passage from the one region to the other during late Cretaceous times.

Such, for example, is the ostrich dinosaur, *Ornithomimus*, which occurs in the Iren Dabasu formation of Mongolia as well as in the Belly River and Lance beds of North America. Again, the gigantic carnosaur, *Tyrannosaurus*, was an inhabitant of the Asiatic region at the end of Cretaceous times, its bones having been found in the upper Cretaceous beds of Mongolia. Other familiar forms that appear in the Asiatic late Cretaceous faunas are the crested duck-bill, *Saurolophus*, the small dome-headed dinosaur, *Stegoceras*, and the horned dinosaur, *Pentaceratops*.

In one respect, namely the well-attested presence of various gigantic sauropod dinosaurs, the Asiatic reptilian faunas of late Cretaceous age are markedly different from those of northern North America. It may be recalled that there are no indications of these great swamp dwellers in the successive reptilian assemblages of the States and provinces on either side of the Canadian–American boundary, and in view of the large size and durable nature of the bones of these dinosaurs, it would seem possible that their lack in the Belly River, Edmonton, Lance sequence is indicative of their absence from these northern latitudes. It may be further recalled that there are bones of sauropods in the Aguja beds of Texas, correlative with the Belly River, and in the Cretaceous formations of New Mexico, correlative with the Lance. So it appears that sauropod dinosaurs were present in the southern portion of North America during late Cretaceous times, but possibly they were not numerous or varied.

In contrast with the scanty evidence of sauropods in the upper Cretaceous beds of North America are the rather numerous and widely established discoveries of sauropod bones in the upper Cretaceous beds of Asia, finds that range from northern China, Manchuria and Japan through the deserts of Mongolia to the peninsula of India. Various genera have been described from this great area, including *Antarctosaurus*, *Laplatasaurus* and *Titanosaurus* – forms that ranged widely over the southern hemisphere. Mention will be made of them again.

In both North America and eastern Asia are upper Cretaceous turtles and crocodilians which, like the dinosaurs, give evidence as to the close relationships between these regions during the final years of Mesozoic history. Of particular interest in this respect are the late Cretaceous mammals discovered in Asia. It was here that the fossil remains of insectivores were found some decades ago by the expeditions of the American Museum of Natural History. It was an exciting discovery because several skulls and jaws were found in the Djadochta beds at Shabarakh Usu, where the bones and the eggs of the ancestral horned dinosaur, *Protoceratops*, occur in such great abundance. These remains of tiny mammals include the skull of *Deltatheridium*, a shrew-like insectivore, and *Zalambdalestes*, an early forerunner of the Old World hedgehogs.

As one journeys away from this North American–eastern Asiatic center of reptilian life, especially of dinosaurian life, differences of the reptilian faunas from those with which we have been concerned become increasingly apparent. Of course, there are resemblances, too. South America, Africa and Europe were habitats favorable to large sauropod dinosaurs, as was eastern Asia, and the giant predators stalked the late Cretaceous landscapes of these widely separated continental regions, clear proof of the ubiquity of these dinosaurs. Likewise there were armored dinosaurs. But with the exception of

Figure 65. One of the first of the horned dinosaurs, *Protoceratops*, from the Cretaceous of Mongolia. This dinosaur, about six feet in length, shows the distinctive characters that were to become so highly developed in its later Cretaceous descendants, the giant ceratopsians.

one genus in Europe, there are no indications of duck-billed dinosaurs in regions beyond North America and eastern Asia. Moreover, there are no absolute proofs of horned dinosaurs outside of this area.

Of course, such gaps in the fossil record of other continents may be owing in part to the accidents of preservation and discovery. In Europe, especially, where there is an abundance of late Cretaceous marine deposits, but a notable scarcity of continental beds, this is a factor which must be given considerable weight. But the lack of water-loving duck-billed dinosaurs in Africa and South America, where water-loving sauropods are preserved, and the lack of upland horned dinosaurs in all continental areas beyond western North America and eastern Asia, where none the less the remains of other upland dinosaurs are found, lends weight to the supposition that

187

perhaps in late Cretaceous times these particular dinosaurs were rather restricted in distribution.

What about the swamp-dwelling dinosaurs, which lived not only in Asia, but also in Europe, Africa and South America during the late Cretaceous ? The genera *Antarctosaurus*, *Laplatasaurus* and *Titanosaurus*, previously mentioned, are of particular interest to the paleontologist because of their very wide distribution. *Antarctosaurus*, first named from the upper Cretaceous beds of Patagonia, also occurs in the Lameta formation of peninsular India, *Laplatasaurus*, another South American dinosaur, as is indicated by its name, has been found in the upper Cretaceous sediments of Madagascar, and *Titanosaurus*, known from abundant fossils found in Patagonia, occurs as well in the Lameta beds of India and in the uppermost Cretaceous sediments of south-eastern Europe. These are indeed enormous ranges for single reptilian genera, and if the identifications are in all cases correct they show that the sauropods were wandering widely at the close of the Mesozoic. Moreover, in Europe and North America are closely related genera, for instance *Hypselosaurus* and *Alamosaurus* respectively, to reinforce the evidence of wide-ranging late Cretaceous sauropods. Thus these dinosaurs show cosmopolitan ranges, seemingly in contrast to some of the other dinosaurian groups.

As for reptiles other than the dinosaurs, turtles and crocodilians were widely distributed throughout the world. It is probable, too, that birds and primitive mammals, particularly multituberculates, marsupials and insectivores, were of world-wide extent, and were numerous in the faunas of the various continents, just as the fossil record shows them to have been in North America. There is still much to be learned about the distributions of these small and fragile animals in the late Cretaceous world.

What is to be gleaned from this survey of late Cretaceous reptilian life beyond the facts of the distributions and associations of these animals across the surface of the globe ? Many things, it may be said, which are of importance to the student interested in the life of the past and the world of the past. A few of these things can be briefly mentioned.

For example, the faunas of the late Cretaceous show very clearly that rates of evolution among the ornithischian dinosaurs were remarkably rapid. Some groups of these dinosaurs expanded and advanced in most spectacular ways, as is shown by their variety, and by the anatomical changes that took place in some of their evolutionary lines within the confines of late Cretaceous time. The great increase of these dinosaurs during the latter part of the Cretaceous period was of such magnitude that it resulted in the numbers of dinosaurs of that age being more than double those of the dinosaurs of any previous stage in Mesozoic history. Moreover, the rapid rate of ornithischian evolution in late Cretaceous time is indicated by the diversity among these reptiles, as exemplified particularly among the hooded hadrosaurs and the horned dinosaurs. Certainly the ultimate in rapid evolutionary rate among the dinosaurs was achieved by the ceratopsians, which developed in great complexity during the late Cretaceous. Seldom in geologic history has the entire history of an animal group of this dimension been encompassed within so small a fraction of a geologic period.

Continuing these considerations, the distribution of reptiles in upper Cretaceous sediments show that in the late Cretaceous, as was so frequently the case during Mesozoic history, the climates of the world seemingly were remarkably uniform over great latitudes. Dinosaurs and other reptiles ranged far to the north and the south on the continents[*], and great marine reptiles swam widely in the oceans. Only tropical and subtropical climates of wide extent could have made possible such broad distributions of the reptiles on the land and in the sea.

Reptilian distributions near the end of the Mesozoic era have other implications, too. They show that there were land connections which allowed various reptiles to wander widely from one continent to another. Certainly there was a bridge between North America and Asia, very probably in the Bering region. There were other land connections that allowed the sauropods to migrate from South America to Asia and Europe. But where were these connections? Was there a land bridge across the South Atlantic? Or was South America closely joined to Africa at this time, as is maintained by many advocates of the theory of drifting continents? These are questions not easily answered. Perhaps the sauropods may have gone from South America up through North America, across to Asia and from there into Africa and Europe. But there is no fossil evidence in the upper Cretaceous beds of North America to support such a route of migration. So it may be that these reptiles moved back and forth between the eastern and western hemispheres along some other path. Future discoveries may help to solve this problem.

[*]See 'Page Corrections and Emendations' in Addendum.

Whether or not the continents resembled modern continents in shape and position, it would seem that the world was in many respects becoming a modern world. True enough, it was still largely a tropical, subtropical and warm temperate world full of strange animals. Yet it was a world in which flowering plants covered the lands, where they were pollinated by many diverse insects; a world in which the waters were teeming with bony fishes. It was a world that would have seemed familiar to us in many respects.

In this world the dinosaurs reigned supreme on the land, and the various marine reptiles ruled the oceans. Life seemed to be set in a well-established pattern, a pattern of reptilian dominance, which to all appearances might have continued indefinitely. The world belonged to the reptiles, and the mammals, numerous as they might have been, were small and of insignificant appearance, seemingly minor elements in the faunas of that day.

Yet this world of gigantic reptiles and small mammals was soon to undergo a great change. The end of the Cretaceous period was drawing near, and with it the end of dinosaurs on land, of pterosaurs in the air and of plesiosaurs and mosasaurs in the sea. A profound change in the complexion of vertebrate life was soon to take place, to make the world of post-Cretaceous times quite different from the world that had so long existed. The great extinction which marked the change from the Mesozoic to the Cenozoic world brought the Age of Reptiles to an end.

Chapter 11

The Great Extinction

THE GREAT EXTINCTION that wiped out all of the dinosaurs, large and small, in all parts of the world, and at the same time brought to an end various other lines of reptilian evolution, was one of the outstanding events in the history of life and in the history of the earth. It forms one of the major lines of demarcation in the record of the rocks, indicating in a rather spectacular and certainly in a very definite manner the end of a long chapter in the complex story of life through the ages. It was an event that has defied all attempts at a satisfactory explanation, for which reason, among others, it has fascinated paleontologists for decades.

One may quite correctly term the disappearance of the dinosaurs at the close of Cretaceous times as the great extinction, because that is what it was. There were other extinctions before it – the extinction that so affected the reptiles and amphibians at the close of the Permian period, and particularly at the end of the Triassic period, and after it – the wave of extinctions at the end of the Ice Age some ten thousand years or so ago that brought to their doom the mammoths and mastodons and woolly rhinoceroses and giant ground sloths with which our stone-age forebears shared the land. And there were others. But none of these extinctions had quite the finality of the extinction, or rather the several parallel extinctions, that marked the end of the Mesozoic world.

The extinctions that took place at the close of Triassic times, for example, brought to an end several reptilian dynasties and an amphibian dynasty as well, but after the disappearance of these animals from the earth their places were taken for the most part by other reptiles. Reptiles succeeded reptiles. And the relatively recent extinctions that resulted in the disappearance of various great Ice Age mammals served in effect to impoverish the life of the earth, but not to change it in any profound way. The world is poorer, now that great herds of mammoths do not wander widely across most of the continents of the world, but there are still elephants in Africa and Asia. Life in Eurasia is less exciting than it used to be, now that the woolly rhinoceros is gone, but there are other rhinoceroses elsewhere. Mammals are still the rulers of the earth, particularly one mammal, man.

But the great extinction of the dinosaurs, and the extinctions of the large reptilian denizens of the oceans, brought about truly profound changes in the life of the earth. Giant reptiles disappeared from the face of the world. They left empty places on the lands and in the seas, and these places were soon filled by quite different animals, the mammals. It is this change in the character of dominant life – from reptiles to mammals – that makes the great extinction at the close of Cretaceous times so very important to the student of earth history and to the student of evolution.

The extinction of the dinosaurs was an evolutionary event, a fact to be kept in mind. It should be remembered, as all too frequently is not the case, that extinctions are evolutionary processes, just as are origins. There would be no evolution without the origin of species, which replaces the old with the new, and at the same time there would be no evolution without the extinction of species, which removes the old to make room for the new. The world is now a very different world from what it was some seventy million years or so ago, when the last dinosaurs were at the pinnacle of their power, and it is different to a very considerable degree because these dinosaurs became extinct.

One might continue at length with generalities about extinction as a phenomenon and with discussions and suppositions about the disappearance of various reptiles at the end of Cretaceous times. There are many interesting aspects to this latter subject, about which much can be said. But first of all it might be helpful to survey the nature and the extent of the extinction that took place during the transition from Cretaceous to Tertiary times.

There are some fifteen or sixteen orders and about fifty-seven families, perhaps a few more, of air-breathing vertebrates preserved in the known record of upper Cretaceous rocks. If this statement seems just a bit vague as to numbers, it must be remembered that discussions based upon classifications are dependent upon the fallibilities of human judgments. The general relationships of animals, past and present, are rather well understood, but there are naturally differences of opinion as to details. Some students will be inclined to 'split' groups of organisms – others to 'lump' them. One authority on modern reptiles will, for example, separate the crocodiles, the alligators and the long-snouted gavial into three separate families; another man of equal ability in his field and of equally sound judgment will indicate these reptiles as subfamily divisions within a single family. So it is that when we consider the numbers of orders, or families, or genera and species of tetrapods that inhabited the earth during late Cretaceous times a certain amount of subjectivity enters into our reflections and qualifying words are necessary. However, it is reasonably accurate to say that about fifteen orders and almost sixty families of tetrapods, within which are contained many hundreds of genera and species, have been exhumed from rocks of late Cretaceous age.

Such is the extent of our knowledge of the tetrapods that inhabited the earth during the final days of dinosaurian dominance, knowledge that is admittedly incomplete. For it is quite certain on all reasonable grounds to think that various groups of animals not found in upper Cretaceous rocks were none the less living when the sediments composing those rocks were deposited. These were the animals which for one reason or another were rarely, perhaps in some cases never, fossilized.

For example there are the salamanders and the coecilians[*]. Fossils of the former of these two amphibian groups are known only from rocks of post-Cretaceous age and the latter group is unknown in the fossil record, yet there is good reason to think that salamanders and coecilians have been on the earth for a long time; their origins must go far back in the geologic record. Again, although lizards and snakes and birds are known from upper Cretaceous rocks, their rather scant fossil record in no way reflects their abundance on the earth in those days. Some of these same considerations apply to certain mammals – the monotremes for instance – which do not appear in the Cretaceous record, but which very probably were living in the days of the dinosaurs. These were all fragile-boned animals, living in environments where they were not often fossilized. We may be sure that if the record were complete many families, genera and species would be added to the roster of upper Cretaceous land-living animals.

The paleontologist must do as best he can with what he has, and certainly what we have in the way of fossils of larger air-breathing vertebrates of late Cretaceous age is considerable, probably a fairly

[*] See 'Page Corrections and Emendations' in Addendum.

good but not completely balanced representation of their presence and abundance upon the earth in the days when they were living. With all of these preliminary remarks in mind let us turn now to an evaluation of the extinctions that took place at the end of Cretaceous history, limiting ourselves to the reptiles, and remembering that any conclusions bearing on the lizards and snakes are necessarily incomplete.

There are definitely ten reptilian orders*, containing about fifty families, known from upper Cretaceous rocks. It seems very probable that the ten orders of reptiles so known make up a complete roster of reptilian orders living at that time; it is not likely that any orders other than these ten were then in existence. These ten orders embrace the turtles, the eosuchians (a limited group destined to suffer extinction soon after the close of the Cretaceous), the rhynchocephalians, the squamates or lizards (including the mosasaurs) and snakes, the crocodilians, the saurischian dinosaurs, the ornithischian dinosaurs, the pterosaurs or flying reptiles, the fish-like ichthyosaurs and the marine plesiosaurs. These animals filled the lands and seas in Cretaceous time, and half of them, counting by orders, the half that are so distinctive and typical of the Age of Reptiles, disappeared from the earth during the days when the Cretaceous period was drawing to a close. At the beginning of Tertiary history the two orders of dinosaurs, the flying reptiles and the marine reptiles had vanished, leaving only the reptiles inhabiting the earth today, plus the short-lived eosuchians. It was indeed a great extinction.

This becomes evident when one turns to an examination of the lesser groups of Cretaceous reptiles. According to the classification on which these remarks are based (essentially a classification recently published by Professor Romer and founded on his lifetime of study), of the fifty families of reptiles known from upper Cretaceous sediments, thirty-five became extinct at the end of Cretaceous time. This is a high degree of mortality indeed. Moreover, it is even higher when one realizes that of the fifteen reptilian families surviving the end of the Cretaceous, five more failed to survive it by very much time, geologically speaking, all dying out during the Eocene. These five groups of reptiles, two families of turtles, the eosuchians already mentioned, a family of lizards and one of crocodilians, were essentially Cretaceous animals that managed to hold on for a time, only to succumb to more successful relatives during early Tertiary history.

*See 'Page Corrections and Emendations' in Addendum.

Thus only ten of the fifty families of late Cretaceous reptiles were truly successful after the end of Cretaceous times, and even one of these, the meiolanid turtles, disappeared during the Pleistocene epoch, the time of the great Ice Age. So it is that the record shows four-fifths of the families of late Cretaceous reptiles becoming extinct at the end of the Cretaceous period, or not long thereafter.

Of course, if the record were complete it would not be quite so striking, because, as already pointed out, there must have been many lizards and snakes on the earth during late Cretaceous time for which there is no fossil evidence. Consequently the numbers of families, and especially of genera and species of these reptiles that survived the Cretaceous–Tertiary transition, was probably considerable. Yet as balanced against this there is the distinct possibility that a great majority of our modern lizards and snakes had their origins after the close of Cretaceous history, that they are comparative newcomers to the earth. Therefore, even though the survival of lizards and snakes from Cretaceous into later history may have been large, it almost certainly did not involve more than a fraction of the numbers of families and genera of these reptiles living today.

Table 14 shows the extinction of reptilian families that took place at the close of Cretaceous history.

Table 14. *Extinction of reptilian families at the close of the Cretaceous*[*]

	NUMBER OF UPPER CRETACEOUS FAMILIES	NUMBER SURVIVING END OF CRETACEOUS	NUMBER LIVING TODAY
Turtles	15	8	9
Eosuchians	1	1	0
Rhynchocephalians	1	1	1
Lizards and snakes	6	3	28
Crocodilians	6	2	1
Saurischians	6	0	0
Ornithischians	9	0	0
Pterosaurs	1	0	0
Ichthyosaurs	1	0	0
Plesiosaurs	4	0	0
	50	15	39

Before going on with our discussion of the extinction that took place among the reptiles at the end of the Cretaceous period, it may be of interest to pause briefly for a look at the evolutionary fate of the reptiles that lived beyond the Cretaceous. Here are the bare facts.

[*]See 'Page Corrections and Emendations' and 'Tables and Diagrams' in Addendum.

Although eight families of turtles lived from Cretaceous into Tertiary times, of these only five persist today. During the interval since the end of the Cretaceous period, in which three families of turtles became extinct, two of them at the relatively early stage of the Eocene, four new families of these reptiles appeared, to bring the total of present-day turtle families to nine. The largest group, by far, of these new lines of turtle evolution is that of the testudinids, the varied pond and swamp turtles and the tortoises. These are the turtles that have, in effect, ecologically replaced many of the turtles that became extinct at the close of the Cretaceous, thereby ensuring the wide-spread radiation of modern turtles across the continental land masses to make them very successful reptiles indeed. The snapping turtles and their relatives, the marine dermochelids, and one group of southern hemisphere side-neck turtles were the other turtle families that seemingly arose after the great reptilian extinction. Thus by a series of replacements the turtles have carried on their long story of evolutionary persistence into modern times, so that even though they may not be as numerous or as varied as they were during the Age of Reptiles, they are none the less important reptilian components of animal life throughout the tropical and temperate regions of the world.

The rhynchocephalians today are represented by a single species, the famous tuatera, now confined to a few islands off the New Zealand coast, where it enjoys the complete protection of the government. This little reptile is the persistent survivor of a group that seemingly was never very numerous after the close of Triassic times, yet a group that was sufficiently endowed to continue throughout the world in spite of competition from the ecologically and physically similar lizards. The same cannot be said for the eosuchians, also lizard-like in form and perhaps in some aspects of life habits, for this group of reptiles disappeared during Eocene time.

It may be that the eosuchians and the rhynchocephalians were under strong pressure from competing lizards during the latter part of the Mesozoic era and in the years subsequent to the Age of Reptiles. Certainly the restriction of these two groups is countered by the great proliferation of the lizards. The lizards very probably were present in large numbers on all continents when the dinosaurs were supreme, but it seems likely that their numbers and variety at the present time far surpass those of past geologic history. And the same may be said with even greater emphasis for the snakes.

As for the crocodilians, it is evident from Table 14 that these interesting cousins of the dinosaurs suffered a marked decline at the end of the Cretaceous period. Almost all of the varied crocodilians that had shared the land with the dinosaurs for so many successive millennia disappeared into limbo, but one group, well established in the days when the dinosaurs were at the climax of their own development, survived and continued very successfully in the tropical and subtropical regions of the world, to the present day. This is the group embracing our familiar crocodiles, alligators and caimans, and gavials.

So it is apparent that there has been much evolution since the end of the Age of Reptiles among the survivors from that distant era. The turtles and the crocodiles continue, to a large degree with replacing forms, the roles they played during the age of dinosaurs. The tuatera barely hangs on, and within the course of a few centuries may become extinct. The lizards and snakes, among all of the reptiles, have radiated widely and variously in this modern Age of Mammals, and have become numerous and successful by living for the most part their lives as small or secretive animals, the lesser beings in a world where giant dinosaurs are no longer supreme.

To get back to the great extinction, this event wiped out almost all of the reptiles which gave to late Cretaceous environments their characteristic appearance. The dinosaurs and the pterosaurs on land, the ichthyosaurs and plesiosaurs, and the mosasaurs, too, in the sea, made the late Mesozoic scene what it was – rather different from any associations of life before and very different from anything afterwards. Then these reptiles disappeared.

Was their extinction sudden – as it so often appears to have been when the geologic record is examined, or was it a gradual decline through the final years of the Cretaceous period*? The answer to this question depends to a large degree upon our definition of terms, upon what is meant by the words sudden and gradual. In terms of human experience the extinction of the dinosaurs and of various other reptiles probably was a gradual phenomenon that extended over many thousands of years, very possibly over many hundreds of thousands of years. Unfortunately it is not possible for us to read the geologic record with a degree of precision sufficiently fine to determine the sequence of Cretaceous events which were separated from each other by a mere hundred thousand years. Thus the final decline of the dinosaurs may have lasted through many millennia without

197

*See 'Page Corrections and Emendations' in Addendum.

our being able to detect it. What we can see from the record of the rocks is that the last of the dinosaurs appear to have vanished rather suddenly and simultaneously all over the world, and the same may have been true for some of the reptiles living in the Cretaceous oceans.

Yet in spite of the uncertainties of time and the interpretation of past time, of fossilization and the preservation of the fossils through the ages, of the accidents of discovery and the difficulties of study, the remains of reptiles that have been found in late upper Cretaceous rocks do give us some clues as to the patterns of evolution and decline during the final several million years of Mesozoic history. It is possible to analyze the fossils from successive rock units of late Cretaceous age, and thus to see what trends in reptilian history may be revealed. Such an analysis is best applied to the upper Cretaceous dinosaurs, the record of which is reasonably complete, and capable of logical interpretation.

If the genera of dinosaurs that lived some time before the end of the Cretaceous, those found in North America in the Belly River sediments of North America and correlative sediments elsewhere, be compared with the Lance and other uppermost Cretaceous dinosaurs, some striking differences in numbers are revealed. The genera of these two ages can be listed, by subordinal groups.

Table 15. *Diminution in the number of dinosaurian genera during late Cretaceous time* *

	BELLY RIVER AGE	LANCE AGE
Theropods – carnivores great and small	15	14
Sauropods – the giants	2	7
Ornithopods – duck-bills and their relatives	29	7
Ankylosaurs – armored dinosaurs	19	6
Ceratopsians – horned dinosaurs	16	7

Of course, the striking thing about these figures is the great decline of plant-eating dinosaurs with the passage of time toward the end of the Cretaceous period. It might be argued that such figures are illusory; that they reflect accidents of preservation, of discovery and of collecting. A good rebuttal may, however, be advanced. For example, there are abundant fossils of horned dinosaurs in both the

*See 'Tables and Diagrams' in Addendum.

Belly River, and the Lance and Hell Creek sediments of North
America, yet the Belly River ceratopsians are quite varied, whereas

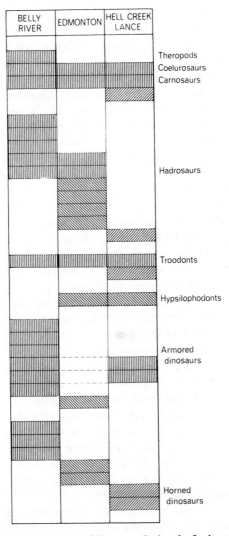

Figure 66. An example of the decline of dinosaurs during the final stages of
Cretaceous history in North America. Each horizontal bar indicates a genus. The
patterns are distinctive for the Belly River, Edmonton and Lance stages, and
indicate either the restriction of genera to these stages, or their continuation from
earlier into later stages.*

199

*See 'Tables and Diagrams' in Addendum.

those of the Lance stage at the end of Cretaceous times are limited to a few generic types. And even though the Lance ceratopsians are thus limited in diversity, they are not at all limited in abundance, for their fossil bones are found in great numbers. Indeed the Lance ceratopsian, *Triceratops*, is known from many skeletons and skulls and innumerable bone fragments; evidence that this dinosaur must have wandered across the lands of western North America in Lance time in large herds, as do elephants in some parts of Africa today. In view of the abundance of fossils, it seems reasonable to think that if there had been numerous genera of horned dinosaurs living in Lance time they would be preserved in the record. Therefore, one may argue with force and logic that the horned dinosaurs had declined in diversity during the passage of time from the Belly River to the Lance stage, and one may speculate on good grounds that the final disappearance of these dinosaurs at the close of the Lance was foreshadowed by the restriction of pre-Lance genera. It was a sequence of evolutionary events similar to what may be seen at closer hand among modern elephants. During the great Ice Age, a half-million years and less in the past, there were many genera of elephants (we call them mammoths) which roamed widely across all of the continents except South America. Today there are just two – the African and the Asiatic elephants. The pattern of development and extinction among these giant mammals during the past half-million years is strikingly similar to that for the dinosaurs seventy million years ago. Similar considerations apply to the armored dinosaurs and the duck-billed dinosaurs, as is apparent from the figures in the list above and from the occurrence of fossils in the field.

As for the great sauropods, the figures show an increase in genera between the two stages of Cretaceous history with which we are concerned. Here we almost certainly encounter results of the accidents of preservation and of discovery. These dinosaurs had in the Cretaceous period declined from their Jurassic eminence, and were seemingly not as numerous nor as varied as they formerly had been. Consequently their record is erratic.

The meat-eating dinosaurs show little change, as is evident. Perhaps the factors that led to the decline of the herbivorous dinosaurs did not affect the carnivores, so that these latter reptiles continued in undiminished diversity, preying upon an abundant but a more monotonous food supply. This is but one of several suppositions that might be made.

The important fact apparent from these comparisons is that there was an initial decline of the herbivorous dinosaurs in late Cretaceous time, so that during the final years of this period the world of the dinosaurs was not as rich as it formerly had been; it had been impoverished by the disappearance of many genera from the Cretaceous scene. This initial decline preceded by a considerable margin in years the final disappearance of all dinosaurs.

Interestingly, this pattern of late Cretaceous development may be seen among reptiles other than the herbivorous dinosaurs, even among those reptiles that survived the close of the Cretaceous period. It may be remembered from page 195 that there were fifteen families of turtles living during late Cretaceous time, of which seven families failed to survive into post-Cretaceous time. But of these seven, four seemingly died out before the Lance stage. Similarly, of the four families of crocodilians failing to extend their range into Tertiary time, two seemingly fell by the way before the beginning of the Lance stage. Such is the evidence of the fossil record as we now know it.

But what about those orders of reptiles, specifically the pterosaurs, the ichthyosaurs and the plesiosaurs, which, like the dinosaurs, disappeared from the earth as the Cretaceous period drew to a close. Did they show this same pattern of decline before extinction? The answer to this question is not as readily apparent as for the reptiles already discussed, because the marine sediments in which the bones of pterosaurs, ichthyosaurs and plesiosaurs are found do not occur as a sequence that can be traced through the final stages of Cretaceous history. Nevertheless the evidence at hand would seem to suggest patterns of development similar to those already seen. It would appear as if the ichthyosaurs may have become extinct before the end of Cretaceous times, because if the fossil evidence has any validity these reptiles had become very much restricted by the Belly River stage – perhaps to a single genus. The records of the flying reptiles, represented in upper Cretaceous sediments by a single family, and the plesiosaurs, represented by four families, do not continue into the uppermost stage of Cretaceous history which may (or may not) indicate the extinction of these reptiles, too, before the close of the period*.

Even though there were declines in the fortunes of many reptilian groups before the Cretaceous period had run its full course, there were none the less enough of these reptiles persisting into the final

*See 'Page Corrections and Emendations' in Addendum.

stage of Cretaceous history for the world to be abundantly populated by them almost to the very end of the Mesozoic. Perhaps they were not as varied as they had been in former ages, but they were certainly numerous. To return to a question put forward earlier in this chapter, was the extinction of these late-persisting forms sudden? The answer in geological terms can be illustrated by some examples.

In Utah there is a sequence of sediments known as the North Horn formation. This is a continuous series of sandstones and clays, without any visible break, without any evidence of disturbances that might have interfered with the steady accumulation of muds and

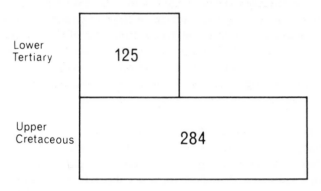

Figure 67. A comparison of the number of genera of upper Cretaceous tetrapods with those known from the lower Tertiary. The extensive extinction of Cretaceous reptiles is evident.*

sands year in and year out. By all ordinary geological criteria the North Horn formation seems to show a single cycle of sedimentation, yet in its lower part are the bones of dinosaurs and in its upper part the bones of mammals. There is no extension of the dinosaurs up into the mammal zone. The separation between the uppermost dinosaurs and the lowermost mammals is no more than thirty-five feet, surely not a great hiatus in the geological sense, but this small gap in the fossil record would seem to record the extinction of the dinosaurs. Here we see the physical evidence for the short time span during which the ruling reptiles vanished from the earth. Certainly it was a sudden event in geologic terms in ancient Utah, and so in general terms it would seem to have been all over the world. The last of the dinosaurs lived at the very end of Cretaceous times, but not beyond that end.

*See 'Tables and Diagrams' in Addendum.

Although the replacement of dinosaurs by mammals within the apparently continuous sedimentary beds of the North Horn formation seems to show a rather abrupt disappearance of these reptiles at the close of Mesozoic history, some impression that this extinction may have been drawn out through an appreciable time span is to be had from the occurrence of fossils in Wyoming in the top of the Lance and in the bottom of the overlying Fort Union formation. As one progresses upward through the highest sediments of the Lance formation the remains of dinosaurs become rare and finally absent; evidently we see here a record of the decline of these dominant Cretaceous reptiles, their gradual diminution in numbers until the last of their kind succumbed. About sixty feet above the highest sandstones in the Lance formation containing the bones of dinosaurs are beds of black lignites and coals, and above these the typical Fort Union sediments, in which the remains of primitive mammals are found.

So in these two examples, which might be repeated, but always with differences in detail, at other places in the world, we see the exit of the rulers of the Mesozoic. We see the end of a long and important chapter of earth history.

This brings us to the great question – why did the dinosaurs and their contemporaries, the pterosaurs, the ichthyosaurs and the plesiosaurs, become extinct? This, one of the great questions of geologic history, has gone unanswered for many decades.

It may be said that the extinction of animals and plants is the result of their inability to become adapted to changing conditions. This is a good statement of a very general kind, but it doesn't help us to understand just what happened in any particular case of extinction.

An obvious and an all too easy explanation is the catastrophic one. Did some great event take place that wiped out these reptiles? If so, why should a great catastrophe be so selective – why should it have caused the extinction of five orders of reptiles and allowed the continuation of five others? Why should all families and genera and species belonging to these five orders have disappeared completely? Moreover, if it was a physical catastrophe of some sort, why is it not recorded in the rocks? The continuity of sediments to be seen in certain localities as Cretaceous beds are succeeded by Tertiary beds indicates an orderly world in those distant days, like the orderly world we know. And indeed this is an expression of the principle of uniformitarianism, so important to the science of geology. From all of the records of the rocks, the world around, there is ample reason to think that earth processes and life processes in the past were as they are today; that events of past ages must be explained by the forces which we see acting in Nature at the present time. There is no place for world-wide catastrophes in the world of the past or of the present if the principle of uniformitarianism has any validity.

But if there were no world-wide catastrophes at the close of Cretaceous history there probably were some changes. The end of the Mesozoic era was marked by the beginning of the Laramide Revolution, the uplift of the lands that gave birth to our modern mountain chains. Would the Laramide Revolution have brought about the extinction of various reptiles at the end of Cretaceous times? It is difficult to visualize any real instance of cause and effect here, because the Laramide Revolution stretched through a long span of geologic time. It began in the Cretaceous, but it continued through a considerable part of Cenozoic time; it was a geologic process that lasted through millions of years of earth history. So it would seem that this long-drawn-out event could hardly in itself have brought about the end of the dinosaurs and of other reptiles, because evolutionary adaptations could surely have been made to such slowly changing conditions. Certainly this would seem to have been the case for the five orders of reptiles that survived beyond the end of the Cretaceous period.

If the making of mountains was on such a grand and sustained scale, is it possible that climates were affected by these uplifts of the land through time, to the detriment of some groups of reptiles? Reptiles are sensitive to temperatures, lacking as they do any internal mechanisms for temperature control, and in view of this it has been suggested that if there were a general cooling of climates during the transition from the Cretaceous into the Tertiary period, such might have led to the disappearance of the dinosaurs and of some other reptiles that had for so long flourished on the earth. Once again the question may be asked why, if the extinctions at the close of the Cretaceous period were the result of a cooling of the earth's temperatures, on land and in the sea, the disappearance of the reptiles should have been so strictly selective on a zoological basis? Why did not some of the dinosaurs survive – at least some of the smaller ones, which, it would seem, might have been as fully adapted for continuation beyond the end of the Cretaceous period as were the crocodiles*. Furthermore, the evidence of the fossils would seem to indicate that

*See 'Page Corrections and Emendations' in Addendum.

the early Tertiary years were not so very different from those of the late Cretaceous, as far as climates and environments were concerned. One would therefore think that the dinosaurs of the tropical and subtropical lands, so widely spread and characteristic of late Cretaceous time, could very easily have continued and lived in the similarly widely spread tropical and subtropical lands of early Tertiary time. The transition from the one period to the next was gradual, and the conditions were not very greatly changed.

Perhaps there was no drop in world temperatures at the end of the Cretaceous period, but rather a rise that brought the dinosaurs, the pterosaurs and the great marine reptiles to the end of their long histories. This suggestion has been advanced and supported by strong arguments. The principal consideration in favor of the theory of reptilian extinctions by rising temperatures is based upon the known temperature tolerances of modern reptiles. The American alligator, for example, will perish if the body temperature reaches the level of thirty-eight degrees Centrigrade (approximately one hundred degrees Fahrenheit). Is it possible that environmental temperatures rose to such levels during the Cretaceous–Tertiary transition that the dinosaurs and certain other reptiles were unable to survive ? The great dinosaurs may have found it frequently difficult to protect themselves, as do many smaller reptiles, being unable to burrow in the ground because of their size. But if the large dinosaurs were thus wiped out by high temperatures, why did not the smaller ones survive, since they presumably could get away from adverse environmental conditions. Why did many of the large crocodilians continue ? If high temperatures are to be invoked, why was the extinction along definite zoological lines ? This is the sticking point.

It has been argued that perhaps high temperatures which may have developed at the end of the Cretaceous period did not bring about the extinction of the dinosaurs because of any effect upon the body temperatures of the adults, but rather because of deleterious effects, producing sterility, that these high temperatures would have had upon the reproductive cells. Here again, how is one to explain such selectivity in the extinctions that took place ? Even supposing that there were shifts of temperatures, either up or down, that would have affected the land-living reptiles, would such shifts have had the same effects on the ocean-dwelling reptiles ? Would not the oceans, in which temperatures are less extreme and less variable than on land, afford havens in which the marine reptiles might have continued ? Why did the ichthyosaurs, plesiosaurs and mosasaurs become extinct along with the dinosaurs and pterosaurs ?

Moreover, and this cannot be ignored, there is no evidence whatsoever in the geologic record to indicate any appreciable raising of temperatures at the close of the Cretaceous period. The fossils seem to show that early Tertiary environments may have been somewhat cooler than those of the late Cretaceous (but not by any great margin) but they certainly do not show that the environments of the later period were warmer than those of the earlier one.

The suggestion has been made that the Cretaceous reptiles which became extinct suffered from competition with the early mammals. It is difficult to visualize any direct competition between the ruling reptiles and the contemporary mammals, all of which were small. But there might have been more subtle types of competition. Did the Cretaceous mammals eat dinosaur eggs ? Very likely they did, but such predation would hardly have brought about the extinction of the dinosaurs. Many modern reptiles continue in undiminished numbers, year after year, in spite of the fact that their eggs are considered as desirable delicacies by numerous animals which roam across the reptilian breeding grounds. The same very probably was true for the Cretaceous reptiles. Like all reptiles through the ages they must have laid eggs in great numbers, so that there were good statistical chances for a certain proportion of the eggs to hatch and the young to survive.

Moreover, how could predation of reptile eggs have been a factor in the extinction of the late Cretaceous marine reptiles, all of which probably reproduced by live births ?

It has even been suggested that the eggs of the late Cretaceous reptiles for some reason were not viable, an argument based upon the large quantities of dinosaurian egg shells found in certain upper Cretaceous sediments. But one must remember that egg shell fragments by the thousands (which have been found) and unhatched eggs by the hundreds (which have also been found) are but an infinitesimal fraction of the numbers of eggs laid by millions of late Cretaceous dinosaurs, living through many successive millennia.

Even though the eggs were normally fertile, is it possible that the dinosaurs, the pterosaurs and the marine reptiles were wiped out by some epidemic at the end of the Cretaceous period ? Hardly, if our knowledge of modern epidemics is at all valid as applied to past history. Epidemics are usually quite specific in their effect, or at most they affect only a limited number of closely related or closely associated organisms. If the various reptiles that disappeared at the end of Cretaceous history were eliminated from the earth by this cause they must have suffered from a wave of parallel epidemics, all sweeping across the earth more or less together. It seems like too strong a coincidence of events to seem very plausible.

What about radiation? This suggested cause for reptilian extinctions, like some others, is difficult to envisage because of its probable wide effect upon many animals rather than its selective effect upon a few reptilian orders. But is it not possible that the surviving reptiles owed their continuation to an ability to protect themselves from extraterrestrial radiation – by burrowing in the ground or by remaining in the waters of rivers, lakes and oceans? Here again, many exceptions can be cited. Of course, the giant dinosaurs were exposed to the untoward events of environmental changes or catastrophes, but there were small dinosaurs that should have been able to survive. And other large reptiles as well as small ones did live through from the Cretaceous into the Tertiary period. With this theory we have come a full circle back to the idea of catastrophes as the cause of extinctions. And in making the circle there have been many ingenious proposals encountered, all of which are inadequate, for one or many reasons, to account for the extinction at the end of Cretaceous time of the dinosaurs, the pterosaurs and the marine reptiles.

Very probably the extinction that brought the Age of Reptiles to a close was complex in nature, the result of many subtle and interacting causes. Very probably we shall never be able to fathom the nature of the extinction, removed as we are from the end of the Cretaceous period by some seventy million years of time. All that we can do is to note the extent and the patterns of this extinction and to speculate about its probable causes. Certainly it was real enough, as we have seen, and was extensive enough to bring about a profound change in the life of the earth.

The dinosaurs disappeared from the lands, as did the flying reptiles from the air and the several groups of marine reptiles from the oceans. From that time when the final years of Cretaceous history merged into the initial years of Tertiary history the long dominance of the reptiles, extending back through two hundred million years of geologic time, came to an end. The Age of Reptiles had vanished into the lost years of the distant past.

Bibliography

The presentation of this bibliography involves some problems and requires some explanations. The problems are inherent in the contents of a book which cuts across the subjects that comprise other books, monographs and papers. The Age of Reptiles as here presented has been a theme composed in part of historical geology, in part of vertebrate paleontology, in part of paleogeography and in part of some other subjects. Consequently the references listed below are of various kinds and concerned with various subjects, for which reason the explanations are in order.

Of course, the literature pertinent in one way or another to the subject of this book is vast, and no attempt can be made to list the many references upon which the text has been based. It is possible only to give a sampling, and to hope that the sample is reasonably representative. The works selected are standard texts, and more specialized contributions – books, monographs and shorter papers.

The listing naturally includes some books on historical geology, in which tetrapods are usually casually mentioned, and some books on systematic paleontology, in which faunas generally are only briefly considered, if at all. It includes zoology texts in which tetrapod relationships are considered, but usually not their evolutionary history through time. It includes books in which evolutionary principles are elucidated, and other books of such theoretical nature. And, of course, it includes technical papers of more limited scope, these being selected to give as nearly as possible some background information on the tetrapods, the faunas and the formations that make up the Age of Reptiles. It also includes some very useful bibliographies.

As has been implied, no one work exactly covers the field of this book. Thus the reader must choose the subject he may wish to follow in more detail, and try to pick a reference from the list that will be helpful. Needless to say almost all of the works in the bibliography that follows have bibliographies of their own, so one thing leads to another.

Books

ANDREWS, H. N. Jr., *Studies in Paleobotany*. New York, 1961: Wiley.
    An excellent text on the evolution of plant life as interpreted from the fossils.
AUGUSTA, J., *Prehistoric Animals*. Illus. Z. Burian; transl. G. Horn. London, 1956: Spring Books.
    A large book with superb restorations of past life, including many late Paleozoic and Mesozoic scenes.

AUGUSTA, J., *Prehistoric Reptiles and Birds*. Illus. Z. Burian; transl. M. Schierl. London, 1961: Hamlyn.
> Pterosaurs and Mesozoic birds. Outstanding restorations.

BEERBOWER, J. R., *Search for the Past*. Englewood Cliffs, New Jersey, 1960: Prentice-Hall.
> A most original treatment of paleontology, with particular emphasis on the interpretation of past life as based upon the principles of heredity, speciation and evolution.

BELLAIRS, A. d'A, *Reptiles*. London, 1957: Hutchinson.

BELLAIRS, A. d'A., *Reptiles: Life History, Evolution and Structure*. New York, 1960: Harper Torchbook 520. (Paperback edition of above.)
> A small but extraordinarily comprehensive and valuable book on the reptiles, living and fossil.

BRINKMANN, R., *Geologic Evolution of Europe*. Transl. J. E. Sanders. Stuttgart, 1960: Ferdinand Enke Verlag.
> A condensed version of a standard textbook on historical geology for European students. It is limited to the historical geology of Europe.

BROOKS, C. E. P., *Climate through the Ages. A Study of the Climatic Factors and their Variations*. New York and Toronto, 1949: McGraw-Hill.
> A standard text on past climates.

BROOM, R., *The Mammal-Like Reptiles of South Africa and the Origin of Mammals*. London, 1932: Witherby.
> The mammal-like reptiles of the Karroo series, as they were known thirty years ago, are summarized by a man who studied them in field and laboratory through a long lifetime.

CARRINGTON, R., *The Study of our Earth*. New York, 1956: Harper.

CARRINGTON, R., *A Guide to Earth History*. New York, 1961: The New American Library of World Literature. (Paperback edition of the above.)
> Historical geology, simply told.

CARTER, G. S., *Animal Evolution*. London, 1951: Sidgwick and Jackson.
> A concise presentation of evolution, as understood by present-day zoologists.

COLBERT, E. H., *The Dinosaur Book*. 2nd ed. New York, 1951: McGraw-Hill.
> This is, in spite of its title, essentially a book on tetrapods that lived during the Age of Reptiles.

COLBERT, E. H., *Evolution of the Vertebrates*. New York, 1955: Wiley.
> A review of vertebrate evolution based largely on the fossil evidence.

COLBERT, E. H., *Evolution of the Vertebrates*. New York, 1961: Science.
> A paperback edition, complete.

COLBERT, E. H., *Dinosaurs. Their Discovery and their World*. New York, 1961: Dutton.
> A book for the general reader.

DU TOIT, A. L., *Our Wandering Continents*. Edinburgh, 1937: Oliver and Boyd.
> The thesis of continental drift by one of its most vigorous champions.

DU TOIT, A. L., *The Geology of South Africa*. Edinburgh, 1954: Constable; New York, Hafner.
> A necessary reference for the student of Karroo reptiles.

EFREMOV, I. A., *Doroga Vetrov*. Moscow, 1956.
   The narrative account, in Russian, of Russian paleontological exploration in Central Asia.
GIGNOUX, M., *Géologie stratigraphique*. 4th ed. revised. Paris, 1950: Masson.
   One of the standard classics.
GREGORY, W. K., *Evolution Emerging: A Survey of Changing Patterns from Primeval Life to Man*. New York, 1951: Macmillan.
   A monumental essay on vertebrate evolution by a great scholar.
HEILMANN, G., *The Origin of Birds*. London and New York, 1926: Appleton.
   A well-presented account of the origin and evolution of the birds, with particular attention given to Jurassic and Cretaceous birds.
KUHN-SCHNYDER, E., *Geschichte der Wirbeltiere*. Basil, 1953: Schwabe.
   A general account.
KUMMEL, B., *History of the Earth*. San Francisco and London, 1961: Freeman.
   An excellent, comprehensive historical geology centered on North America, but of world-wide scope.
MATTHEW, W. D., *Climate and Evolution*. Vol. I, New York, 1939: New York Academy of Sciences, Special Publ.
   A classic study, first published in 1915. It is especially concerned with the distribution of tetrapods and past continental relations.
NAIRN, A. E. M. (ed.), *Descriptive Palaeoclimatology*. New York and London, 1961: Interscience.
   A symposium by outstanding authorities that attempts to interpret climates of the past.
PEYER, B., *Geschichte der Tierwelt*. Zürich, 1950: Büchergilde Gutenberg.
   Not a textbook, but rather paleontological essays.
PIVETEAU, J. (ed.), *Traité de Paléontologie: Tome V, Amphibiens, Reptiles, Oiseaux*. Paris, 1955: Masson.
   One volume of a series on paleontology. The various chapters are written by authorities who have special knowledge of the subject being treated. Mammal-like reptiles are not included in this, but in the following volume.
PIVETEAU, J., *Traité de Paléontologie: Tome VI, volume 1, L'Origine des Mammifères et les Aspects Fondamentaux de leur Évolution*. Paris, 1955: Masson.
   The mammal-like reptiles are included in this volume, also Mesozoic mammals.
READ, H. H., *Geology*. London, 1949: Oxford University Press.
   A standard text.
ROMER, A. S., *Vertebrate Paleontology*. Chicago, 1945: University of Chicago Press.
   The standard work in English on fossil vertebrates. Three chapters are devoted to the distribution, and the age relationships, of vertebrates, during the Paleozoic, Mesozoic and Cenozoic eras. Includes a bibliography.
ROMER, A. S., *Osteology of the Reptiles*. Chicago, 1956: University of Chicago Press.
   A comprehensive survey of reptilian osteology. Fossil forms are emphasized. An invaluable classification of reptiles down to genera is a major feature of this book. Includes a bibliography.
ROZHDESTVENSKY, A. K., *Auf Dinosaurierjagd in der Gobi*. Leipzig, 1958: Brockhaus Verlag. (A German translation, from the original Russian.)
   A narrative, parallel to that by Efremov, of Russian paleontological exploration in Central Asia.

SHERLOCK, R. L., *The Permo-Triassic Formations. A World Review.* London and New York, 1947: Hutchinson.
   A survey.
SIMPSON, G. G., *The Meaning of Evolution.* New Haven, 1949: Yale University Press.
   An interpretation by one of the foremost authorities of the present time.
SIMPSON, G. G., *The Major Features of Evolution.* New York, 1953: Columbia University Press.
   Searching analyses of the processes and results of evolution through time.
SIMPSON, G. G., *Life of the Past.* New Haven, 1953: Yale University Press.
   The paleontological story, simply and effectively told, with illustrations by the author.
SIMPSON, G. G., PITTENDRIGH, C. S. & TIFFANY, L. H., *Life. An Introduction to Biology.* New York, 1957: Harcourt, Brace.
   A book without parallel, the standard for students at the University level. Perhaps no other book covers the subject so thoroughly.
STOKES, W. L., *Essentials of Earth History.* Englewood Cliffs, New Jersey, 1950: Prentice-Hall.
   A book particularly concerned with the principles governing the evolution of the earth and of life. Fossil vertebrates receive more attention than is usual in a book on historical geology.
SWINTON, W. E., *The Dinosaurs.* London, 1934: Murby.
   A valuable survey of the dinosaurs. Now out of print.
WEGENER, A., *The Origin of Continents and Oceans.* London, 1924: Methuen.
   Wegener, although not the originator of the theory of drift, was the man who above all others developed it. This is his classic work on the subject.
WILLISTON, S. W., *Water Reptiles of the Past and Present.* Chicago, 1914: University of Chicago Press.
   A popular book on Mesozoic and other aquatic reptiles, by a great authority.
WILLS, L. J., *A Palaeogeographical Atlas of the British Isles and Adjacent Parts of Europe.* London and Glasgow, 1951: Blackie.
   Ancient land and sea areas.
YOUNG, J. Z., *The Life of the Vertebrates.* London, 1950: Oxford University Press.
   A book useful to all students of the vertebrates. Adaptations, relationships and behavior (where known) of vertebrates, recent and extinct.

Monographs

ALLEN, P., 1949. Notes on Wealden Bone-Beds. *Proceedings of the Geological Association,* **60**, 275.
   The lower Cretaceous of Europe.
ANDREWS, C. W., *A Descriptive Catalogue of the Marine Reptiles of the Oxford Clay.* London, 1910–1913: printed by Order of the Trustees of the British Museum.
   The marine tetrapod fauna of England in late Jurassic time, as known from the fossils.
ARAMBOURG, C., 1952. La Paléontologie des Vertébrés en Afrique du Nord Française. *XIX Congrès Géologique International. Monographies Régionales, Hors Série.*
   A resumé in which attention is given to reptiles of the Mesozoic. There is a valuable bibliography.

ARKELL, W. J., 1935. On the Nature, Origin and Climatic Significance of the Coral Reefs in the Vicinity of Oxford. *Quarterly Journal of the Geological Society of London*, **91**, 77.
   Evidence on late Jurassic climates in northern Europe.
ARKELL, W. J., *Jurassic Geology of the World*. New York, 1956: Hafner.
   The first attempt at a synthesis of one system on the basis of marine faunas.
BRINK, A. S., 1956. Speculations on Some Advanced Mammalian Characters in the Higher Mammal-Like Reptiles. *Paleontologia Africana*, **4**, 77.
   A philosophical paper, by one of the active modern students of the Karroo fauna, that supplements his many excellent descriptions.
BROILI, F. & SCHROEDER, J., 1934–1937, *Beobachtungen an Wirbeltieren der Karrooformation. I–XXVIII*. München. Bayerische Akademie der Wissenschaften.
   A series of papers on the tetrapods of the Karroo beds.
BROOM, R., 1910. A Comparison of the Permian Reptiles of North America with those of South Africa. *Bulletin of the American Museum of Natural History*, **28**, 197.
BROOM, R., 1913. On the Relationship of the South African Permian Reptiles to those of Russia. *Journal of Geology*, **21**, 728.
   These are but two among a very large series of papers by Broom on Karroo tetrapods. Much of his vast knowledge on this subject is summed up in his book of 1932, cited under Books.
BROWN, B. & SCHLAIKJER, E. M., 1940. The Structure and Relationships of *Protoceratops*. *Annals of the New York Academy of Sciences*, **40**, 133.
   Analysis of a primitive ceratopsian.
BUCHER, W. H., 1952. Continental Drift versus Land Bridges. *Bulletin of the American Museum of Natural History*, **99**, 93.
   The evidence against continental drift.
CAMP, C. L., 1936. A New Type of Small Bipedal Dinosaur from the Navajo Sandstone of Arizona. *University of California Publications, Bulletin of the Department of Geological Sciences*, **24**, 39.
   A fleeting glimpse of early Jurassic (possibly late Triassic) life in North America.
CAMP, C. L., 1945. *Prolacerta* and the Protorosaurian Reptiles. *American Journal of Science*, **243**, 18, 84.
   Relationships of these reptiles.
CASE, E. C., 1919. The Environment of Vertebrate Life in the Late Paleozoic in North America: a Paleogeographic Study. *Publications of the Carnegie Institution of Washington*, no. 283.
CASE, E. C., 1926. Environment of Tetrapod Life in the Late Paleozoic of Regions other than North America. *Publications of the Carnegie Institution of Washington*, no. 375.
   Two large monographs on late Paleozoic climates, as deduced largely from tetrapod evidence.
CASIER, E., *Les Iguanodons de Bernissart*. Brussels, 1960: Edition au Patrimoine de l'Institut Royal des Sciences Naturelles de Belgique.
   A very readable account of the discovery, restoration and interpretation of a large series of *Iguanodon* skeletons.

COLBERT, E. H., 1951. Environment and Adaptations of Certain Dinosaurs. *Biological Review*, **26**, 265.
An essay on probable dinosaurian adaptations correlated with probable climates.
COLBERT, E. H., 1952. The Mesozoic Tetrapods of South America. *Bulletin of the American Museum of Natural History*, **99**, 237.
Bearing of fossil reptiles on the avenues of overland migration between South America and other continents during the Mesozoic.
COLBERT, E. H., 1958. Tetrapod Extinctions at the End of the Triassic Period. *Proceedings of the National Academy of Sciences*, **44**, 973.
A comparison of Triassic tetrapod extinctions with those that occurred at the end of the Cretaceous.
COLBERT, E. H. & GREGORY, J. T., 1957. Correlation of Continental Triassic Sediments by Vertebrate Fossils. *Bulletin of the Geological Society of America*, **68**, 1,456.
A review of the age relationships of Triassic vertebrate-bearing sediments in North America.
COTT, H. B., 1961. Scientific results of an enquiry into the ecology and economic status of the Nile crocodile (*Crocodilus niloticus*) in Uganda and Northern Rhodesia. *Transactions of the Zoological Society of London*, **29**, iv, 211.
This study gives much insight into the life of modern crocodilians, and is therefore useful as a base for an interpretation of the life of extinct archosaurian reptiles.
CROMPTON, A. W. & CHARIG, A. J., 1962. A New Ornithischian from the Upper Triassic of South Africa. *Nature*, **196**, 1,074.
An important announcement, establishing the beginning of ornithischian evolution in the Triassic – as had long been suspected.
CROMPTON, A. W. & ELLENBERGER, F., 1957. On a New Cynodont from the Molteno Beds and the Origin of the Tritylodontids. *Annals of the South African Museum*, **44**, 1.
A study of advanced therapsids.
DUNBAR, C. O. *et al* 1960. Correlation of the Permian Formations of North America. *Bulletin of the Geological Society of America*, **71**, 1,763.
The report of a committee of experts in this field.
DU TOIT, A. L., 1927. A Geological Comparison of South America with South Africa. *Carnegie Institution of Washington*, publ. 381.
The resemblances of the two great southern hemisphere continents are noted in detail, as arguments in favor of drift.
DU TOIT, A. L., 1948. The Climatic Setting of the Vertebrate Faunas of the Karroo System and its Significance. *Robert Broom Commemorative Volume, Special Publ. of the Royal Society of South Africa*, 113.
The environments of the Karroo reptiles.
EFREMOV, I. A., 1940. Preliminary Description of the New Permian and Triassic Tetrapods from U.S.S.R. *Travaux Institute Paléontologie Academie Sciences U.R.S.S.*, **10**, ii.
One of many descriptions of the Permian–Triassic tetrapod fauna of northern Russia.

EFREMOV, I. A., 1940. Die Mesen-Fauna der permischen Reptilien. *Neues Jahrbuch für Mineralogie, Geologie und Paläontologie. Beilage-Band Abt. B*, **84**, 379.
The fauna of the second zone in the Russian sequence.

EFREMOV, I. A., 1957. The Gondwana System of India and the Vertebrate Life History in the Late Paleozoic. *Journal of the Paleontological Society of India, D. N. Wadia Jubilee Number*, **2**, 24.
Gondwanaland and the evidence of late Paleozoic tetrapods in India and other parts of Asia.

FRAAS, E., 1889. Die Labyrinthodonten der schwäbischen Trias. *Palaeontographica*, **36**, 1.
The last of the labyrinthodonts.

FRITSCH, A., *Fauna der Gaskohle und der Kalksteine der Permformation Böhmens*. Prague, 1879–1901.
An elaborate monograph describing an early tetrapod fauna from central Europe.

GILMORE, C. W., 1914. Osteology of the Armored Dinosauria in the United States National Museum, with Special Reference to the Genus *Stegosaurus*. *Bulletin of the United States National Museum*, **89**, 1.
Monographic treatment of the stegosaurs.

GILMORE, C. W., 1926. The Fauna of the Arundel Formation of Maryland. *Proceedings of the United States National Museum*, **59**, 581.
Cretaceous reptiles from eastern North America.

GILMORE, C. W., 1933. On the Dinosaurian Fauna of the Iren Dabasu Formation. *Bulletin of the American Museum of Natural History*, **67**, 23.
Description of a Mongolian Cretaceous fauna.

GILMORE, C. W., 1946. Reptilian Fauna of the North Horn Formation of Central Utah. *United States Geological Survey*, Professional Paper no. 210–C, i, 29.
The last of the dinosaurs.

GRACHT, W. van W. van der, et al., 1928. Theory of Continental Drift. *American Association of Petroleum Geologists, Tulsa, Oklahoma*.
A symposium on the subject.

HAUGHTON, S. H., 1919. A Review of the Reptilian Fauna of the Karroo System *Transactions of the Geological Society of South Africa*, **22**, 1.
A very useful review.

HAUGHTON, S. H., 1924. The Fauna and Stratigraphy of the Stormberg Series. *Annals of the South African Museum*, **12**, 323.
The upper Triassic stratigraphy and fossil reptiles of South Africa are summarized.

HAUGHTON, S. H., 1953. Gondwanaland and the Distribution of Early Reptiles. *Geological Society of South Africa, Alex L. du Toit Memorial Lectures*, **56** (Annexure), 1.
The relationships of southern continents in the light of the distribution of early reptiles.

HENBEST, L. G. (ed.), et al., 1952. Distribution of Evolutionary Explosions in Geologic Time. *Journal of Paleontology*, **36**, 298.
Review by a panel of experts of the reasons why organisms suddenly appear in great numbers in the geologic record.

HUENE, F. von, *Die Ichthyosaurier des Lias und ihre Zusammenhänge*. Berlin, 1922: Evolution of the ichthyosaurs.

HUENE, F. von, 1929. Los Saurisquios y Ornitisquios del Cretáceo Argentino. *Annales Museum La Plata*, **3**, (Series 2a), 1.
A large and detailed monograph on the Cretaceous dinosaurs of Patagonia.

HUENE, F. von, *Die Fossile Reptil-Ordnung Saurischia, ihre Entwicklung und Geschichte*. Leipzig, 1932: Gebrüder Borntraeger. Monographien zur Geologie und Palaeontologie, series 1, heft 4.
This is a large monograph on the saurischian dinosaurs, with emphasis on Triassic forms.

HUENE, F. von, 1940. Die Saurier der Karroo-, Gondwana-und verwandten Ablagerungen in faunistischer, biologischer und phylogenetischer Hinsicht. *Neues Jahrbuch f. Min.*, etc., **83**, 246.
A useful comparison of Permian–Triassic faunas throughout the world.

HUENE, F. von, 1940. The Tetrapod Fauna of the Upper Triassic Maleri Beds. *Memoirs of the Geological Survey of India*, N.S., **32** (no. 1), 1.
A monographic description.

HUENE, F. von, *Die Fossilen Reptilien des Südamerikanischen Gondwanalands*. München, 1935–1942: Beck'sche Verlagsbuch-handlungen, i, 1.
A detailed study of the Triassic reptiles of southern Brazil.

HUENE, F. von, Die Fauna der Panchet-Schichten in Bengalen. *Zentralblatt für Mineralogie*, etc., *Abteilung B*, no. 11, 354.
The lower Triassic tetrapods of India.

HUENE, F. von, *Paläontologie und Phylogenie der Niederen Tetrapoden*, Jena, 1956: Fischer Verlag.
A systematic treatment of fossil amphibians and reptiles by a great scholar who has devoted a long life to this subject.

JANENSCH, W., 1914. Übersicht über die Wirbeltierfauna der Tendaguru-Schichten, etc. *Archiv für Biontologie*, **3**, i, 81.
An early account of the upper Jurassic reptilian fauna of Africa.

JANENSCH, W., 1935. Die Schädel der Sauropoden *Brachiosaurus*, *Barosaurus* und *Dicraeosaurus* aus den Tendaguru-Schichten Deutsch-Ostafrikas. *Palaeontographica* (Suppl. 7), **1**, ii, 147.
Elucidation of part of the Tendaguru fauna. One of a series of papers devoted to this subject.

JUST, T., 1952. Fossil Floras of the Southern Hemisphere and their Phytogeographical Significance. *Bulletin of the American Museum of Natural History*, **99**, 189.
Southern continents and the evidence of the fossil plants.

KAY, M., 1952. Stratigraphic Evidence Bearing on the Hypothesis of Continental Drift. *Bulletin of the American Museum of Natural History*, **99**, 159.
Discussion by a stratigrapher of continental drift.

KUHN, E., 1952. Die Triasfauna der Tessiner Kalkalpen. XVII. *Askeptosaurus italicus* Nopcsa. *Schweizerischen Paläontologischen Abhandlungen*, **69**, 1.
Description of an important member of the Triassic fauna found in southern Switzerland.

KUHN-SCHNYDER, E. & VONDERSCHMITT, L., 1954. Geologische und paläonto-
logische probleme des Südtessins. *Eclogae Geological Helvetiae*, **46**, 223.
A review.

LAPPARENT, A. F. de, 1954. Etat actuel de nos connaissances sur la stratigraphie,
la paléontologie et la tectonique des – Gres de Nubie – du Sahara central.
Congrès géologique international. XIX Session, Alger, **21**, 113.
Review of work being done in North Africa.

LEHMAN, P. P., 1961. Les Stegocéphales du Trias de Madagascar. *Annales de
Paléontologie*, **47**, 111.
Relationships of Triassic amphibians of Madagascar to those of South Africa
and Russia.

LULL, R. S., 1933. A Revision of the Ceratopsia or Horned Dinosaurs. *Memoirs of
the Peabody Museum of Natural History*, **3**, iii.
The evolution of the horned dinosaurs.

LULL, R. S., 1953. Triassic Life of the Connecticut Valley. *Connecticut Geological
and Natural History Survey Bulletin*, no. 81.
An account of the animals and plants that lived in New England during late
Triassic times, as known from fossils found in the Newark beds. Much attention is given to tetrapod footprints.

LULL, R. S. & WRIGHT, N., 1942. Hadrosaurian Dinosaurs of North America.
Geological Society of America Special Papers, no. 40.
A comprehensive and detailed study of the late upper Cretaceous duck-billed
dinosaurs, showing adaptations and evolutionary trends.

MAYR, E. (ed.), *et al.*, 1952. The Problem of Land Connections Across the South
Atlantic, with Special Reference to the Mesozoic. *Bulletin of the American
Museum of Natural History*, **99**, 79.
A symposium largely devoted to the theories of continental relationships dur-
ing Mesozoic and earlier times, as deduced from various lines of evidence.
Certain individual papers especially pertinent to the Age of Reptiles are sepa-
rately listed in this bibliography.

MCKEE, E. D., *et al.*, 1956. Paleotectonic Maps Jurassic System. *United States
Geological Survey: Miscellaneous Investigations*.
A large folio compiled with great care from an immense background of know-
ledge and experience.

MCKEE, E. D., *et al.*, 1959. Paleotectonic Maps Triassic System. *United States
Geological Survey: Miscellaneous Investigations*.
A companion to the Jurassic folio.

OLSON, E. C., 1951. The Evolution of a Permian Vertebrate Chronofauna. *Evolution*, **6**, 181.
An interesting study of the evolution of successive faunas in one locality.

OLSON, E. C., 1957. Catalogue of Localities of Permian and Triassic Terrestrial
Vertebrates of the Territories of the U.S.S.R. *The Journal of Geology*, **65**, 196.
Presentation in English of a summary of the vertebrates and stratigraphy of the
continental Permian–Triassic red beds of Russia. Done by a leading authority
not only on the reptiles of this age, but also on the Russian scientific literature,
collections and localities.

OLSON, E. C., 1962. Late Permian Terrestrial Vertebrates, U.S.A. and U.S.S.R. *Transactions of the American Philosophical Society, N.S.*, **52**, ii, 1.
A comprehensive comparison of great significance.

OLSON, E. C. & BEERBOWER, J. R., 1953. The San Angelo Formation, Permian of Texas, and its Vertebrates. *Journal of Geology*, **61**, 389.
Tetrapods from the base of the middle Permian in North America.

PARRINGTON, F. R., 1948. Labyrinthodonts of South Africa. *Proceedings of the Zoological Society of London*, **118**, ii, 426.
The Karroo amphibians; one of a considerable series of papers on Karroo tetrapods by a leading authority.

PARRINGTON, F. R. and WESTOLL, T. S., 1940. On the Evolution of the Mammalian Palate. *Philosophical Transactions of the Royal Society of London, Series B*, **230**, 305.
An important contribution on the transition from reptile to mammal that took place in early Mesozoic times, by two outstanding authorities on primitive tetrapods.

PATTERSON, B., 1956. Early Cretaceous Mammals and the Evolution of Mammalian Molar Teeth. *Fieldiana*, **13**, 1.
Evidence on the mammals that lived in Cretaceous times, and the course of their evolutionary development.

PEABODY, F., 1948. Reptile and Amphibian Trackways from the Lower Triassic Moenkopi Formation of Arizona and Utah. *University of California, Bulletin of the Department of Geological Science*, **27**, 295.
Careful interpretations from footprints of Triassic tetrapods and the environments in which they lived.

PEYER, B., 1931–1937. Die Triasfauna der Tessiner Kalkalpen. I–XII. *Abhandlungen Schweizerischen Paläontolgischen Gesellschaft*, **50–59**.
A series of monographs on a well-preserved fauna, containing some unusual reptiles, from southern Switzerland.

PRICE, L. I., 1946. Sôbre um Novo Pseudosuquio do Triássico Superior do Rio Grande do Sul. *Departamento Nacional da Produção Mineral, Divisão de Geologia e Mineralogia Boletim*, no. 120.
Additional evidence on the Triassic tetrapod fauna of Brazil.

PRICE, L. I., 1950. Os Crocodilideos da Fauna Formação Baurú do Cretáceo Terrestre do Brasil Meridional. *Anais da Academia Brasileira de Ciencias*, **22**, 473.
The continental Cretaceous of Brazil, and some of its tetrapods.

REESIDE, J. B., Jr., *et al.*, 1957. Correlation of the Triassic Formations of North America Exclusive of Canada. *Bulletin of the Geological Society of America*, **68**,
Report of a committee of experts in this field.   [1,451.

ROBINSON, P. L., 1962. Gliding Lizards from the Upper Keuper of Great Britain. *Proceedings of the Geological Society, London*, no. 1601, 137.
Some of the earliest known lizards, surprisingly highly specialized for gliding.

ROMER, A. S., 1930. The Pennsylvanian Tetrapods of Linton, Ohio. *Bulletin of the American Museum of Natural History*, **59**, 77.
Study of an early tetrapod fauna, composed mainly of amphibians. A parallel study of similar fossils in the British Museum collections, by M. Steen, was published in 1930 in the *Proceedings of the Zoological Society of London*.

ROMER, A. S., 1935. Early History of Texas Redbeds Vertebrates. *Bulletin of the Geological Society of America*, **46**, 1,597.

A survey of the Wichita and Clear Fork faunas by a paleontologist who has spent much time exploring the Texas redbeds, and studying the fossils from them.

ROMER, A. S., 1947. Review of the Labyrinthodontia. *Bulletin of the Museum of Comparative Zoology at Harvard College*, **99**, 1.

The definitive monograph on the labyrinthodont amphibians.

ROMER, A. S., 1960. Vertebrate-Bearing Continental Triassic Strata in Mendoza Region, Argentina. *Bulletin of the Geological Society of America*, **71**, 1,279.

A preliminary account of a Triassic region of immense importance.

ROMER, A. S. & PRICE, L. L., 1940. Review of the Pelycosauria. *Geological Society of America, Special Papers*, no. 28.

A detailed monograph on the mammal-like reptiles of the Wichita and Clear Fork beds of Texas, and associated formations.

ROSENKRANTZ, A. & BROTZEN, F. (eds), 1960. The Cretaceous–Tertiary Boundary. *International Geological Congress, Report of the Twenty-First Session, Norden. Part V, proceedings of section 5*.

A symposium with many valuable papers by students of the subject. The paper by William A. Clemens on the stratigraphy of the type Lance formation is especially pertinent.

RUSSELL, L. S., 1930. Upper Cretaceous Dinosaur Faunas of North America. *Proceedings of the American Philosophical Society*, **69**, 133.

A useful summary.

RUSSELL, L. S., 1932. The Cretaceous–Tertiary Transition of Alberta. *Transactions of the Royal Society of Canada, Third Series*, **26**, iv, 121.

The end of the Age of Reptiles and the beginning of the Age of Mammals as recorded in the rocks.

RUSSELL, L. S., 1939. Land and Sea Movements in the Late Cretaceous of Western Canada. *Transactions of the Royal Society of Canada, Third Series*, **33**, iv, 81.

The delineation of Cretaceous lands and seas in an area where dinosaurs were abundant.

SCHUCHERT, C., 1918. Age of the American Morrison and East African Tendaguru Formations. *Bulletin of the Geological Society of America*, **29**, 245.

A comparison of the upper Jurassic dinosaur-bearing formations.

SCHUCHERT, C., 1929. Review of the Late Paleozoic Formations and Faunas, with Special Reference to the Ice Age of Middle Permian Time. *Bulletin of the Geological Society of America*, **39**, 769.

An important paper.

SCHUCHERT, C., 1932. Gondwana Land Bridges. *Bulletin of the Geological Society of America*, **43**, 875.

The evidence in favor of land bridges between southern continents.

SIMPSON, G. G., *A Catalogue of the Mesozoic Mammalia in the Geological Department of the British Museum*. London, 1928: printed by Order of the Trustees of the British Museum.

A monographic study of the archaic mammals that were contemporaneous with the dinosaurs.

SIMPSON, G. G., 1929. American Mesozoic Mammals. *Memoirs of the Peabody Museum of Yale University*, **3**, i.
A study parallel to the one previously cited, but based on fossils from North America, especially those collected by O. C. Marsh and his associates.

SIMPSON, G. G., 1935. The First Mammals. *Quarterly Review of Biology*, **10**, 154.
Review of the subject by the leading authority.

STEEN, M., 1934. The Amphibian Fauna from the South Joggins, Nova Scotia. *Proceedings of the Royal Society of London, 1934*, 465.
The record of early labyrinthodont amphibians, living in an ancient forest, set within a swamp.

STEEN, M., 1938. On the Fossil Amphibia from the Gas Coal of Nyrany and Other Deposits in Czechslovakia. *Proceedings of the Zoological Society of London, B*, **108**, 205.
A primitive tetrapod fauna.

STERNBERG, C. M., 1949. The Edmonton Fauna and Description of a New Triceratops from the Upper Edmonton Member: Phylogeny of the Ceratopsidae. *Annual Report of the National Museum of Canada for the Fiscal Year 1947–1948*, Bulletin no. 113, 33.
Stratigraphic occurrences of some dinosaurs and their interpretation.

STOKES, W. L., 1944. Morrison and Related Deposits in and Adjacent to the Colorado Plateau. *Bulletin of the Geological Society of America*, **55**, 951.
A modern stratigraphic study of the Morrison formation.

TEICHERT, C. (ed.), *et al.*, 1952. Symposium sur les Séries de Gondwana. *XIX Congrès Géologique International. Alger 1952*.
Views of authorities from all over the world on the past relationships of the southern continents.

WALKER, A. D., 1961. Triassic Reptiles from the Elgin Area: *Stagonolepis, Dasygnathus* and their Allies. *Philosophical Transactions of the Royal Society of London, Series B* (no. 709), **244**, 103.
Entirely new light is thrown upon some of the upper Triassic reptiles of northern Europe. More is to follow.

WATSON, D. M. S., 1913. The Beaufort Beds of the Karroo System of South Africa. *Geological Magazine, N.S.*, **10**, 388.
Discussion by an authority.

WATSON, D. M. S., 1926. The Evolution and Origin of the Amphibia. *Philosophical Transactions of the Royal Society of London, B*, **214**, 189.
A comprehensive study and interpretation of Paleozoic amphibians.

WATSON, D. M. S., 1942. On Permian and Triassic Tetrapods. *Geological Magazine*, **79**, 81.
An essay on tritylodonts and other contemporaneous reptiles.

WEEKS, L. G., 1947. Paleogeography of South America. *Bulletin of the American Association of Petroleum Geologists*, **31**, 1,194.
A comprehensive review of the limits of land and ocean in and around South America through the ages.

WELLES, S. P., 1943. Elasmosaurid Plesiosaurs with Description of New Material from California and Colorado. *Memoirs of the University of California*, **13**, 125.
Cretaceous plesiosaurs – their adaptations and evolution.

WELLES, S. P., 1947. Vertebrates from the Upper Moenkopi Formation of Northern Arizona. *University of California Publications, Bulletin of the Department of Geological Science*, **27**, 241.
   A description of lower or middle Triassic tetrapods.
WILLIS, B., 1932. Isthmian Links. *Bulletin of the Geological Society of America*, **43**, 917.
   The concept of narrow isthmian links between continents is developed, in opposition to the theory of drift.
WIMAN, C., 1929. Die Kreide-Dinosaurier aus Shantung. *Paleontologia Sinica, Series C*, **6**, i, 1.
   Cretaceous dinosaurs of East Asia.
YOUNG, Chung-Chien, 1940. Preliminary Notes on the Mesozoic Mammals of Lufeng, Yunnan. *Bulletin of the Geological Society of China*, **20**, 93.
   Description of tritylodonts from China.
YOUNG, Chung-Chien, 1951. The Lufeng Saurischian Fauna in China. *Palaeontologica Sinica*, no. 134, 19.
   The upper Triassic reptiles of western China.
ZANGERL, R., 1935. *Pachypleurosaurus edwardsi, Cornalia* sp. Osteologie – Variationsbreite – Biologie. *Abhandlungen Schweizerischen Paläontologischen Gesellschaft*, **55**, 1.
   One of the series of monographs by Peyer and his associates on the Triassic reptiles found in southern Switzerland.

Bibliographies

CAMP, C. L. & VANDERHOOF, V. L., 1940. Bibliography of Fossil Vertebrates, 1928–1933. *Geological Society of America*, Special Paper no. 27.
CAMP, C. L., TAYLOR, D. N. & WELLES, S. P., 1942. Bibliography of Fossil Vertebrates, 1934–1938. *Geological Society of America*, Special Paper no. 42.
CAMP, C. L., WELLES, S. P. & GREEN, M., 1949. Bibliography of Fossil Vertebrates, 1939–1943. *Geological Society of America*, Memoir 37.
CAMP, C. L., WELLES, S. P. & GREEN, M., 1953. Bibliography of Fossil Vertebrates, 1944–1948. *Geological Society of America*, Memoir 57.
HAY, O. P., 1902. Bibliography and Catalogue of the Fossil Vertebrata of North America. *Bulletin of the United States Geological Survey*, no. 179.
HAY, O. P., 1929. Second Bibliography and Catalogue of the Fossil Vertebrata of North America. *Carnegie Institution of Washington*, publ. no. 390, **1**.
HAY, O. P., 1930. Second Bibliography and Catalogue of the Fossil Vertebrata of North America. *Carnegie Institution of Washington*, publ. no. 390, **2**.
ROMER, A. S., WRIGHT, N. E., EDINGER, T. & VAN FRANK, R., 1962. Bibliography of Fossil Vertebrates Exclusive of North America, 1509–1927. *Geological Society of America*, Memoir 87, **1**, **2**.

Addendum

Introduction

THREE GENERAL TOPICS will be addressed in this Addendum:
1. Large aspects of tetrapod taxonomy.
2. Plate Tectonics, in the early literature of this subject referred to as 'Continental Drift'.
3. The distributions of late Paleozoic and Mesozoic tetrapods, as interpreted from our present knowledge of Plate Tectonics.

In addition, brief remarks will be made concerning details on specified pages that require corrections or emendations.

At first glance this list may appear formidable, demanding perhaps such critical reexamining and questioning of the original text as to raise queries concerning the validity of what was written thirty years ago. But there need not be deprecating doubts about earlier views of a past world. From whatever viewpoint we may look at fossils and at the rocks within which they are contained, the basic facts are there. Thus there can be no denying the validity of a good fossil with proper, well-authenticated data concerning locality and stratigraphic occurrence. There can be no denying the nature of rocks, of rock strata, and where they occur. Our present-day understanding of rocks and fossils is a matter of learning how they accord with or are at variance with other aspects of geology and biology. In short, our new knowledge as developed during the past three decades is largely incremental to what we knew before, and it is primarily this incremental knowledge that will be discussed in these pages. Where new knowledge has invalidated former concepts, such replacement of the old by the new must be freely acknowledged.

The Large Aspects of Tetrapod Taxonomy

Our concepts concerning the relationships of organisms have developed through the years largely as the result of new knowledge acquired in field and laboratory. So far as animals are concerned, Carl von Linné (Linnaeus) laid the foundation for our understanding of basic zoological relationships in 1758, with the publication of the tenth, definitive edition of his great *Systema Naturae*—the fountainhead for binomial taxonomy (which he invented) and for the classification of organisms, fossil and recent. The Linnaean system has withstood the test of time, and today, with its range of categories from highest to lowest, is the basis for the classification of tetrapods published in the 1965 edition of *The Age of Reptiles*, as well as of revisions, to be discussed in these pages.

It should be mentioned here that a new and in many respects a revolutionary system of analysis and classification, known as *cladistics*, has arisen during the past three decades. Cladistics stems from the publication of a book entitled *Grundzüge einer Theorie der phylogenetischen Systematik* by W. Hennig in 1950. The system of cladistics has been variously received by modern zoologists and paleontologists, enthusiastically embraced by some, completely rejected by others. It has its virtues, which should be recognized, and its shortcomings, which also should be recognized. Since it is a very complex subject, to which even the briefest and simplest explanation would be a disconcerting side issue at this point, no attempt at a discussion will be presented.

Rather, immediate attention will be addressed to a revised classification along Linnaean lines, as intimated in a previous paragraph, devoted to the tetrapods that lived during the Age of Reptiles. For practical purposes the categories in descending grades to be considered in this classification are restricted from the full hierarchy as shown herewith:

Phylum
Subphylum
Class
Subclass
Infraclass
Superorder
Order
Superfamily
Family
Genus
Species

In the classification here set forth, the two highest categories, namely Phylum and Subphylum, may be taken for granted. At the lower end of the listing the categories of Superfamily, Family, Genus and Species are not included for the sake of simplicity. The subject of taxonomic relationships is being considered here in their larger aspects; therefore the status of taxons (as individual categories are designated) below the rank of Orders is purposely not considered.

A Restricted Classification of Tetrapods

PHYLUM Chordata
  SUBPHYLUM Vertebrata
    CLASS Amphibia
      SUBCLASS Labyrinthodontia
        ORDER Ichthyostegalia: Devonian–Carboniferous
        ORDER Temnospondyli: Carboniferous–Triassic
        ORDER Anthracosauria: Carboniferous–Triassic
      SUBCLASS Lepospondyli
        ORDER Aistopoda: Carboniferous–Permian
        ORDER Nectridia: Carboniferous–Permian
        ORDER Microsauria: Carboniferous–Permian
        ORDER Lysorophia: Carboniferous–Permian
      SUBCLASS Lissamphibia
        ORDER Gymnophiona: Paleocene–Recent
        ORDER Caudata: Jurassic–Recent
        ORDER Proanura: Triassic
        ORDER Anura: Jurassic–Recent

    [Amphibia or Reptilia (uncertain) Diadectids: Carboniferous–Permian]
    CLASS Reptilia
      SUBCLASS Anapsida
        ORDER Captorhinida: Carboniferous–Triassic
        ORDER Mesosauria: Carboniferous–Permian
      SUBCLASS Testudinata
        ORDER Chelonia: Triassic–Recent
      SUBCLASS Diapsida
        ORDER Araeoscilida: Carboniferous–Permian
        ORDER Choristodera: Cretaceous–Eocene
      INFRACLASS Lepidosauromorpha
        ORDER Eosuchia: Permian–Triassic
        ORDER Sphenodontida: Triassic–Recent
        ORDER Squamata: Triassic–Recent
      INFRACLASS Archosauromorpha
        ORDER Rhynchosauria: Triassic
        ORDER Thalattosauria: Triassic

ORDER Trilophosauria: Triassic
ORDER Protorosauria: Triassic
SUPERORDER Archosauria
ORDER Thecodontia: (Permian)–Triassic*
ORDER Crocodylia: Triassic–Recent
ORDER Pterosauria: Triassic–Cretaceous
ORDER Saurischia: Triassic–Cretaceous
ORDER Ornithischia: Triassic–Cretaceous
SUPERORDER Sauropterygia
ORDER Nothosauria: Triassic
ORDER Plesiosauria: Jurassic–Cretaceous
SUPERORDER Placodontia: Triassic
SUBCLASS Ichthyopterygia: Triassic–Cretaceous
SUBCLASS Synapsida
ORDER Pelycosauria: Carboniferous–Permian
ORDER Therapsida: Permian–Jurassic
CLASS Aves
SUBCLASS Archaeornithes: Jurassic
SUBCLASS Ornithurae: Cretaceous–Recent
CLASS Mammalia
SUBCLASS Prototheria
ORDER Monotremata: Cretaceous–Recent
ORDER Triconodonta: Triassic–Cretaceous
SUBCLASS Allotheria
ORDER Multituberculata: Triassic–Eocene
SUBCLASS Theria
INFRACLASS Trituberculata
ORDER Symmetrodonta: Triassic–Cretaceous
ORDER Eupantotheria: Jurassic–Cretaceous
INFRACLASS Metatheria: Cretaceous–Recent
INFRACLASS Eutheria: Cretaceous–Recent

Amphibia—Discussion
(See pages 12–13, 25–26)

It now seems proper to accept a three-fold division of the amphibians, rather than the two-fold arrangement published in the original edition of

---

*Some paleontologists maintain that the name Thecodontia should be abandoned, because of the diversity among genera comprising this order.

The Age of Reptiles. This is effected by placing the modern amphibian groups, the caecilians, salamanders, and frogs and toads, in a separate category, the Lissamphibia, at the subclass level. One strong argument for this grouping is that the lissamphibians, in decided contrast to all other amphibians, have *pedicellate* teeth, in which the base and crown of each tooth are separated by a zone of fibrous tissue.

In this revised arrangement the two other subclasses are retained, but with most of the labyrinthodonts included within an expanded Order of temnospondyls. Those labyrinthodonts designated as embolomeres, gephyrostegids, and seymouriamorphs (this latter frequently placed among the primitive reptiles) are separated from the temnospondyls in the Order Anthracosauria. The two Orders can be distinguished each from the other by, among other things, the nature of their vertebral structures: interlocking blocks in the temnospondyls, secondarily simplified in the anthracosaurs.

The lepospondyls retain their previous status as small, quite varied aquatic amphibians.

Reptilia—Discussion
(See pages 14–22, 26–27)

The reptiles are composed of a rather diverse assemblage of *amniotes*, tetrapods reproductively advanced beyond the amphibians by reason of direct development of the embryo without the interposition of a larval (or 'pollywog') stage within an aquatic environment. The two other components of the amniotes are the birds and the mammals.

The reptiles are here envisaged as being contained within five major divisions having the rank of subclasses. They may be broadly but not completely defined by the patterns (or the lack thereof) of openings in the skull roof behind the orbits.

The most primitive skull pattern, a direct inheritance from labyrinthodont ancestors, is that of the anapsid reptiles, in which the skull roof consists of solidly articulated bones behind the eyes, the only opening in this bony skull roof being the small pineal foramen, located on the suture between the two parietal bones. This opening housed the pineal organ, a light receptor characteristic of many amphibians and reptiles.

Such solid-skulled tetrapods belonging to the subclass Anapsida, the most primitive of reptiles, range in geologic age from the Carboniferous through the Triassic.

The second subclass of reptiles is the Testudinata or turtles, which also have an anapsid skull pattern. In many classifications the turtles are included within the Anapsida, but modern evidence would seem to indicate that the turtles (or testudines) had a comparatively late origin from primitive captorhinids, thereafter following an evolutionary trend very different from all other reptiles. Therefore it is logical to place the testudines within a separate subclass, extending from Triassic into modern times.

The third and largest reptilian subclass is the Diapsida, in which there are two openings on each side of the skull behind the eyes, these being the superior and lateral temporal fenestrae, separated from each other by a bar composed of the postorbital and squamosal bones.

The diapsids may be subdivided into two great moieties—the lepidosauromorphs (lizards and snakes, sphenodonts and certain early primitive diapsids) and the archosauromorphs (various Triassic reptiles dominated by a large diverse order known as the thecodonts, the crocodilians, two orders of dinosaurs designated as the saurischians and ornithischians and the flying reptiles or pterosaurs). These were the dominant Mesozoic reptiles, arising in Carboniferous times, some of them persisting into our modern world.

The Mesozoic nothosaurs, plesiosaurs, placodonts and ichthyosaurs have often been included within a major group designated as the Euryapsida (as in the 1965 edition of *The Age of Reptiles*). The skull is distinguished by a single large opening or fenestra behind the eyes on each side, bounded *below* by the postorbital and squamosal bones—obviously the homolog of the upper skull opening of the diapsids.

These reptiles are now considered as modified diapsids. The nothosaurs and plesiosaurs may be included within the Diapsida as a major group, perhaps of superorder status, designated as the Sauropterygia. The placodonts are likewise to be included within the Diapsida, perhaps as a separate order.

The ichthyosaurs, even though characterized by an euryapsid type of skull, with an upper temporal opening, are so isolated from all other reptiles, and of such obscure origins, that it is logical to place them in a separate fourth subclass, the Ichthyopterygia.

The fifth reptilian subclass is a well-knit group, the Synapsida, ranging in geologic age from the Carboniferous into the Jurassic. In these reptiles there is a single temporal opening on each side behind the eyes, quite obviously homologous with the lateral opening of the diapsids. Certain advanced synapsids are the direct ancestors of the mammals.

Aves—Discussion
(See pages 22–23, 27)

The birds are essentially of diapsid relationships, probably descended from certain theropod dinosaurs, or alternatively derived in common with the theropods from thecodont diapsids.

Mammalia—Discussion
(See pages 22–24, 27)

Finally there are the mammals, of synapsid origin. Three groups of mammals lived during the Mesozoic era, the age of reptiles. And some of these primitive mammals lived into early Cenozoic and recent times. The three mammalian groups were the prototheres, including the Mesozoic triconodonts and the modern monotremes (the platypus and echidna); the allotheres, composed of the multituberculates ('rodent-like' mammals persisting into basal Cenozoic times); and the therians—essentially the mammals as we know them in our modern world. The therians may in turn be subdivided into three groups: the trituberculates, primitive mammals of Jurassic age, some of which, the eupantotheres, were ancestral to modern mammals; the metatherians, the pouched marsupials; and the eutherians, the placental mammals that comprise the overwhelming bulk of modern mammals. These last two groups, marsupials and placentals, range in geologic age from the late Cretaceous period to modern times.

Plate Tectonics

In 1964, when *The Age of Reptiles* was being written, a profound revolution in geological thinking was under way, a revolution emanating from studies being made in the fields of geophysics, structural geology and other aspects of the earth sciences. It was based upon the premise of a mobile earth on which ancient continents were perpetually migrating from one position to another across the surface of the globe. The idea, put forward by a German meteorologist, Alfred Wegener, in 1912, was originally called 'continental drift'. It is now more properly known as Plate Tectonics.

As propounded by Wegener, continental drift seemed to many paleontologists to be at odds with the prevailing ideas about the distributions of organisms on stable continents through geologic time. So it was that *The Age of Reptiles* was written without any references to continental drift and the effect that moving continents might have had on the distributions of late Paleozoic and Mesozoic tetrapods.

Yet in those days significant geophysical studies of the continents and particularly of the ocean basins were being prosecuted at various universities and research institutes throughout the world. The evidence for a mobile earth according to the precepts of Plate Tectonics was becoming increasingly convincing.

Then, paleontologically speaking, the final unequivocal evidence supporting the reality of Plate Tectonics was the discovery and excavation in 1968 and 1969–1970 of Lower Triassic amphibians and reptiles in the Transantarctic Mountains, about four hundred miles from the South Pole. These fossils are not only generically but often specifically identical to fossils found in the Karroo sediments of South Africa. All of which points without doubt to the fact that in early Triassic times the particular assemblage represented by the Antarctic fossils, a strictly terrestrial fauna known in South Africa as the *Lystrosaurus* fauna, inhabited southern Africa and eastern Antarctica when these two continental areas, now separated from each other by some six thousand miles of ocean, were part of a single land mass.

Perhaps it is ironic that I was the leader of the paleontological crew that excavated the first Triassic tetrapods to be found in Antarctica. Today numerous Mesozoic amphibians and reptiles, including dinosaurs, are being found in the South Polar continent.

Thanks to the fossil tetrapods of Antarctica, supplementing as they do the indisputable evidence from physical geology and geophysics, Plate Tectonics is now so firmly established as to be factual rather than theoretical geology.

Ancient Continents and Tetrapods

There is no point in expounding the facts of Plate Tectonics at length here. Suffice it to say that the crust of the earth is clearly seen to consist of a series of large plates that are constantly in motion. Some plate borders are separating from each other, as seen in the Midatlantic ridge running from north to south through the middle of the North and South Atlantic oceans, while others are colliding, as seen in the impact between the great Pacific Plate and the western borders of North and South America.

Such is the evidence revealed by the arrangements and the movements of the plates as we see them today. When earth-science research is carried back through geologic time, a dynamic and awesome view of our mobile sphere through the ages becomes evident.

Thus it is clear that in mid-Paleozoic times there existed one great supercontinent, which has been named Pangaea. This enormous land mass stretched north and south essentially from pole to pole, and east and west across some 200 degrees of latitude. Its northern-hemisphere part, which is called Laurasia, consisted of what was to become North America and Eurasia, lacking peninsular India. Its southern hemisphere, which is called Gondwanaland, or Gondwana, was made up of what would be Africa, South America, peninsular India, Australia and Antarctica. During and after the Mesozoic era, the several components of the great supercontinent broke away from their primordial attachments and drifted to the positions that the continents occupy today.

Of course the movements of plates with their included continental blocks and oceanic basins have had profound effects through the millennia on the distributions and relationships of terrestrial plants and animals, from mid-Paleozoic times to the present day.

This brings us to the distributional maps published on pages 39, 73, 124 and 166 of *The Age of Reptiles*. These maps show the prime localities for Permian, Triassic, Jurassic and Cretaceous tetrapods as known in 1965, and as plotted on a world map, with the continents in their present positions.

Maps of Pangaea During the Age of Reptiles

The four maps in the present section are simplified renditions, based upon but modified from Dietz and Holden, 1970 (see 'Additions to Bibliography' at end of Addendum)*. They are intended to give some insight into the supposed spatial relationships of continental blocks during the Age of Reptiles, namely during the Permian, Triassic, Jurassic and Cretaceous periods of earth history, according to the concept and evidence of Plate Tectonics.

During Permian times it would seem that Pangaea was truly a unified supercontinent, with broad ligations between the several blocks that eventually were to separate into the continents as we know them.

---

*In the form in which the maps in the present section now appear, they were originally published in *Evolution of the Vertebrates*, by Edwin H. Colbert and Michael Morales, copyright © 1991 by Wiley-Liss, Inc. They are reprinted here by permission of Wiley-Liss, Inc., a division of John Wiley & Sons, Inc.

The beginning of rifting is apparent in the Triassic map, where the clockwise rotations of the two Americas resulted in the initial openings, from south to north, of the North and South Atlantic oceans. Yet the continental ligations were sufficiently close to allow, for example, the wide distribution of the *Lystrosaurus* fauna.

In Jurassic times the separation between Laurasia and Gondwanaland became broader, yet continental connections were still of such dimensions as to allow the worldwide distributions of numerous diverse dinosaurs.

By Cretaceous times the continental blocks were assuming the shapes and approaching the locations of the modern continents. Of particular significance was the separation of peninsular India from its primordial position as a wedge between Africa and Antarctica and the beginning of its rapid drift toward, and eventual collision with, southern Asia, thereby elevating the Himalayan barrier. South America was on its way to becoming a Cenozoic island continent on which unique mammals were to

Permian Pangaea, according to the evidence of Plate Tectonics. In this reconstruction, as in the maps of Triassic, Jurassic and Cretaceous Pangaea, Laurasia is composed of North America (left) and Eurasia minus peninsular India (right). Gondwana is composed of South America (left), Africa (right), Antarctica (below Africa), Australia (to the right of Antarctica) and peninsular India (between Africa and Antarctica).

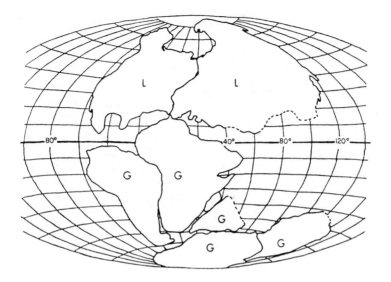

Triassic Pangaea. Abbreviations: G—Gondwana, L—Laurasia.

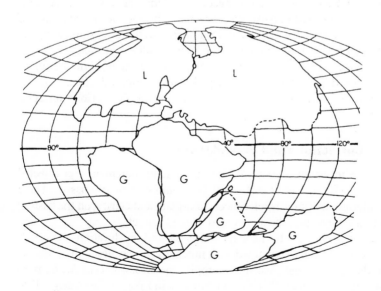

Jurassic Pangaea. Abbreviations: G—Gondwana, L—Laurasia.

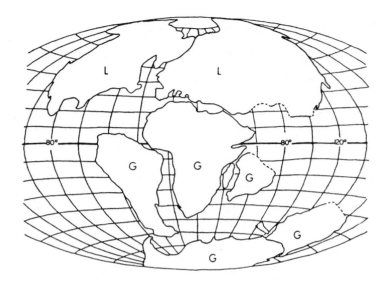

Cretaceous Pangaea. Abbreviations: G—Gondwana, L—Laurasia.

evolve, with the South Atlantic becoming a long, narrow ocean. Antarctica, still connected to Australia, served as a bridge for the expansion of early South American marsupials into Australia, thereby establishing the marsupial fauna so distinctive of the 'down-under' continent.

It is quite evident that the progressive differentiations of the continental blocks during the Age of Reptiles had profound effects on the evolution of tetrapods and the composition of the various tetrapod faunas.

Page Corrections and Emendations

In the following paragraphs certain salient statements on selected pages of *The Age of Reptiles* will be mentioned or discussed. These remarks are intended as references, to explain and clarify, on the basis of modern knowledge, the subjects to which they refer.

Page 5. Since 1965 the geologic time scale and the durations of periods in years have been determined with much greater accuracy than was the case thirty years ago. See, for example, the *Geologic Time Scale*, published by the Geological Society of America in 1983, or the *Geologic Time Scale* by Harland, Armstrong, Cox, Craig, Smith and Smith, published by Cambridge University Press in 1989. However the more recent determinations of period durations do not for the most part significantly alter the *relative* dimensions of the geological time scale as presented in 1965. A comparison of the geological time scale as published in the 1965 edition of *The Age of Reptiles* with that of Harland *et al.*, 1989, is shown below in the section 'Tables and Diagrams'.

Page 10. Research during the past three decades suggests that the differences in metabolism and body temperatures between the ectotherms (amphibians and reptiles) on the one hand, and the endotherms (birds and mammals) on the other, are and were not as clear-cut as formerly was thought to be the case.

Page 12. Recent discoveries indicate that labyrinthodont amphibians persisted beyond the Upper Triassic boundary.

Page 21. The pterosaurs are now known to have arisen in late Triassic times.

Page 43. At the present time there is an unresolved controversy as to whether *Diadectes* was an amphibian or a reptile.

Page 51. Much research has been carried on in recent years, especially by A. W. Crompton, concerning the jaw mechanics and diet in the dicynodont reptiles.

Pages 61–62. Much of the discussion on these and adjacent pages has been resolved by geophysical and paleontological studies prosecuted during the past three decades. The evidence now indicates, quite unequivocally, that the modern evidence of Plate Tectonics is the key to continental relationships and the distributions of land-living tetrapods during the long interval from Permian to modern times. The reality of a one-time Pangaea, its subsequent fragmentation and the eventual movements of its several components—the ancestors of our modern continents—is now so firmly established as to transcend the limits of theory and become recognized as probable geological facts. Furthermore, the distributions of terrestrial tetrapods from the Permian to recent times are in full accord with geophysical evidence.

Page 63. The existence of a great Pangaean supercontinent that extended in Permian times across all latitudes north and south, from the one polar region to the other, and was inhabited throughout by a remarkable panoply of amphibians and reptiles, bespeaks a world of seemingly benign environments. Yet the presence of Permo-Carboniferous tillites, old, consolidated glacial rubble often showing oriented grooves (the record of glacial ice advancing across rock surfaces), indicates the existence of a glacial regime centered in southern Africa and extending into what are now South America, India, Antarctica and Australia. Therefore some paleontologists have advocated that certain Gondwana reptiles, notably the synapsids, were 'warm-blooded' and protected by a covering of hair.

Page 64. It should be noted here that there were significant extinctions among the tetrapods marking the transition from Permian to Triassic times (see pages 66, 112–113).

Page 65. The stereospondyl labyrinthodonts are now generally included within the temnospondyli (see the section of the Addendum 'A Restricted Classification of Tetrapods').

Page 66. The position of eosuchians as ultimate ancestors of the archosaurian reptiles may now be questioned. The eosuchians probably are more logically placed as lepidosaur progenitors.

Page 67. As the result of new discoveries and attendant research, *Eunotosaurus* is now regarded as belonging to a distinct suborder of reptiles, perhaps only distantly related to the turtles. The ancestry of turtles probably is to be found among primitive captorhinids.

Page 68. The ancestry of the ichthyosaurs is still as obscure as ever. Any suggestions, such as the one on this page, are highly speculative.

Pages 69–70. The earliest thecodont, *Archosaurus*, is from the Upper Permian of Europe, but except for this lonesome forerunner, the thecodonts are strictly Triassic archosaurs. The classification of these reptiles is being much debated, and assignment of the pseudosuchians as representing a comprehensive group of primitive thecodonts is no longer utilized.

Page 82. Several Lower Triassic therocephalian genera are now recognized. As for *Prolacerta*, recent discoveries and research show that the affinities of this reptile are with the archosaurs rather than with early lizards.

Page 84. According to our more recent knowledge pertaining to the mammal-like reptiles, the diademodonts, in the strict sense, are of early Triassic age. But related cynodonts, particularly those belonging to an evolutionary advanced family, the Tritylodontidae, range upward into sediments of late Triassic and even early Jurassic age.

Page 92. The view, prevalent for many years, that the rhynchosaurs were closely related to the modern rhynchocephalian *Sphenodon* has now been replaced by the generally accepted opinion that the presence of certain primitive features in the skulls of rhynchosaurs and sphenodonts denote a common ancestry among primitive diapsid reptiles.

Page 93. *Hesperosuchus*, originally described as a thecodont, is now widely viewed as an early crocodilian.

Page 95. *Teratosaurus* may questionably be a thecodont rather than a dinosaur.

Page 96. *Eupelor* is now considered synonymous with *Metoposaurus*.

Pages 102, 105. The arguments on these pages concerning past continental relationships are made obsolete by the modern evidence of Plate Tectonics.

Page 116. The description of a watery Jurassic world does not contravene the evidence of Plate Tectonics. Many of the Jurassic waterways were shallow incursions across continental blocks.

Page 121. During recent years new Liassic dinosaurs have been discovered in various parts of the world.

Page 123. The Kayenta formation is now almost universally regarded as of early Jurassic age.

Page 129. The fossil record of Lower and Middle Jurassic tetrapods is today far more abundant than might be assumed from what was written thirty years ago.

Page 130. In addition to the three general regions cited as localities where Upper Jurassic dinosaurs have been collected, there might be mentioned the southwestern United States, northern Mexico, additional regions in Africa, widely distributed areas in Asia and localities in South America and Australia.

Page 137. There are now six known skeletons of *Archaeopteryx*.

Page 140. The Plate Tectonic evidence for the broad ligations between the several large segments of Pangaea explains the wide distributions of dinosaurs and other land-living tetrapods during Mesozoic times.

Page 141. Beautifully preserved and abundant dinosaurian fossils have been unearthed in western China since 1965.

Page 145. A large body of literature has been produced during the past three decades concerning Mesozoic climates and the possible physiology of large dinosaurs and other reptiles. Numerous debates have erupted at scientific meetings and in print devoted to the 'cold-blooded' versus 'warm-blooded' dinosaurs. The arguments still go on. Could the dinosaurs have lived in other than tropical climates? A very large book might be written devoted to what is said on this page of *The Age of Reptiles*. Indeed such a book appeared in 1980, entitled *A Cold Look at the Warm-Blooded Dinosaurs* and edited by D. K. Thomas and Everett C. Olson.

Page 148. As is the case with the evidence for lower and middle Jurassic tetrapods, that for lower Cretaceous vertebrates has been greatly expanded during the past thirty years. Therefore, the third paragraph on this page should be read with the above remark in mind.

Page 155. The fossil record does provide information about the various Wealden vertebrates, for example *Dryolestes*, a small mammal.

Page 156. *Pachyophis* is not necessarily the first snake known in the fossil record. *Lapparentophis* is from the lower Cretaceous of northern Africa.

Pages 156–157. A veritable eruption of dinosaurs has issued from China and Mongolia during the past thirty years to augment with remarkable detail our knowledge of dinosaurian evolution and distribution.

Page 161. Because of recent discoveries the Wealden fauna no longer is so isolated in the lower Cretaceous fossil record as was formerly the case.

Page 163. The pachycephalosaurs or 'dome-headed' ornithischians should be added to the roster of dinosaurs that arose and prospered during Cretaceous times.

Page 169. The troödonts, originally described from non-diagnostic teeth, are now questionably placed among the theropods.

Page 170. The discovery of late Cretaceous dinosaurs in northern Alaska adds some interesting fossils as well as attendant problems to the history of dinosaurs in North America.

Page 173. See preceding comment concerning troödonts. It is now widely assumed that the thick, bony dome comprising the top of the skull in the pachycephalosaurs or 'dome-headed' dinosaurs may have been for butting, analogous to the heavy horns in the modern bighorn sheep.

Page 174. *Albertosaurus* now supersedes 'Gorgosaurus' as the proper name for this theropod.

Page 183. *Quetzalcoatlus*, from the Upper Cretaceous of Texas, with a wingspan of 35 to 40 feet, was the giant among pterosaurs.

Page 189. See preceding discussions of Plate Tectonics. Dinosaurs are now known from localities throughout the earth, from as far north as Spitzbergen and from as far south as central Antarctica.

Page 193. 'Salamanders' in the broad sense of the word, are known from Mesozoic sediments, while the record of caecilians goes back to the Paleocene. Monotremes are known from the Cretaceous of Australia.

Page 194. 'Definitely ten reptilian orders'. In Robert Carroll's comprehensive textbook, *Vertebrate Paleontology and Evolution* (1988) there are twenty-three named reptilian orders, and several of uncertain relationships.

Page 195. Again, using Carroll's book as a source, and hoping that my counts are accurate, the following figures are presented as an update of those published in 1965. Number of Upper Cretaceous families of reptiles, 71. Number surviving at end of Cretaceous, 21. Number living today, 29. This last figure probably would be modified by herpetologists.

Page 197. The extinction of the dinosaurs is being hotly debated today between two schools of thought. On the one hand are the proponents of a sudden, dramatic event causing the extinction of the dinosaurs—probably a huge bolide, a comet or meteorite, striking the earth at the end of Cretaceous times. This idea is favored by many geologists, geophysicists and physicists. On the other hand are those, including most vertebrate paleontologists, who maintain that the dinosaurs suffered a slow decline during late Cretaceous times, resulting in the extinction of the ruling reptiles. At the present time there does not seem to be any prospect of a solution of the argument. Table 15 and Figure 66 are graphic representations interpreting the latter argument.

Page 201. It is now evident that some plesiosaurs and pterosaurs did continue into the final stages of Cretaceous history.

Page 204. There is a nagging question that remains throughout all of the discussions and arguments pertaining to the extinction of the dinosaurs: why did not some of the dinosaurs, particularly the smaller forms, continue past the close of Cretaceous history, as did turtles, crocodilians, lizards and snakes, and sphenodonts? Why was the extinction so strictly defined along zoological relationships? This question is a stumbling block to the theory of a great, catastrophic, sudden extinction.

Tables and Diagrams

INTRODUCTION

The various tables and diagrams published in the 1965 edition of *The Age of Reptiles*, although dated, are still useful in presenting the information for which they were designed. Unlike the four new maps that illustrate a concept of earth history that was little understood and less appreciated thirty years ago, the tables showing the distributions of tetrapods and the correlations of sediments with their included fossil faunas convey information that has been augmented rather than superseded by discoveries and research of the past three decades. Of course there are details in these tables and diagrams that need to be upgraded, while there are certain aspects of information that were presented in those years long past with which some paleontologists and geologists today will disagree. The disagreements may in part be based upon new knowledge, in part upon the inevitable differences of opinion that are integral to scientific research.

However, the tables and diagrams are retained as they were originally published—without apologies. In cases where there are significant discrepancies between information as set forth in the published tables and diagrams, and our present-day knowledge of such information, some explanatory remarks will be made in the following paragraphs. It is to be hoped that in this way the reader will be brought up-to-date concerning certain facts having to do with the evolution, relationships and distribution of terrestrial tetrapods that inhabited Pangaea during the Age of Reptiles, while at the same time this reader will gain some appreciation of the advances in our knowledge of life on the earth that have resulted from thirty years of intensive paleontological research.

TABLES 1–15—REMARKS

A discussion of the Geologic Time Scale has been presented in the remarks on page 5 in the section 'Page Corrections and Emendations'. At this place is a comparison of determinations of the lengths of periods in millions of years recently published.

	'AGE OF REPTILES' 1965	GEOL. SOC. AMERICA 1983	HARLAND ET AL. 1989
Cenozoic	70	66.4	65.64
Cretaceous	65	78	91
Jurassic	45	64	70.5
Triassic	35	37	37
Permian	45	41	45
Carboniferous	80	74	60
Devonian	50	48	56
Silurian	40	30	28
Ordovician	60	67	71
Cambrian	100	65	60
	590	570	583

Table 2 (page 40)

In recent years formational names have been applied to the previously named zones of the South African Sequence (see Table 3).

Table 3 (page 60)

PREVIOUS NOMENCLATURE			REVISED NOMENCLATURE

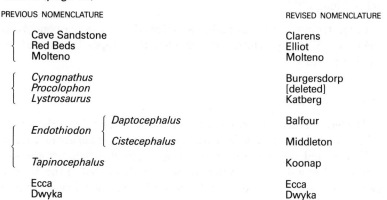

PREVIOUS NOMENCLATURE — REVISED NOMENCLATURE

⎰ Cave Sandstone — Clarens
⎱ Red Beds — Elliot
  Molteno — Molteno

⎰ *Cynognathus* — Burgersdorp
⎱ *Procolophon* — [deleted]
  Lystrosaurus — Katberg

⎰ *Endothiodon* ⎰ *Daptocephalus* — Balfour
⎱   ⎱ *Cistecephalus* — Middleton

  Tapinocephalus — Koonap

Ecca — Ecca
Dwyka — Dwyka

Table 4 (page 77)

The Wingate, Moenave and Kayenta formations of North America are now regarded as of Lower Jurassic affinities. Likewise, the Lufeng beds of China are now seen as extending into the Jurassic. The Triassic of Germany may now be subdivided as follows:

Rhaetic

Keuper	Knollenmergel Stubensandstein Buntemergel Schilfsandstein Gipskeuper Lettenkohle

Table 5 (page 104)

In this table the Kayenta, according to recent evidence, should be shifted up into the Jurassic. The Moenave and the Wingate may be considered as of Rhaetic age. In the European column the Keuper should not extend up to include the Rhaetic. As for the 'Lettenkohle' (Lettenkohl) and 'Gypskeuper' (Gipskeuper), see the comments above concerning Table 4.

Table 6 (page 107)

Large temnospondyl amphibians, referred to as stereospondyls in 1965, as well as phytosaurs, have been found in Upper Triassic beds in northern Africa.

Table 7 (page 108)

The term rhynchocephalians, as used in this table, includes the sphenodonts as well as the rhynchosaurs. The sphenodonts appear in Triassic sediments and continue into recent times. The rhynchosaurs are now considered as a distinct reptilian order, strictly limited to the Triassic period. The line for the pterosaurs should be extended downward into the Upper Triassic.

Table 8 (page 110)

The placodonts probably were bottom feeders in shallow, coastal waters. The marine turtles were and are inhabitants of the open ocean. The rhynchosaurs may have fed upon underground rhizomes and roots.

Table 9 (page 117)

The fossil record is sparse as to the presence of Lower Jurassic turtles, ichthyosaurs, plesiosaurs and pterosaurs outside of Europe. However, Lower Jurassic crocodilians are widely represented not only in Europe, but also in North America, South America, Asia and southern Africa. Theropod dinosaurs of this age are known from Africa, as well as from Europe and North America. Sauropod-type dinosaurs (including prosauropods) are recorded from North America and Asia in addition to the localities shown in the table. Ornithopod dinosaurs have been found in South Africa and Asia.

Table 10 (page 119)

The presence of giant sauropods in the Lower Jurassic Kota formation of India clearly shows that the trend to giantism was established at an early stage in the evolution of these dinosaurs.

Table 11 (page 142)

This table demonstrates the ubiquity of the dinosaurs in late Jurassic times. Not shown in the table are: frogs and crocodilians in South America, pterosaurs in North America and Asia, and mammals in Asia.

Table 12 (page 151)

Since this correlation table was published, a revealing series of theropod dinosaurs has been collected in the Lower Cretaceous Cloverly formation.

Table 13 (page 168)

Extensive and intensive field work in Mongolia has revealed a rich kingdom of Upper Cretaceous tetrapods, dominated by dinosaurs, many of which are new. This has led to a revised interpretation of the Upper Cretaceous sequence in Mongolia, which may be generally expressed in the following manner:

Nemeget
Bain Shire
Barun Goyot
Bain Dzak
Iren Dabasu
Oshih

Table 14 (page 195)

Today the number of reptilian families of late Cretaceous age, the number that became extinct during the transition from Cretaceous to Cenozoic times and the number existing at present will be different from the numbers published in 1965. This is owing, of course, to new discoveries and to changes in classification, all to be expected in three decades of paleontological endeavor. A count, based upon the classification in Carroll (1988), shows 80 families of late Cretaceous age, 23 families that survived the Cretaceous–Tertiary boundary and 42 families existing today. According to this count 35 families of Cretaceous reptiles (dinosaurs, pterosaurs, plesiosaurs and ichthyosaurs) failed to survive at the end of Cretaceous times.

Table 15 (page 198)

Clemens in 1986 published a comparison of the decline of dinosaurian genera in the western interior region of North America between Judithian times (roughly equivalent to the Belly River as used in the 1965 edition of this book) and Lancian times (equivalent to the Lance in that edition). His figures show a diminution of about 33 percent among the saurischian dinosaurs and of about 30 percent among the ornithischian dinosaurs during the final years of Cretaceous history. It would thus appear that some dinosaurs (at least) were 'on their way out' before the great extinction at the end of the Cretaceous.

CHARTS AND DIAGRAMS—REMARKS

Figure 20 (page 28)

The configuration for pterosaurs should extend down into the Upper Triassic.

Figure 21 (page 31)

An error in this diagram shows the ichthyosaurs as extending up into Tertiary times. These reptiles, of course, became extinct near the end of the Cretaceous period.

Figure 33 (page 66), Figure 44 (page 109), Figure 67 (page 202)

The figures for the disappearance of tetrapod genera during the three great extinctions—Upper Permian to Lower Triassic, Upper Triassic to Lower Jurassic and Upper Cretaceous to Lower Tertiary—are considerably larger as based upon counts of the classification published by Carroll in 1988. This is to be expected, owing in part to the increase of knowledge during a thirty-year period of very active paleontological field work and research and in part to increased and more sophisticated sources in the literature. The newer figures for the tetrapod genera are as follows:

Upper Permian 230, Lower Triassic 142
Upper Triassic 134, Lower Jurassic 64
Upper Cretaceous 346, Lower Tertiary 168

In short, there was an extinction rate for tetrapod genera from late Permian to early Triassic times of about 40 percent; from late Triassic to early Jurassic times, of about 50 percent; and from late Cretaceous to early Tertiary times, also of about 50 percent.

Figure 45 (pages 112–113)

This illustration, showing the ranges and abundance of tetrapods that lived during the Age of Reptiles, is still probably reasonably valid. As in previous charts or diagrams, the term rhynchocephalians is too inclusive by modern criteria, while the pterosaurs should be extended down into the Upper Triassic.

Figure 66 (page 199)

This illustration is a pictorial representation of the figures set forth in Table 15.

Additions to Bibliography

Needless to say a great many books and scientific papers pertinent to the subject of this volume have appeared during the past thirty years. Of particular interest has been the great outpouring of books and other contributions devoted to dinosaurs. Indeed, the recent interest in dinosaurs, not only among paleontologists, but among the general public—of all ages and persuasions—is one of the cultural phenomena of our modern world.

The bibliographical additions presented here reflect the wide interest in dinosaurs by including a few of the books that have been written. There are also a few other paleontological citations, as well as some dealing with Plate Tectonics.

The additions are, however, restricted; this is not the place to present even a modest attempt at a comprehensive list of books.

ALEXANDER, R. McN., *Dynamics of Dinosaurs and Other Extinct Giants*. New York, 1989: Columbia University Press.

CALDER, N., *The Restless Earth. A Report on the New Geology*. New York, 1972: The Viking Press.

CARPENTER, K. & CURRIE, J. (eds.), *Dinosaur Systematics. Approaches and Perspectives*. Cambridge, 1990: Cambridge University Press.

CARROLL, R. L., *Vertebrate Paleontology and Evolution*. New York, 1988: W. H. Freeman and Company.

CLEMENS, W. A., *In Dynamics of Extinction*. David K. Elliott (ed.) New York, 1986: John Wiley and Sons, Inc.

COLBERT, E. H., *Dinosaurs. An Illustrated History*. Maplewood, New Jersey, and New York, 1983: A Dembner Book, Hammond Incorporated.

COLBERT, E. H., *Wandering Lands and Animals. The Story of Continental Drift and Animal Populations*. New York, 1985: Dover Publications, Inc.

COLBERT, E. H. & MORALES, M., *Evolution of the Vertebrates. A History of the Backboned Animals Through Time*. New York, 1991: John Wiley and Sons, Inc.

DESMOND, A. J., *The Hot-Blooded Dinosaurs. A Revolution in Paleontology*. New York, 1975: The Dial Press.

DIETZ, R. S. & HOLDEN, J. C., *The Breakup of Pangaea*. New York, 1970: Scientific American, Vol. 223, pp. 30–41.

ELLIOTT, D. K. (ed.), *Dynamics of Extinction*. New York, 1986: John Wiley and Sons, Inc.

HALLAM, A., *A Revolution in the Earth Sciences. From Continental Drift to Plate Tectonics*. Oxford, 1973: Clarendon Press.

HOTTON, N., MacLEAN, P. D., ROTH, J. J. & ROTH, E. C., (eds.), *The Ecology and Biology of Mammal-Like Reptiles*. Washington, 1986: Smithsonian Institution Press.

KURTEN, B., *The Age of Dinosaurs*. New York, 1968: McGraw-Hill Book Company, World University Press.

NORMAN, D., *The Illustrated Encyclopedia of Dinosaurs*. New York, 1985: Crescent Books.

NORMAN, D. B., *Dinosaurs!* London, 1991: Boxtree Limited.

PADIAN, K. (ed.), *The Beginning of the Age of Dinosaurs*. Cambridge, 1986: Cambridge University Press.

RUSSELL, D. A., *A Vanished World. The Dinosaurs of Western Canada*. Ottawa, Canada, 1977: National Museum of Natural Sciences; Natural History Series No. 4.

SULLIVAN, W., *Continents in Motion. The New Earth Debate*. New York, 1974: McGraw-Hill Book Company.

THOMAS, D. K. & OLSON, E. C. (eds.), *A Cold Look at the Warm-Blooded Dinosaurs*. Boulder, Colorado, 1980: Westview Press.

WEISHAMPEL, D. B., DODSON, P. & OSMOLSKA, H. (eds.), *The Dinosauria*. Berkeley, 1990: University of California Press.

WILFORD, J. N., *The Riddle of the Dinosaur*. New York, 1985: Alfred A. Knopf.

Index

Abo-Cutler beds, 40
Abundance of Upper Cretaceous reptiles, 161–4
Acanthopholis, 155
Admiral formation, 42
Aetosaurus, 94
Age of Amphibians, 2
Age of Fishes, 2
Age of Mammals, 3
Age of Man, 3
Age of Reptiles, beginning of, 3; defined, 1, 6–7; duration of, 3
Agua Zarca member (of Chinle), 104
Aguja fauna, 175–6; formation, 165, 168, 175–6, 186
Aistopoda, 25
Alamosaurus, 179, 188
Alberti, H. von, 72
Alcova formation, 77, 104
Alligator, fig. 13
Allosaurus, 133, 136, 140; pl. 13
Allotheria, 27
Amniote egg, 3
Amphibia, 25
Amphibians, at end of Triassic, 106; contrast between Paleozoic and Mesozoic, 65–6; modern, 14; reproduction in, 2
Amphibians and Reptiles at transition from Triassic to Jurassic, 108
Amur beds, 168
American Museum of Natural History, 132, 186
Anapsida, 26
Anatosaurus, 179; fig. 60
Ancestral dinosaurs, 70
Anchiceratops, 178; fig. 60
Andrews, C. W., 16, 17
Angiosperms, Cretaceous radiation, 149
Animas formation, 165, 168
Ankylosaurus, 173, 178; pl. 18
Anning, Mary, 120
Anoa, 144
Anomoiodon, 78
Antarctosaurus, 186, 188

Antrodemus, 133; pl. 13
Anura, 25
Apatosaurus, 32; pl. 13
Apoda, 26
Apsidospondyli, 25
Archaeopteryges, 27
Archaeopteryx, 27, 137; figs. 18, 51
Archaeornithes, 27
Archaic mammals, 22–4
Archelon, 184
Archosauria, 26
Arrhinoceratops, 178; fig. 60
Arroyo formation, 42
Arundel formation, 150, 151, 156
Autun beds, 40
Aves, 27

Baharija beds, 167, 168
Bain Shire beds, 168
Bauru formation, 167, 168
Beaufort (Lower), 40, 49–57; characters of faunas, 49–50; therapsids of, 50–2; pl. 2
Beaufort (Upper), 60, 77
Beaufort zones, sequence of, 84
Belesodon, 102
Belle Plains formation, 42
Belly River, 179; environment, 169; fauna, 169–75; plains, 184
Belly River group, 164, 165, 168–79, 181, 185, 186, 198–201; pl. 16
Benton formation, 181, 182
Benthosuchus, 80
Bijori beds, 40, 59
Binomial system, 11
Birds, characters, 22; Upper Cretaceous, 183
Blaine formation, 42
Bone Cabin Quarry, 132; pl. 12
Bothriceps, 89
Bothriospondylus, 126, 136
Brachiosaurus, 32, 133, 140
Bradysaurus, 52; fig. 29
Brown, Barnum, pls. 17, 19
Brunswick formation, 104
Brushy Basin member (of Morrison), 132

Bunter, 76–7; tetrapods of, 78–80
Bunter amphibians, habitats of, 76–8
Bushmanland beds, 168

Caenagnathus, 175
Calamites, 33
Camptosaurus, 133, 136, 140
Candelaria, 101
Capitosaurus, 76, 80, 87
Carboniferous, environments, 33–5; glaciation, 34; lack of zoned climates, 34
Carnegie Museum, 131
Categories of classification, 12
Cave Sandstone formation, 60, 77, 100; pl. 4
Ceratopsians, horns of, 172–3
Ceratosaurus, 133, 140
Cetiosaurus, 126, 136, 140
Chalk, Southern England, 167, 168; pl. 15
Champsosaurus, 174
Chasmatosuchus, 80
Chasmosaurus, 172; fig. 60
Chelonia, 26
Cheneosaurus, fig. 60
Chialangosaurus, 142
Chienkosaurus, 141
Chinle formation, 75, 77, 96–8, 104; pls. 6, 7
Chiweta beds, 40, 57
Chordata, 25
Choza formation, 42
Chugwater group, 104
Church Rock member (of Chinle), 104
Cistecephalus zone, 40, 49, 56, 57, 59, 60, 82; pl. 2
Classes of vertebrates, 8; fig. 1
Clear Fork group, 40, 42
Cloverly formation, 151, 156
Clyde formation, 42
Coelophysis, 97; pls. 7, 8
Colbert, E. H., 21
Comparison of Permo-Triassic in Russia and South Africa, 60
Compsognathus, 136
Conemaugh formation, 40
Continental Intercalaire Saharien beds, 168
Cope, Edward Drinker, 131
Cordaites, 33
Correlation of Jurassic Vertebrate horizons, 119
Correlation of Lower Cretaceous Vertebrate horizons, 151
Correlation of Permo-Carboniferous Vertebrate horizons, 40
Correlation of Triassic Vertebrate horizons, 77
Correlation of Upper Cretaceous Vertebrate horizons, 168
Correlation of Upper Triassic Vertebrate horizons of North America, 104

Correo member (of Chinle), 104
Corythosaurus, 172, 177; fig. 60; pl. 18
Cotylorhynchus, 48, 52; fig. 27
Cotylosauria, 26
Cotylosaurs, defined, 14
Crests in hadrosaurs, 171–2
Cretaceous angiosperms, 149
Cretaceous, decline of dinosaurs, 198–201; decline of non-dinosaurian reptiles, 201–2; end of, 190; primitive placentals, 24; teleost fishes, 148–9; tetrapod localities, 166
Cretaceous extinctions, 192–5; causes of, 203–7; rates of, 197–8
Cretaceous (lower), life of, 158–60; reptiles of Asia, 156–7; reptiles of Australia, 157–8; seas, 147–8; tetrapods of North America, 156
Cretaceous (upper), abundance of reptiles, 161–4; birds, 183; climates, 189; continents, 189–90; diminution of dinosaurian genera, 198; distribution of dinosaurs, 187–8; localities, 164–7; marine reptiles, 180–4; rates of evolution in dinosaurs, 188–9; reptiles, 161–4; reptiles of Asia, 185–6
Cretaceous vertebrate horizons, correlations, 151
Crocodilia, 26
Crocodilians, 20
Crow Mountain formation, 77, 104
Cryptodraco, 136
Cutler formation, 40
Cuttie's Hillock beds, 40
Cyclotosaurus, 87
Cymbospondylus, 86
Cynognathus, 83, 102; fig. 37
Cynognathus zone, 60, 74, 77, 82–4, 102

Dacentrurus, 136
Dakota formation, 151; pl. 7
Darwin, Charles, 30
Decline of Cretaceous dinosaurs, 198–201
Decline of non-dinosaurian reptiles in late Cretaceous, 201–2
Deltatheridium, 186
Desmatosuchus, 97; pl. 8
Destruction of eggs as a factor in reptilian extinctions, 206
Diadectes, 43; figs. 4, 25
Diademodon, 83–4
Diapsid reptiles, 16
Diapsida, 26
Diarthrognathus, 100
Dicraeosaurus, 140
Dicynodon, 84
Dicynodonts, great numbers of, 53–4
Difunta formation, 165, 168, 176

Dimetrodon, 46; fig. 26
Diminution of dinosaur genera during late Cretaceous, 198
Dimorphodon, 122, 123; fig. 48
Dinosaur Canyon member (of Moenave), 104
Dinosaur National Monument, 131
Diplocaulus, fig. 3; pl. 3
Diplodocus, 133, 140, 141
Djadochta formation, 168, 186; pl. 14
Dockum group, 75, 77, 96, 98, 104
Dog Creek beds, 42
Dogger, 118, 119
Dogger seas, 125
Dolores formation, 104
Dorygnathus, 122
Draco, 92
Dunkard formation, 40
Durham Downs beds, 119
Dvina River, 57
Dwyka formation, 40, 60
Dysalatosaurus, 140

East Berlin formation, 104
Ecca formation, 40, 60
Edaphosaurus, pl. 3
Edmonton fauna, 177–8
Edmonton formation, 164, 168, 177–9, 185, 186, 199; pl. 17
Edmontonia, 178
Edmontosaurus, fig. 60
Elaphrosaurus, 140
Elasmosaurus, fig. 61
Elginia, 59
Embolomeri, 25
Endothiodon, 55; fig. 31
Endothiodon zone, 40, 49, 55, 57, 60, 67
English coal fields, 40
Entrada sandstone, pl. 7
Eoanura, 25
Eodelphis, 175
Eosuchia, 26
Eosuchians defined, 16
Epidemics as a factor in reptilian extinctions, 206–7
Eryops, 44; figs. 2, 24
Eupelor, 96; pl. 8
Euryapsida, 26
Eusthenopteron, fig. 22
Eutheria, 27
Expansion of seas in early Cretaceous, 147–8
Extinction, a complex process, 207; as an evolutionary process, 192
Extinction of reptiles, early mammals as factor, 206; epidemics as factor, 206–7; destruction of eggs as factor, 206; radiation as factor, 207; temperature tolerances as factor, 204–6

Extinctions, and catastrophes, 203–4; at end of Cretaceous—causes, 203–7; at end of Triassic—causes, 109–13; compared, 191–192
Extinctions in late Cretaceous, rates of, 197–8
Extinctions of Cretaceous tetrapod orders and families, 192–5; Table 14

Flowerpot formation, 42, 48
Foremost formation, 168, 169
Forest Marble, 118, 126
Formation, definition of, 30–2; correlation of, 32
Fort Union formation, 203
Fossils, definition of, 28–9
Fredericksburg formation, 151
Fruitland formation, 165, 168

Gault formation, 151
Geography of late Jurassic, Europe, 135
Geologic Eras, names of, 4
Geologic Periods, measurement of duration, 6; names of, 4–6
Geologic time, 5; table of, 5
Geosaurus, fig. 52
Giants, dominance of in late Jurassic, 144–5
Glaciation in Carboniferous, 34
Gondwanaland, 60, 62, 103
Gorgonopsians, 55
Gorgosaurus, 174, 178, 179; pl. 18
Grallator, 97
Granger, Walter, pl. 12
Greensand beds, 150, 151
Gregory, J. T., 16
Gregory, W. K., 13, 14, 15, 20
Gyps-Keuper beds, 77, 104

Hadrosaurs, crests in, 171–2
Halticosaurus, 95
Hampden Volcanics, 104
Hawkesbury beds, 74, 77, 89
Heilmann, G., 23
Hell Creek formation, 164, 168, 179, 199; pl. 20
Helopus, 157
Hennessey formation, 40, 48
Henodus, 91; fig. 40
Hesperornis, 183; fig. 63
Hesperornithes, 27
Hesperosuchus, 93–4, 95, 96; pl. 8
Holyoke Volcanics, 104
Holzmaden beds, 119
Hook Mountain Volcanics, 104
Hoplitosaurus, 156
Horns, of ceratopsians, 172–3
Hsiosuchus, 142
Hypacrosaurus, 177; fig. 60
Hypselosaurus, 188

Hypsilophodon, 153–4, 178; fig. 55
Hypsognathus, 98

Ichthyornithes, 27
Ichthyosaur, figs. 6, 46
Ichthyosauria, 26
Ichthyosaurs, defined, 14; Triassic, 68
Ichthyostega, fig. 22
Ichthyostegalia, 25
Ictidosaurs, 22
Iguanodon, 152, 153, 155; fig. 54
Inostrancevia, 59
Insectivora, 27
Iren Dabasu formation, 151, 185
Ischigualasto beds, 74, 77
Itarare beds, 40

Joggins formation, 40
Judith River formation, 168, 175
Jura, Black, 118; Brown, 118; White, 118
Jurassic, climates of, 117–8; correlation of
  vertebrate horizons, 119; end of, 146;
  replacements at beginning of, 110; reptiles
  of English Lias, 120–2; reptiles of German
  Lias, 123; spread of seas, 116–7; tetrapod
  localities, 124; fig. 49; tetrapod localities,
  lower and middle, 118; tetrapods in Asia,
  141–2
Jurassic (lower), distribution of reptiles, 117
Jurassic (middle), reptiles of Morocco, 126;
  reptilian life, 126–8; tetrapods, 126–9;
  tetrapods of England, 125–6
Jurassic (upper), dominance of giants, 144–5;
  geography of Europe, 135; marine reptiles,
  142–3; tetrapods, 142; Table 11; tetrapods
  in Asia, 141–2; tetrapods in Europe, 136–
  138; unknown in certain regions, 143–4

Kaisen, Peter, pl. 12
Kannemeyeria, 84
Kansu beds, 165, 168
Karoomys, 84
Karroo basin, 49
Kashmir beds, 40
Kayenta formation, 77, 98, 104, 123 (foot-
  note)
Kentrosaurus, 140
Keuper beds, 77, 104
Keuper, characteristic tetrapods, 75–6; dino-
  saurs, 95–6; tetrapods, 90–6
Kimmeridge formation, 32, 119, 130, 136,
  139, 140
Kingori sandstone, 101
Kirtland formation, 165, 168
Koiloskiosaurus, 78
Komodo lizard, resemblance to mosasaurs,
  183
Kota beds, 119, 125

Kotlassia, 59
Kounova beds, 40
Kritosaurus, 171; fig. 60
Kronosaurus, 158; fig. 58
Kuangyuan beds, 119
Kuehneosaurus, 92
Kupferschiefer beds, 38, 40

Labyrinthodontia, 25
Labyrinthodonts, defined, 12–13
Lambeosaurus, 172, 177; fig. 60
Lameta beds, 165, 168
Lance fauna, 178–80
Lance formation, 164, 165, 168, 185, 186,
  198–201, 203; pl. 19
Lance mammals, 180
Laplatasaurus, 186, 188
Laramide Revolution, 162–3, 204
Lepidodendron, 33
Lepidosauria, 26
Lepospondyli, 25
Lepospondyls, defined, 13
Leptoceratops, 178
Leptopleuron, 90
Lettenkohle beds, 77, 104
Leuders formation, 42
Lias, 118, 119
Liassic beds, pl. 9
Life of the Early Permian in Texas, pl. 3
Life of the Late Cretaceous in Western
  Canada, pl. 18
Life of the Late Jurassic in Western North
  America, pl. 13
Life of the Late Triassic in Western North
  America, pl. 8
Linnaeus, 11
Linné, Carl von, 11
Linton formation, 40
Lizards, appearance in Triassic, 69
Lockatong formation, 104
Lufeng formation, 76, 77, 99
Lufengosaurus, 99, 100
Lukachukai member (of Wingate), 104
Lull, Richard Swann, pl. 12
Lycaenops, 55; figs. 16, 32
Lystrosaurus, 82, 84; fig. 36
Lystrosaurus zone, 60, 74, 77, 80–4

Madagascar, Cretaceous of, 167, 168;
  Jurassic of, 119
Maestrichtian, 167
Magothy formation, 168
Maleri formation, 76, 77, 99
Malm, 118, 119
Mamenchisaurus, 141
Mammalia, 27
Manda beds, 75, 101
Mangwa beds, 57

Mantell, Gideon, 152
Marine reptiles of late Jurassic, 142–3
Marsh, Othniel Charles, 131, 132
Marsupialia, 27
Mastodonsaurus, 87
Matawan formation, 168
Mazon Creek beds, 40
Megalosaurus, 125, 126, 136, 140, 154
Megalosaurus wetherelli, 123 (footnote)
Mesa Verde formation, 165, 168; 174 (footnote)
Mesen River, 57
Mesosauria, 26
Mesosaurus, 62
Metatheria, 27
Metoposaurus, 90, 96
Microcnemus, 80
Microsauria, 26
Middle Triassic, end of, 89
Milk River formation, 168
Mixosaurus, 86
Moenave formation, 77, 104
Moenkopi formation, 74, 77, 85
Molteno formation, 60, 77, 100
Mongolosaurus, 157
Monitor Butte member (of Chinle), 104
Monjurosuchus, 142
Monmouth formation, 168
Monoclonius, 172; figs. 12, 60
Monongahela, 40
Monotremes, 24
Moran formation, 42
Morocco, Cretaceous of, 167, 168; Jurassic of, 119
Morrison dinosaurs, 132–4
Morrison formation, 32, 119, 130–6, 139, 144, 145; pls. 7, 11, 12
Morrison mammals, 134–5
Mosasaurs, 167
Moschops, 53; fig. 30
Moss Back member (of Chinle), 104
Multituberculata, 27
Multituberculates, 24
Muraenosaurus, fig. 8
Murchison, Roderick Impey, 37, 57
Muschelkalk beds, 77; sea, 86; tetrapods, 86–9

Narrabeen beds, 74, 77
Nautilus, 120
Navajo sandstone, 118, 119, 123
Nectridia, 25
Nemegetu formation, 168
Neornithes, 27
Nequen beds, 151
New Haven arkose, 104
New tetrapods arising in Triassic, 71
Newark group, 75, 77, 96–8, 104

Newcastle beds, upper, 40, 59
Niobrara formation, 165, 168, 181, 182, 183
North Horn formation, continuity of Cretaceous and Tertiary sediments, 201–3; record of dinosaurian extinction in, 202–3
Nothosaurs, 68
Nothosaurus, 78, 87; fig. 35
Nugget sandstone, 104
Nyasaland, 57
Nyřany, 40

Oldman formation, 168, 169; pl. 16
Oligokyphus, 122
Olson, E. C., 13
Olson, E. C. and Broom, R., 17
Omeisaurus, 141
Omosaurus, 126, 136
Ondai Sair formation, 151
On Gong formation, 151, 152, 157
Oolites, 118, 126
Opal beds, 167, 168
Ophiacodon, pl. 3
Ornithischia, 27
Ornithischian dinosaurs, defined, 19
Ornitholestes, 133, 136, 140; pl. 13
Ornithomimus, 174, 178, 179, 185; fig. 11
Osborn, H. F., 18
Oshih formation, 151, 152, 156
Owl Rock member (of Chinle), 104
Oxford clays, 119, 130, 136; pl. 10

Pachycephalosaurus, 179
Pachyophis, 155
Palaeoscincus, 173, 178
Panchet beds, 74, 77
Pantotheres, 24
Pantotheria, 27
Paracyclotosaurus, 102
Parapsida, 26
Parasaurolophus, 172, 178; fig. 60
Pareiasaurs, 52
Patagonia beds, 167, 168
Pease River group, 40, 42
Pelycosauria, 27
Pelycosaurs, 21, 43–5
Pentaceratops, 186; fig. 60
Permian, beginning of, 36; climates, 63; comparison of Texas and New Mexico, 46; continental relationships in, 60–3; of Russia, 57–9; of Texas, 41–5; 'red beds' of Texas, 41–6; reptiles of Russia, 58–9; seaway separating Texas and New Mexico, 45–6; tetrapod localities, 39; variety of tetrapods in, 37–8
Permian (lower), extent of, 46–7
Permo-Carboniferous correlations, 40
Petrified Forest, 104
Phobosuchus, 175–6

Phytosaurs, 17, 70, 94–5
Phytosaurus, 95, 97; pl. 8
Pierce Canyon formation, 104
Pierre formation, 165, 168, 181
Pierre seas, 184
Pistosaurus, 87
Placerias, 98
Placochelys, 91
Placodonts, 68–9
Placodus, fig. 35
Plateosauravus, 100
Plateosaurus, 95–6, 100; fig. 42
Polacanthus, 153; fig. 56
Poleo member (of Chinle), 104
Popo Agie formation, 75, 77, 96, 104
Portland beds, 104, 119, 130, 136
Primitive placentals, in Cretaceous, 24
Proanura, 25
Proceratosaurus, 126
Procheneosaurus, 172, 177; fig. 60
Procolophon, 83
Procolophon zone, 60, 74, 77, 82–3
Proganochelys, 90
Prolacerta, 82
Prosaurolophus, 171; fig. 60
Protobatrachus, 127
Protoceratops, 186; fig. 65; pl. 14
Protorosauria, 26
Protorosaurs, defined, 15
Protosuchus, 98
Pseudosuchians, 17, 69–70
Psittacosaurus, 156; fig. 57
Pteranodon, 183; fig. 64
Pterodactylus, 140
Pterosauria, 26
Pterosaurs, defined, 21
Pueblo formation, 42
Purbeck beds, 119, 130, 136, 139, 145, 155
Purbeck mammals, 138
Putnam formation, 42

Quarry Nine, 134, 145

Radiation as a factor in reptilian extinctions, 207
Raritan formation, 168
Red Beds formation (of South Africa), 60, 77, 100; pl. 4
Red Peak formation, 77
Redonda formation, 104
Replacements at beginning of Jurassic, 110
Reptiles, compared with amphibians, 7–9; compared with birds and mammals, 9–10; reproduction in, 3; that survived the Cretaceous, 196–7
Reptilia, 26
Reptilian dominance, beginning of, 36
Rachitomi, 25

Rhaetic, 76, 77, 104
Rhamphorhynchus, 137, 140; figs. 14, 50
Rhoetosaurus, 128
Rhynchocephalia, 26
Rhynchocephalians, 16; of Triassic, 69
Rhynchosaurs, 92; in North America, 97–8
Rock Point member (of Wingate), 104
Rolling Downs beds, 151
Romer, Alfred S., 194; pl. 1
Romer, A. S., and L. I. Price, 21
Rothliegende beds, 38, 40
Ruhuhu beds, 40, 57, 75
Russian Triassic zones, 74

Sakamena beds, 77
Salientia, 25
Salitral member (of Chinle), 104
Saltoposuchus, 93, 95, 96
Saltopus, 95
San Angelo formation, 42, 48
Sanpasaurus, 142
Santa Maria formation, 74, 77, 101–2; pl. 5
Santa Rosa formation, 104
Sarcosaurus, 121, 122
Saurischia, 27
Saurischian dinosaurs, defined, 19
Saurolophus, 177, 185; fig. 60
Sauropterygia, 26
Sauropterygians, defined, 15–6
Scaphonyx, 93, 101
Scelidosaurus, 120, 121, 122, 128; fig. 47; pl. 9
Sedimentary rocks, 29–30; succession of, 30
Segisaurus, 123
Serra Geral lavas, pl. 5
Shabarakh Usu, 186
Shansi beds, 77
Shantung beds, 150, 151, 165, 168
Shinarump member (of Chinle), 104
Shuttle Meadow formation, 104
Sigillaria, 33
Simpson, G. G., 24
Sinkiang beds, 150, 151
Sinocoelurus, 142
Sinognathus, 102
Sinokannemeyeria, 85
Smith, William, 4
Solnhofen beds, 119
Species, definition of, 11–12
Sphenacodon, 46; fig. 15
Springdale member (of Moenave), 104
Squamata, 16, 26
Stagonolepis, 94; fig. 10
Stahleckeria, 101
Stegoceras, 173, 186
Stegosaurus, 134, 136; pl. 13
Stenaulorhynchus, 101
Steneosaurus, 126, 140

Steppesaurus, 48
Stereognathus, 125
Stereospondyli, 25
Stockton formation, 104
Stonesfield slate, 118, 125
Stormberg group, 60, 77, 100; pl. 4
Stratigraphic succession, 4
Styracosaurus, 172; fig. 60; pl. 18
Symmetrodonta, 27
Symmetrodonts, 24
Synapsida, 27
Szechuanosaurus, 141

Talbraggar beds, 119
Talcott Volcanics, 104
Tambo beds, 151
Tanga, 57
Tanystrophaeus, 88; fig. 38
Tapinocephalus, 53
Tapinocephalus zone, 40, 49, 52, 60
Taxonomy, 11
Teleost fishes, Cretaceous radiation, 148–9
Temperature tolerances as a factor in reptilian extinctions, 204–6
Tendaguru fauna, 139–41
Tendaguru formation, 32, 119, 130, 139, 140, 141
Tendaguru formation, age of, 139; conditions of deposition, 140
Teratosaurus, 95
Tetrapods, at beginning of Triassic, 70–1; classification of, 25–7; comparisons, 7–10; defined, 7; during Triassic-Jurassic transition, 108; ectothermic, 7; emergence of, 35–6; endothermic, 7
Thecodontia, 26
Thecodontosaurus, 100
Thecodonts, 17, 69–70
Theories of continental relationships, 60–1
Therapsida, 27
Therapsids, defined, 21–2; dominance of in Lower Triassic, 82–4; evolution of, fig. 28
Theria, 27
Thescelosaurus, 178
Thrinaxodon, 82
Thoosuchus, 80
Tienshanosaurus, 157
Titanosaurus, 186, 188
Titanosuchids, 54
Todilto gypsum, pl. 7
Tornieria, 140
Torosaurus, 179; fig. 60
Transylvania beds, 167, 168
Trematosaurus, 80
Triassic, advent of, 64; amphibians, 106; continental connections, 103–5; correlation of vertebrate horizons, 77; end of,

113–5; in Spitzbergen, 76; new reptiles of, 102, 103; problems of fossil collecting, 89; threefold division, 72
Triassic environments, 103
Triassic extinctions, causes, 109–13
Triassic fossils, problems of collecting, 89
Triassic land, restrictions of, 109
Triassic (lower), environments of, 71–2; evolutionary break at end of, 85; dominance of therapsids, 82–4; tetrapods of Asia, 84; tetrapods of North America, 85; tetrapods of South Africa, 80–4
Triassic (middle), outside of Europe, 89
Triassic reptiles, age of in South America, 75; at end of, 106–8; continuing from Permian, 66–7, 71; new types, 67–70
Triassic seas, invasion by reptiles, 67–9
Triassic tetrapod localities, 34
Triassic tetrapods, distribution at end, 107; extinction of, 108–9
Triassic turtles, 67
Triassic (upper), of Asia, 99; reptiles of Africa, 100–1; reptiles of South America, 101–2; tetrapods of North America, 96–9; vertebrate horizons in North America, correlations, 104
Triassochelys, 90; fig. 39
Triceratops, 179; fig. 60; abundance of fossils, 200
Triconodonta, 27
Triconodonts, 24
Trilophosaurus, 98; fig. 7
Trimerorhachis, 44; pl. 3
Trinity formation, 150, 151, 156
Tritylodon, 100
Tritylodonts, possible habits, 98–9
Tröodon, 173
Turtle skeleton, fig. 5
Two Medicine formation, 168, 175
Tylosaurus, fig. 62
Typothorax, 97
Tyrannosaurus, 179, 185

Uitenhage beds, 151, 152
Urodela, 26

Vale formation, 42
Vertebrata, 25
Vertebrates, classes of, 8
Volgosuchus, 80

Walker, A., 18
Walloon beds, 119
Washita formation, 151
Watchung Volcanics, 104
Wealden beds, 150, 151, 152, 178

Wealden fauna, 152–5, 161
Weiyan beds, 119
Wetlugasaurus, 80, 84
Wichita group, 40, 42; pl. 1
Wianamatta beds, 77
Wingate formation, 77, 104
World Map, Cretaceous tetrapod localities, 166; Jurassic tetrapod localities, 124; Triassic tetrapod localities, 73; Permian tetrapod localities, 39

Yabeinosaurus, 142
Yerrapalli formation, 74, 77
Young, C. C., 22
Youngoides, fig. 9

Zalambdalestes, 186; fig. 19
Zechstein, 38, 40
Zones O–IV, 40, 60
Zones V–VII, 60, 74, 77
Zoological classification, 10